PSYCHO"THERAPY"

PSYCHO"THERAPY"

Theory, Practice, Modern and Postmodern Influences

Laurence Simon

PRAEGER

Westport, Connecticut
London

Library of Congress Cataloging-in-Publication Data

Simon, Laurence R.
    Psycho"therapy" : theory, practice, modern and postmodern influences
/ Laurence Simon.
      p.   cm.
    Includes bibliographical references and index.
    ISBN 0–275–94690–8
    1. Psychotherapy—Philosophy. 2. Psychotherapy. I. Title.
RC437.5.S537   1994
616.89′14—dc20   94–1141

British Library Cataloguing in Publication Data is available.

Library of Congress Catalog Card Number: 94–1141
ISBN: 0–275–94690–8

First published in 1994

Praeger Publishers, 88 Post Road West, Westport, CT 06881
An imprint of Greenwood Publishing Group, Inc.

Printed in the United States of America

The paper used in this book complies with the
Permanent Paper Standard issued by the National
Information Standards Organization (Z39.48–1984).

10 9 8 7 6 5 4 3 2 1

This book is dedicated to my wife Rochelle

CONTENTS

PREFACE

My professional life has gone on now for almost three decades, during which time I divided myself between an academic and a clinical career. While still a young psychologist, I could not always see the connection between my role as a professor and my role as psychotherapist. This book reflects my attempts at an integration and began the moment I realized that good psychotherapy was educational and good education was always therapeutic.

I have spent the last twenty-five years teaching a variety of psychology courses at Kingsborough Community College. The demands of teaching have provided one of my main motives to continue to satisfy a voracious appetite for reading in a wide variety of topics. I am grateful for the support I have received from my friend, colleague, and chairperson, Dr. Philip Stander. I am also in the debt of Leon Goldstein, president of Kingsborough Community College since 1970, for creating a harmonious and stable environment in which intellectual activities could take place.

My clinical foundations were developed at Flushing Hospital Mental Health Clinic, where I was encouraged to explore a wide range of therapeutic styles under an equally wide range of therapeutic settings. Over the years I am indebted for the relationships I have had with Dr. Dorit Whitman, Dr. Milton Kornrich, Mr. John Scheffer, and Ms. Rosanne Edelsack, the current director of the Mental Health Clinic.

I should like to thank the many teachers who have helped me see what the true role of educator and scientist might be. Sam Troik, Murray Stahl, Donald Spence, and especially Isidor Chein come to mind as most influential in my professional life. Chein's monumental book *The Science of Behavior and the*

Image of Man remains a constant source of knowledge and inspiration in my life.

Finally, I would like to thank Lennie Adelman, who typed this manuscript and never lost her sense of humor while dealing with the chicken scratch that passes for my handwriting.

PSYCHO"THERAPY"

INTRODUCTION:
MODERNISM AND POSTMODERNISM

The concepts of modernism and postmodernism require definitions, as both play important roles in the present work. The modern era began in Western society with the Enlightenment and the scientific revolution. Modernism is best described as an attitude marked by a number of characteristics, the first of which involves the rejection of a dualistic explanation of causality. Demons, angels, and all other manifestations of a spirit world cannot be utilized as causative agents in any work labeled scientific. All causes have to be of this earth and to have a material basis if they are to appear as truly scientific. Scientists may believe in spirits, but only in their roles as private citizens and not in their professional capacities.

A second factor defining the modern era involves the rise of rationalism and objectivity and the decline of emotionalism as modes of experiencing the world. Inductive and deductive reasoning underlie scientific work, and scientists are expected to be objective as they make their observations and form their conclusions. Objectivity demands that the scientist discover what exists in reality rather than discover the products of his or her own wish fulfillments. Rationalism and objectivity reached a peak when scientists chose mathematics to be the basic language of science.

A third manifestation of modernism involves the rise of technology as both a means of scientific research and a product of that same scientific activity. Much of the success of science can be traced to the development of microscopes, telescopes, computers, and all the other technological equipment that aids in basic discovery and data analysis. Our modern way of life is marked by an explosion of technological devices designed to improve our lives as well as to defend them where deemed necessary.

The rise of modernism, however, has not been without its critics. The totality of attitudes representing this criticism might be called postmodernism. Postmodernism has existed longer than the term that defines it. However, in recent years, particularly in university departments devoted to the humanities, postmodernism has grown more focused, strident, and self-aware. Postmodernism may be defined by a set of related attitudes often critical of modernism.

The first, and perhaps defining attitude of postmodernism is the belief that knowledge is power and hidden concepts may exist in a theory or text that justifies the use of power. These power concepts may allow those who possess knowledge to devalue, subjugate, and otherwise victimize those who do not possess such knowledge. Whenever hidden power exists within a knowledge base danger exists for all concerned.

Postmodernists direct their criticism of organized science at the concepts of rationality and objectivity as they are promulgated by many scientists such as the logical positivists. These scientists have argued that rationality and objectivity afford science a transcendent, supracultural view of truth and reality. Postmodernists counter by stating that all methods of studying reality and all claims of truth are merely socially constructed conventions and therefore reflect the shared values of those utilizing those conventions. By creating a moral hierarchy where scientists are perched above society with regard to truth, the scientific viewpoint easily falls prey to the political, economic, and social needs of the scientist. Science becomes potentially dangerous to the society in which it operates.

Another defining element of postmodernism involves the process of deconstruction—the analysis of the hidden element of power inherent in all organized systems of knowledge. The analysis makes these power relationships clear and explicit allowing all who are involved with a system of knowledge to make choices concerning the goals of their activities. One cannot avoid power but one can be aware of its presence and reduce the chances of it being abused.

Postmodernism is not inherently against science as an activity nor hostile to the empirical methods utilized by scientists. There is nothing in the postmodern philosophy or methodology that seeks to bring society back to a premodern point of view. Most postmodernists accept that modern science is an excellent method for studying the world around us. However, the critics of modernism seek to expose and challenge the modernists' attitude that replaces the "gods" with the scientists.

Further, postmodern criticism of modernism involves the questioning of the notion that unbridled technological development represents either "progress" or an advancement of the human condition. Many who define themelves as postmodernists feel that as the use of machines grows more common we are diminished in our basic self-definition of what it means to be human. We are not the owners and controllers of technology; rather, we are experiencing the diametric opposite. We are controlled by machines and increasingly spend our lives in the service of them.

I agree with many of the tenets of postmodernism. I take the position here that modernism's excesses and failures are the result of ideologies and moral judgments that are extrascientific and form what might be called "scientism" rather than science. I also take the position that many who define themselves as postmodernists are also in need of deconstructing their own ideological and extremist positions. One reads many postmodern tracts that suggest that the very essence of science is reducible to an intolerable and destructive political stance and that any point of view is equally as valid or invalid as any other. I see this wing of postmodernism as not only antiscientific but anti-intellectual as well. Such positions open the door to a return to premodernism.

This book argues that modern psychiatry is not science but rather an example of scientism or pseudoscience. Modern psychiatry treats its human subjects as if they were reducible to the twitching of neurons, biological drives, and conditioned stimuli—and little else. Human consciousness, choice, and dignity count for very little. I believe that a postmodern deconstruction of psychiatry's position can lead to redefinitions of psychology and psychotherapy that are modernistic and scientific and that avoid both the scientism of psychiatry and the scientific nihilisms of extreme postmodernism.

The book is organized in five parts. Part I is comprised of only one chapter, a polemic against modern psychiatry, clinical psychology, and the medical model of "mental illness." Part II is comprised of three chapters, in which psycho"therapy" is defined and the philosophical underpinnings of this endeavor are explicated. Chapter 2 discusses the differences between scientific description and moral judgment and the problems created when one is confused with the other. Chapter 3 discusses a postmodern philosophy of science friendly to psycho"therapy" and then explicates the moral philosophy known as humanism. Chapter 4 discusses the biological and evolutionary underpinning of psychology and sociology, as well as the reciprocal nature of these areas of study. It also defines consciousness and suggests that consciousness and its development are legitimate topics for our scientific interests as "therapists."

Part III is also comprised of three chapters, which contain an outline of a scientific theory of psychology capable of directing the field of psycho"therapy." Chapter 5 lays the foundation of a theory of psychology as a human science rather than as a natural or even a social science. Chapter 6 discusses personality as an adaptive paradigm, while Chapter 7 describes individual variations in human adaptive functioning.

Part IV contains two chapters that attempt to redefine the psychiatric diagnoses as adaptive modes of behavior. In both chapters, the contents of the Psychiatric Diagnostic and Statistical Manual (DSM) are interpreted to be individual differences in personal adaptive strategies rather than as mental illnesses or disorders. Chapter 8 discusses the less serious diagnoses that in previous editions of the DSM were referred to as neuroses, while Chapter 9 reinterprets the psychoses, including schizophrenia, the illness that lies at the very heart of psychiatric justification.

Part V contains three chapters on topics related to the history, context, and procedures that make up the processes of psycho"therapy." Chapter 10 discusses the history and sociological nature of psycho"therapy," as well as problems stemming from the current training of psychotherapists. Chapter 11 explicates some of the techniques that lie at the center of psycho"therapy" as a helping activity. Chapter 12 closes the book with a perusal of several topics including working with children, confidentiality, and the use of myths in human experience.

I

THE PROBLEM

1

PSYCHO"THERAPY"
AND THE MEDICAL MODEL

The goal of this book is to help psychotherapists create a working professional identity free of the medical model that lies, in one way or another, at the heart of their working lives. Why might one want to be free of this model? Simply, it is an incorrect metaphor and paradigm for the problems it purports to help understand and solve. As a result of utilizing the medical model, both individual therapists and the field of psychotherapy are in crisis. To think incorrectly about a problem, to use the wrong language to describe and discuss it, to apply the wrong methods to ameliorate it, and to be unable even to understand that the wrong model is in operation is to create a massive crisis. The present quagmire in which our field finds itself flows from the innumerable unintended and interactive consequences that develop because of the medical metaphor. These consequences destructively affect the therapist, the patient, the field of psychotherapy, and the society in which they all function.

THE MEDICAL MODEL

When individuals will not recognize the nature of various life problems, it is often because they are employing what psychotherapists call *defense mechanisms*. These mechanisms deny and distort the reality of some problem. When life turns harsh, tragic, unjust, and—in the perceptions of various individuals—unmanageable, overwhelming, and uncontrollable, people use defenses to relieve themselves of the anxiety, shame, guilt, and other painful emotions created when they confront such situations. As individuals pretend to solve their real-life problems or fail to solve them because they refuse to recognize that the problems exist, they live lives full of unintended consequences. They find that their lives are full of additional crises, now of their own making. Often these unintended consequences are destructive to these individuals or others involved with them. These self-imposed crises are experienced by these individuals with emotions such as anxiety, rage, and depression. Psychotherapists call such people mentally ill or disordered and call their behavior and powerful emotional states mental illness or disorders.

Psychotherapists soon discover that when they directly confront their patients' use of defenses, these individuals become angry and resistant to further dealings with their therapists. When therapists argue with patients, the patients reveal intense anxiety, anger, and an increase in their already dogmatic insistence that their defensive belief systems are in no way related to their life crises. Unlike nondefensive thinking, which can be confronted and which usually yields to empirical or logical evidence that proves it false, defensive behaviors seem driven and resistant to such logic and empiricism.

By calling unwanted behavior and painful emotions illnesses, mental health professionals have employed the medical model to describe problems in living. In the analysis that follows, I try to demonstrate that mental illness is a myth (Szasz 1974); if not, then the medical model would be the mental illness of the field of psychotherapy. The behaviors of psychotherapists employing their notions of mental illness are identical to those of the therapist's patients employing defense mechanisms, delusions, and other fanciful distortions of reality.

The ideas of Thomas Szasz (1974, 1978) and R. D. Laing (1967b, 1969) and a particularly penetrating and seminal work by Theodore Sarbin and James Mancuso (1980) are, in part, the inspiration of this work. Szasz and Laing have been met by the adherents of the medical model with derision, hatred, and professional rejection. Both have been called mentally ill, and Laing has been accused on numerous occasions of being schizophrenic. Sarbin and Mancuso's work, more logical and empirical and modeled after scientific psychology in its written format, is less angry than Szasz's writings and less poetic and speculative than Laing's. Because Sarbin and Mancuso's writings are framed in a manner more acceptable to American psychology, I believe their work is more dangerous to the "myth" and therefore has been largely ignored by the field.

PARADIGMS

Szasz and Laing are not mentally ill, any more than the patients who will not accept the interpretations of their psychotherapist or the psychotherapists who will not assimilate the ideas of Laing and Szasz. However, if we reject the metaphor of mental illness or disorder, then with what do we replace it? In *Cognition and Affect* (Simon 1986) I developed a personality theory, built in part upon the ideas of George Kelly (1955), that conceives of all people as scientists seeking to describe, explain, predict, and control themselves, others, and the world around them. I continue to develop this argument further by suggesting that, when Thomas Kuhn (1970) discusses the role of paradigms, crisis, and paradigmatic revolution in scientific upheavals, he too is describing a universal process. By explicating the manner in which personal paradigms are created, maintained, defended, discarded, and replaced, we can create a model for explaining human behavior and deviancy that permits replacement of the medical model. We can explain the behavior of the patient and of the mental health professional. We can describe the manner in which human beings, both professional and otherwise, solve or (in the judgment of someone) fail to solve problems in living without calling anyone sick or disordered.

Let me briefly present Kuhn's model and then extend it to the nonprofessional. Kuhn believes that at any moment in time the scientific enterprise is guided by a working paradigm. The paradigm involves a shared theory concerning the subject of scientific interest and a set of procedures by which this subject is to be studied. The purpose of a paradigm is the solution of puzzles or problems that permit an increase in the explanatory value of the paradigmatic theory, as well as improvements in the procedures that allow increases in factual knowledge to take place. Kuhn suggests that eventually a working paradigm uncovers new knowledge that is contradictory to the paradigm that led to its discovery and acceptance. At that point the new knowledge acts as an anomaly in the existing scientific paradigm. An anomaly that cannot be explained or predicted by the existing paradigm threatens to invalidate the existing paradigm, whose function is to explain such events.

Scientists do not abandon or radically revise their existing paradigms in the face of an anomaly; rather, they begin modifying and shifting their paradigms to include the anomaly, thus rendering it consistent with basic existing beliefs and procedures. The anomaly tends to be reinterpreted in such a way as to deny its anomalous nature. If these adjustments in theory cannot be made or if an increasing number of scientists lose faith in the existing paradigm because the paradigm cannot explain the anomaly, then science enters into a period of crisis. Kuhn believes that the crisis is resolved only when an individual scientist or group of scientists replaces the existing paradigm with one believed to be more explanatory and practical. Such a scientific revolution often leads to a radical new view of the world. This new view becomes the basis for ongoing science as younger scientists embrace it and older scientists either retire or die off.

PERSONALITY AND PARADIGM

Kuhn's work is a descriptive epistemology. It does not include a psychological component that can explain the experiential basis of scientific crises or the extreme resistance to changing an existing paradigm once it has lost its usefulness. I attempt to provide a psychological underpinning for Kuhn's work in Chapters 5 and 6, but here I utilize his model and the dynamics that flow from it to begin replacing the medical model of mental illness. In the present theory of the individual as a scientist, personality is comprised of a paradigm that includes a theory of self, others, the surrounding world, and the interaction of all of these. The personal paradigm comprising and defining individual personality also includes a set of skills that permit implementation of the individual's theory. Each person's beliefs, attitudes, knowledge, and motor skills have the goal of solving the individual's problems in living and satisfying the basic human needs that define successful adaptation. (See Chapter 6 for a formal definition of human adaptation.)

Like their scientific counterparts, all human beings confront anomalies that create crises involving the paradigms comprising their personalities. We all confront situations in which our explanations, predictions, and controls fail. We all deal with a physical and social world that defeats our abilities to satisfy our needs and to solve a wide variety of problems. At such times we find ourselves experiencing a crisis. At such a juncture individuals might seek to revise their personality paradigms by increasing knowledge, changing beliefs, and adopting new skills. If successful in accommodating to the demands of a difficult and anomalous reality, such individuals might be said to have undergone a personal scientific revolution.

Also, as do their more formally trained scientific counterparts, individuals may not face the anomaly as it exists but rather may deny and distort the nature of the situation confronting them. Why and how one individual goes through a crisis and revolution and why and how another employs defense mechanisms is one of the crucial questions that psycho"therapists" must try to answer. Though many reasons explain why individuals protect their existing paradigms rather than undergo a transforming revolution, we will deal with only two at this juncture.

The first reason that existing paradigms are defended involves the fact that human beings simply do not recognize their theories as theories, that is, as a series of educated (or uneducated) guesses. The tools of our survival are simply too important to be taken conditionally. The psychological imperatives of survival and meaningful living seem to demand that we protect our personal paradigms, our knowing, even in the face of evidence that is most damning to them. Second, and as important, the personal theories of individuals, the rules that explain and govern behavior, are most often cast as moral imperatives and not merely as descriptions. What we believe we "should" believe; how we behave "should" or "ought" to be our behavior.

The human capacity to experience the world in moral terms and to confuse moral terms with description is universal, but nowhere more true and complete than when one person describes the behavior of another. The source of much human conflict and, as will be described later, the problems of the medical model involve the confusion of moral judgment with factual descriptions. Human beings protect their adaptive paradigms because they are both intellectually and morally committed to them. When evidence is presented, through our own experience or through social interactions, that our paradigm is faulty, the anomalous information is usually resisted with vigor. Such information implies that we are simultaneously morally and intellectually inferior. When persons are told by others that their thoughts and actions are wrong or bad in some way, one can predict intense defensive activities.

Human beings protect their existing paradigm by denying and distorting certain realities (or the truth of others, particularly when they are cast in morally negative terms) that demand change in the existing paradigm. No one learns anything new without risk and psychological pain (crises). Human beings will continue to maintain their defenses until the pain of doing so is greater than the pain of change and until "better" views of reality and skills are discovered or provided them.

The concepts of mental illness and mental disorders have been invented both as attempts to explain and judge and as rationalizations to ameliorate the inevitable conflicts that arise between people when they interact with one another from the lenses of differing individual personal paradigms. Although individuals often share similar features of their paradigms, just as with the human faces they turn to each other, similarities always give way to individual uniqueness. The conflicts that exist between people as they seek to adapt occur on both an individual level and on institutional bases. Conflicts created by antagonistic paradigms exist between and within families, religious groupings, social groups of all kinds, and political entities such as cities, states, and nations.

As human beings interact, they constantly evaluate and criticize the perceptions, thoughts, and actions that comprise the personalities or personal paradigms of their fellow human beings. Such conflicts and criticisms will often lead one individual or group to seek to change or stop entirely the thoughts, speech, and behavior found to be wanting or offensive. The bases of criticism and justifications to seek changing the paradigms of others are as endless as are the means used to affect change.

As societal groups organize themselves, some paradigms emerge as dominant. The dominant viewpoint and modes of adaptive behavior will be defended by participating group members not only as sensible, but as morally correct. In any given society, at any time in its history, there may be more or less tolerance to difference in individual thought and expression. Few, if any, societies fail to find some personal paradigms so wanting in effectiveness and moral worth as not to seek to prevent their continued expression or existence. Such paradigms might be attacked by religious groups as sinful, by civil community standards as criminal, by political evaluators as treasonous, or by the modern psychiatric establishment as mental illness.

Every society has a mechanism for dealing with individual deviance that is built into its political system. The police and the courts are currently this country's constitutionally created institutions for dealing with a wide variety of paradigmatic behavior labeled criminal. Just what is criminal differs from society to society. In some cultures, extreme violence against property or persons is judged criminal; in others, it is considered mere criticism of the state's political system. It is beyond our present discussion to discuss differences in tolerance to deviancy, as well as the various types of political agencies and the methods societies employ to deal with such individual differences.

There is also, in most societies, a range of thought and behavior that is not specifically criminal nor directly politically unacceptable, but that is still socially unacceptable. These deviant paradigms may involve strange, obnoxious, frightening attitudes and actions that are hard to empathize with and explain. They may also be ideas that call into question the truth and validity of society's existing and cherished paradigms. Individuals spouting heretical opinions or behaving counter to existing mores and role expectations are both a general nuisance and a threat to the existing power structure and lifestyle of those comprising the dominant society. People living according to contrary paradigms can be a threat to any social institution in which their deviant ideas and behavior may be taken seriously enough by others to create anomaly and crises. People who fail to succeed according to the economic, educational, and other social norms of society may be so judged.

Every society also has some mechanism to deal with these noncriminal yet deviant paradigms. In our culture it is the so-called mental health professional to whom this task has fallen. Although an increasing number of paradigms hitherto deemed criminal are coming under the jurisdiction of mental health, our profession deals mostly with noncriminal deviancy. We still deal with those who, for a variety of reasons, will not go to school or hold down a "productive" job, who refuse to dress or groom themselves according to social expectation, or who use language in a strange and hard-to-comprehend manner. People who criticize and fail to live according to society's (and, I believe, middle-class) standards are most often called mentally ill and convinced to seek out treatment. Often the patients most requiring the services of mental health professions are errant children who refuse or are unable to learn and apply society's dominant paradigm.

Human beings experience some of their most potent adaptive struggles when dealing with children. Children need a great deal of help in satisfying needs and solving problems. It is the perceived job of parents, teachers, and all those who work with children to see to it not only that children get the help they need but also that they develop a personal paradigm that will allow them to adapt effectively on their own. Parents, teachers, clergy, and others constantly try to influence the development of the paradigm of the children for whose growth they feel responsible. But these adults influence children through the lens of their own paradigms, which they seek to defend on both intellectual and moral grounds. Each of us tends to experience our own theory as truth and our own skills as correct. We invest our knowledge and skills with both passion and pride.

Parents and teachers or others who influence children may see their work as educational, social, or even scientific, but they invariably see such efforts as simultaneously moral in nature. When children do not learn what adults believe is effective behavior, the children are said to be misbehaving and resistant to truth. When children fail to develop paradigms valued by their adult guardians and teachers, some of society's most potent means are utilized to bring them into social compliance. Nothing can be more threatening to a culture than a large number of children who fail to develop attitudes and behavior capable of carrying on their society's most valued paradigms.

When psychotherapists disagree with the thinking, perception, emotions, judgment, and behavior of another, they call such an individual mentally ill or mentally disordered. *Mental disorder* expresses the paradigm of the professional who judges the paradigm of the child (or adult) who is creating problems for family, school, or society at large. What is termed mental illness is a judgment by one person as to both the validity and the morality of the paradigm of another. (At times the patient agrees with the therapist that something is wrong with his or her paradigm; at other times, the patient will disagree and maintain the correctness of his or her personal paradigm.)

There is nothing inherently wrong in the valuation of one paradigm by another; indeed, it is necessary. Scientists constantly evaluate the theories of fellow scientists. The goal of a scientific revolution is the cessation and removal of a paradigm judged to be less worthy and adequate than a competing paradigm. However, both the process of evaluation and the criteria that comprise these processes are often made clear in science. One scientific theory is better than another if it is more logically consistent, more explanatory, and more testable and has greater heuristic value. These and other criteria allow scientists to evaluate the moral nature of their enterprise.

Individuals, as scientists and as citizens, also must evaluate the paradigms of his or her fellows in a society from the perspective of a given paradigm. Any given individual may develop a personal theory or engage in personal problem solving that his or her fellows consider inadequate, obnoxious, disgusting, destructive, strange, uninterpretable, dangerous, or a combination of these and other moral criteria. Moral enterprise exists in all societies, as people evaluate each other's modes of making sense of the world and the manner in which they adapt to that same world.

A problem is immediately created by the use of the medical model because, to most professionals and ordinary people, calling another mentally ill is merely descriptive, not judgmental. As will be argued, mental illness or disorder is clearly a judgment. Compounding the problem, the disguised judgment no longer requires that professionals make explicit the criteria of their judgments. The unintended consequences discussed below flow from this most serious mistake.

Various hidden criteria contained in the judgment qua description justify calling individuals mentally ill. The actual criteria used by therapists in judging the inferiority of the patients' paradigms may be that (1) the patients are merely different in some way or disapproved of by the culture's values; (2) individuals, in their own judgment or that of others, may be deemed incompetent in satisfying needs or solving problems related to their living; (3) patients are experiencing crises in their operating paradigms and suffering emotionally; or (4) individuals may be stubbornly defending their paradigms and utilizing defenses as they experience themselves being attacked both intellectually and morally.

As a result of the rise in the scientific method and scientific materialism expressed in the work of Bacon, Kepler, Galileo, Newton, Darwin, Freud, and others, a belief emerged that deviancy resulted from biological problems rather than spiritual problems. The natural sciences emerged to replace religion and philosophy as the authority seeking to explain human behavior (Giorgi 1970). Society replaced the shared paradigm in which "strange" thought and behavior could be understood and dealt with as demonic possession with the view that these same behaviors could be conceptualized and changed by medically treating flaws in a person's brain and nervous system. The medical model, rooted in the emerging scientific methods and increasingly successful in diagnosing and treating problems in human anatomy and physiology, was now employed to explain and control deviant individual paradigms. The religious rituals and torture employed by the church to save souls were replaced by the "talking cure" of psychoanalysis and with the chemical and physical therapies of a new field of medicine.

THE MYTH OF MENTAL ILLNESS

The creation and revolution of a new paradigm were thus accomplished. The new paradigm, however, was built upon a myth. Mental illness and psychotherapy were the words to describe and replace sin and exorcism (Szasz 1974). However, these new words are as flawed and unscientific as those they replaced. Although the new methods were quite different from the old, they were as often as cruel and invasive. The use of psychosurgery and insulin-induced seizures represents a moral low point in dealing with human beings who have problems in living. A flawed paradigm based on the supernatural was replaced by another flawed paradigm in which moral values were confused with scientific, nonevaluative description and in which psychologically meaningful behavior was confused with the neurological and biochemical factors from which behavior is organized.

Let me briefly describe why mental illness must be a myth and why searching for it is likened by Sarbin and Mancuso to the search for the unicorn. As stated earlier, behavior can be either described or judged. Deviancy can be defined statistically or be evaluated in such a way as to define it as good or bad, acceptable or unacceptable. How people are supposed to live, suggest Perry London (1986) and Laurence Kohlberg (1984), can only be demanded and expressed by the use of the word *should*. Unacceptable thoughts and behavior are those that should not be. Judgments specifically concerning human behavior are moral in nature. While many criteria can be utilized to define why a paradigm should or should not be, the use of the words should and shouldn't, good and bad, is necessarily moral in nature. As such, these words are based on personal opinion. There is no objective way of defining goodness, badness, beauty, ugliness, or a whole panoply of moral terms.

Personal moral opinion, that is, judgments of human behavior, no matter how justified, belongs to the realm of moral philosophy and religion and not to scientific enterprise. It is the confusion of moral judgment with scientific description and of medical judgment with judgments of behavior that leads to so many of the difficulties in the medical model and its failure to comply with scientific standards. When a medical doctor describes my blood pressure in measurably specific terms (e.g., 150/100) and judges my blood pressure to be high, that judgment carries no moral implications concerning the behavior of my coronary vascular system. Moreover, the descriptive criteria of that judgment are explicit. It is a true medical judgment. A psychiatrist who judges the "defiance" by a child of the rules established by authority in school is perforce making a clear moral judgment. In pretending that the "rebellious," "defiant" child is the province of medicine, the psychiatrist hides his moral judgment under the cloak of medical expertise. It takes a great deal of mental manipulation to convince oneself that medical training in the coronary artery system makes one an expert in the moral standards of school children, but this is regularly done in our culture.

When the church dealt with deviancy, it was clear that it did so because of moral authority. While the church explained deviant paradigmatic behavior in supernatural terms, its goal in changing these paradigms was one of changing sinfulness to goodness. When psychiatry replaced the church as the judge and jury in matters of moral deviancy, it created a new metaphor that not only seemed to explain such deviancy but also justified changing or operating on it. Remember, a paradigm consists of both theory and operating procedures. The inherent moral nature of psychiatric goals was hidden and denied by the terms *illness* and *health*. Sin had become medicalized. Mental illness masked a moral "verdict" (Sarbin and Mancuso 1980) concerning unwanted behavior, while mental health became a metaphor for the opposite judgment. Psychological processes considered disordered were those unwanted in the paradigmatic judgment of society (or the individual) and its new moral agency, the growing mental health field spearheaded by psychiatry.

Let me deal for a moment with the theoretical concept that deviant paradigms are the product of biological anomalies and diseases. This supposed fact justifies the inclusion of medicine in the moral management of deviant behavior. No matter the causes of a behavior, if that behavior is purposeful and under the control of the individual, then judgments of it are inherently moral in nature. If the behavior is merely the reflexive result of organic neurological damage, then the behavior represents a true symptom of a physical or real illness. The sneezing involved in a cold or the hiccuping caused by an upset stomach is no more moral than the behavior of the arteries in creating high blood pressure.

Sarbin and Mancuso, quite correctly, call schizophrenia a moral verdict, rather than a disease. These authors review fifteen hundred studies on schizophrenia, which were attempts to prove a biological underpinning of the schizophrenic paradigm with its unacceptable modes of perceptual experience (termed *hallucinations*), thought (called *delusions*), and operating behaviors (termed *bizarre*). Sarbin and Mancuso demonstrate that no studies exist to prove such an underpinning. However, I believe, that Sarbin and Mancuso miss the important point made previously. Were science to prove that the schizophrenic paradigms are merely symptoms of brain injury, then schizophrenia would be no more a mental illness than, say, Parkinson's disease. Parkinsonian paralysis and tremors are never referred to as mental illness, as they are devoid of psychological meaning; thus, judgments of them are never moral in nature. We do not say of a Parkinsonian patient, "He should not shake."

That there is as yet no proof of a clear correlation, let alone a cause-and-effect relationship, between brain injury and schizophrenic thought merely adds weight to the idea that schizophrenia involves psychological and social issues. It suggests that schizophrenia represents meaningful behavior and thus that any judgments of it are moral and not medical in nature. However, if such a cause and effect relationship were established and schizophrenia were to be seen as the same as Parkinson's disease, it would be called a neurological illness (a true medical judgment) and would be treated by neurologists. It would become the province of real science and real medicine and not of the pseudoscience of psychiatry. Schizophrenia, however, to those who deal with it, represents the attempts of an individual (who may have a real bioneurological illness) to adapt to the world. The world may make little sense or different sense to the struggling individual because of the physical illness. To the degree that the hallucinations and delusions are constructed by the individual to provide meaning to his world, they are psychological and social; therefore, judgments of them are moral and not medical. Schizophrenia is thus a moral judgment and not a mental illness. Mental illness is a mythological concept even when schizophrenia is involved to justify its reality. Perhaps a specific example can make this still clearer.

When a man at a party tells a joke considered inappropriate, the joke may well be called sick. "Sick" is metaphorical and could be a synonym for "dirty," "socially inappropriate," and the like. The word sick in this context is recognized as a moral evaluation. However, if we now call the joke teller "sick," a psychiatrist might well "diagnose" him as having an "antisocial personality disorder." Suddenly, the members of the party begin to treat this man differently than before. The metaphorical nature of "sick" is forgotten, and the term is now taken literally. A mental illness has been declared into existence, and a wide variety of confusions and unintended consequences follow. Instead of being asked to leave the gentle company of those offended by the joke, someone might demand that this sick man seek treatment for his mental illness.

Let me make as clear as I can that those of us who argue that mental illness is a myth are not arguing that hallucinations, delusions, bad jokes, and behavior judged incomprehensible and inappropriate do not also exist. The literature makes clear that many who disagree with Szasz believe that when he calls "schizophrenia" a socially created concept he is denying the existence of the behaviors that lead to the diagnosis in the first place. For example, Paul R. McHugh (1992) quotes Szasz as saying "In other words, the identity of an individual as a schizophrenic depends on the existence of the social system or (institutional) psychiatry." McHugh then goes on to write, "The only reply to such commentary is to know the patients for what they are in schizophrenia—people disabled by delusions, hallucination and disruption of thinking capacities and to reject an approach that would trivialize their impairments and deny them their frequent need for hospital care" (499).

Szasz, Laing, and all the rest of us who argue that mental illness is a myth do not for a second disagree that such people suffer and deserve help with their problem. However, we do argue that the real trivialization of the "schizophrenic" takes place when his or her whole phenomenological experience of being in the world is denied by calling such experience an impairment. Moreover, many of us would agree with Laing that the incarceration of the patient in a mental hospital is a "degradation ceremony" after which no real attempts are made to explain the nature of the hallucinations, delusions, and other constructed alternatives in reality that guide the life of the schizophrenic. By employing the faulty psychiatric paradigm that called unwanted behavior sick or disordered, a variety of intellectual, social, scientific, economic, political, and moral forces are unleashed. The unintended consequences of all these factors produce crises for those who use the paradigm and for those labeled by it. I now turn to the nature of some of these unintended consequences and the crises produced by them.

THE CRISES CREATED BY EMPLOYING THE MEDICAL MODEL

The crises created by the medical model involve problems of understanding, knowing, and morality. Niels Bohr has reportedly said that "one can judge a thing or understand a thing, but not at the same time." Although the judgments of the medical model pose as explanations, they remain judgments nonetheless.

Both the judge and the judged have an illusion of understanding that prevents real understanding. There is a simultaneous illusion that the medical model is morally neutral. The pretense of such neutrality invites a warping of the values and morals of all involved. As a result, those involved with the medical model experience crises in both their scientific understanding of one another and the morality of their social and professional relationships. It is my belief that the currently constituted mental health establishment is warping not only the science of human behavior but also the very foundation of societal morality.

Let me begin to describe the crises of many therapists in a personal manner. In 1988 and 1990 I wrote two letters to the editor that were published in the Nassau County Psychological Association's newsletter. I gave voice to some of my personal concerns, as well as to potential solutions to the difficulties that I and my field seem to be experiencing. I wrote, "Many of us are weary of calling the victims of abuse and injustice who come to us for sympathy, understanding and help in sorting out realty from distortion, 'sick' or 'mentally ill.' " I suggested that we, as a field and as individuals, are at our moral and scientific best "when we create a non-judgmental atmosphere in which individuals 'depoliticize' (Laing 1982) their experiences and come to understand the perception, thoughts, memories, interpretations, as well as emotions and drives that comprise experience. Individuals sort out realities from fantasy, lie from truth, justice from injustice, and thus live lives of meaning and purpose which are of their own choosing."

I closed my second letter by asking, "Are there other members in NCPA who would like to . . . return Psychotherapy to its rightful roots? Are there others who might be interested in meeting once a month, at a mutually convenient time, to discuss the growing literature critical of the medical model, as well as attempt to heal the intrapsychic and interpersonal rifts created by our common professional 'mental disorder'?" I concluded by providing my name and phone number.

The calls I received were many. People were often joyful that someone had given voice to their own doubts, confusion, angers, and frustration. Others were sad as they poignantly described the personal pain of signing insurance forms that labeled people sick whom they otherwise liked and respected. Still, others grew enraged describing the processes of labeling school children disordered at "Committee of the Handicapped" meetings, when they knew that calling these children bad names only adds stigma and pain to already tenuous school adjustments. In the end, one colleague remarked "that the child is given to a teacher to work with. No medical care is either needed or available." Still others described the humiliation of working in hospital settings in which medical directors made decisions better made by the psychologist and social worker therapists, who ultimately were to work with the patients assigned them.

In many of my discussions, therapists spoke of confusions resulting from the fact that they knew they were neither involved with a medical procedure nor working with patients; yet they were unable to find the alternative words to describe these phenomena. However, no matter how great the pain, confusion, fear, anxiety, and loathing professed, no one wished to meet regularly because to change things was fraught with too many dangers cast in economic, political, moral, and intellectual terms. "If the insurance companies stop paying us, how will I earn a living?" "If I express these ideas to my supervisor, I will be either called crazy, fired, or both." "Keep up the good fight, but you needn't call me back. This is too much for me to take on."

Three consistent themes of conflict emerged from my discussions with my colleagues, in addition to fears of reprisal and economic deprivation. Hinted at previously, they can be explicated and discussed at this juncture. The first conflict is created by the therapist's desire to understand his patients and foster understanding in the patient, which is blocked by the very act of diagnosing a patient with a moral judgment. The second conflict involves the therapist's struggle to see patients in humanistic terms. Humanism demands that all human beings be taken seriously as to their thoughts and feelings, the choices they make, and the responsibilities that accrue from those choices. The third conflict involves the therapist's prevalent desire to be the patient's advocate. The institutions that pay the therapist are those that are judging the patient mentally ill according to their institutional standards. When the therapist is paid by parents, school, and so on to cure someone, that is, to change the behavior unwanted by the institution to behavior wanted by the institution, the therapist can hardly be an advocate of the client.

I will return to these three related conflicts in subsequent chapters, but wish to expand upon them just briefly here. To understand another human being, one must begin by comprehending and accepting that human being's experience of reality. Experience is provided by the perception, thoughts, anticipations, needs, and emotions as they relate to real and imagined constructions of experience. To understand others is to understand them in the context in which they live. To comprehend another is to see the world from that person's point of view. It is "to walk a mile in another's shoes." Therapists often do this when they either ignore or refuse to employ the judgments inherent in the medical metaphor.

Once diagnosed, however, the individual's perceptions, thought, and memories are invalidated as sick or disordered. The individual is not seen through his own experiences. The "sick" individual is described free of the context in which thoughts, emotions, and behavior occur. Thinking is always about something. Behavior is goal directed and purposeful only within a given context. Both the context and the history of the context are ignored, as the diagnosed individual becomes motivated by his sickness, rather than toward or away from the goals provided by environmental, social, historical, political, economic, and familial contexts. Finally, the sick individuals are not responsible for their behavior. If one is not responsible because one is not capable of choice, then one is a puppet, a programmed machine or a collection of twitching neurons. How can one understand, advocate for, and humanize individuals and, at the same moment, make them into "nonpersons" (Sarbin and Mancuso 1980)?

All of these conflicts are especially accelerated in the case of children brought by frustrated parents or referred by an exasperated school. How often have I heard school psychologists rage against "irrational teachers," "tyrannical principals," "dysfunctional abusive families," and yet work with a child diagnosed with "Oppositional Defiant Disorder." (I wonder why the DSM does not have a category of "Overly Conformist Disorder"?) The diagnosed child is sick because he breaks minor rules and opposes adult authority. What crises are produced in the therapist under these inherently conflicted, tension-laden situations?

The unintended consequences of the medical paradigm involve more than just the intrapsychic crises of therapists. As I have suggested, the whole field is involved, as well as society itself. Let me turn to a brief description of what might be described as the macrocrises of the field of therapy engendered by the use of the medical model. The inconsistencies and hypocrisies created by the use of pseudomedicine are reflected in a number of related areas: (1) There can be no agreement as to who does psychotherapy. Does medicine, social work, or psychology provide its trainees with superior credentials to decide the moral worth of an individual's thought and behavior? (2) There can be no agreement as to what constitutes mental illness. The number of diagnostic categories grows exponentially, as anyone may declare any behavior considered unwanted to be a new mental illness. (3) There can be no agreement as to what constitutes treatment. There are, at last count, hundreds of competing therapies. New treatments are being added continuously. Let us examine each crisis in turn.

When psychologists gained a foothold in the field of psychotherapy during World War II, they initiated a battle with medical psychiatry that goes on today. These battles deplete the assets in both fields as M.D.'s and Ph.D.'s contest for control over clinics and hospital, vie for private practices and third-party insurance payments, and struggle to be considered for state aid and federally funded programs. The struggle has largely been decided in favor of the psychologists, but medicine attempts to retaliate all the time. Psychologists still find themselves wedded to the Diagnostic and Statistical Manual (DSM); and if psychiatry does issue forth a promised handbook of prescribed treatment, they will once again be determining the battlefield in which psychology must go to war.

As a psychologist, I have found it to be a source of continuous professional distress that I, until recently, could not define my professional roles in terms positive to psychology. Instead, I had to pretend to be a "little doctor" infringing on the medical prerogative of those trained in medicine. I have watched my colleagues lose their souls in this battle as they publicly claim to be experts in a medical procedure, while privately recognizing their expertise in psychological understanding of their patients. Many now watch with rising concern a segment of psychologists vie for the right to dispense psychotropic medication. Although this new venture might lead to increased privileges and enhanced income, it represents a total capitulation to the medical model. Arthur Kovacs (1988) has eloquently and passionately advised psychotherapists to "say, No! to drugs" and reclassify psychotherapy as a social science, rather than a health science. Voices are raised here and there against psychology's final embrace of medicine, but by and large the bulk of psychologists seem oblivious to the dangers inherent in this latest and rather extreme betrayal of psychologically defined psychotherapy.

When a physician prescribes a real medicine for a real illness, he has in mind a chemical that will change the function of an organ of the body, either by reducing the pathogenic effects of bacteria or by altering the biochemistry of that organ. When a psychiatrist prescribes a drug, he is attempting to change unwanted behavior. It is the unconscious awareness that medicine has nothing to do with morality that opened the door to psychology in the first place. As psychologists can understand and change unwanted behavior as well as psychiatrists, why should they not also utilize drugs to deal with moral verdicts?

The intrusion of psychology into the mental health profession led social workers to be trained in clinical techniques. There are now more M.S.W.'s practicing psychotherapy than the combined total of M.D.'s and Ph.D.'s. Clinical social workers are included in health insurance plans and establish and maintain psychoanalytic training programs too numerous to count. M.S.W.'s direct clinics, wards, and mental hospitals. Because they are now as expert as any others in making moral verdicts and changing unwanted behavior, can it be long before they, too, claim the right to dispense psychotropic medicine?

The illogical nature of the present trend can be elucidated with still another example. If Ph.D.'s and M.S.W.'s do, indeed, practice medicine when they diagnose and treat mentally ill patients, why do they not seek also to work in the operating room as surgeons or practice internal medicine? Would the reader take an electrocardiogram from a psychologist or allow a social worker to perform a sigmoidoscopy? Would anyone in society ever entertain the idea of such behavior? The absurdity of non-M.D.'s practicing medicine is somehow missed when we insist that psychotherapy is a medical procedure.

If there is no agreement as to who can do psychotherapy, there is certainly no end to the proliferation of mental illness. DSM I contained sixty "mental illnesses"; DSM III contains 230. How many new "illnesses" will exist when DSM IV, V, and VI are published? Any unwanted behavior can be declared to be an illness or disorder. Anyone can make a verdict and declare into existence a new treatable problem. The effects of a couple of cups of coffee are now mental disorders. Was the Inquisition ever as conservative in its definition of sin as the American Psychiatric Association is in its?

A newspaper article reports that a Long Beach, California, psychiatrist has suggested that individuals working out ninety minutes a day may be suffering from "hypergymnasia." I believe the good doctor missed one here. People who do not go to the gym at all must suffer from "hypogymnasia." In a humorous article, Stuart A. Kirk (1986) writes of his discovery that he had "Restless Legs Sleep Disorder." He suggests that the current proliferation of mental illness representing any and all deviation from middle-class norms may ultimately provide every man, woman, and child with his or her own diagnosis. Democracy in action!

Mental disorders can be canceled out of existence as quickly as they are created. Cunnilingus and fellatio, two serious perversions when I was in clinical training, are now proper techniques of foreplay. Thirty years ago people sought psychotherapy for wanting oral sex; now, they seek it because they don't. Homosexuality began as a mental illness, progressed to an alternative lifestyle, and, under the political pressures of gay groups, was dropped as an illness from the latest DSM. In fact, if one does not like homosexuals, one can be diagnosed as "homophobic." I will not belabor the point. Anyone can make a moral judgment about any aspect of human paradigm and declare himself the discoverer of a new disorder. A scientific field deserves better than such mockery.

Finally, we turn to the issues of what constitutes legitimate "psychotherapeutic" techniques. It must be clear to the reader by now that a field that cannot agree as to who should solve a problem and cannot properly define the problem can in no way adequately describe what should be done about it. The proliferation in explanatory paradigms has led to a proliferation of paradigmatic techniques. There are psychoanalytic therapies, behavior therapies, chemotherapies, and physical therapies all competing with one another, none with more evidence of success or failure than any other. Within the field of psychoanalysis, literally dozens of schools of therapy argue as to which is the legitimate group even to be called psychoanalysis. There are literally hundreds of ways in which professionals and nonprofessionals try to change unwanted behavior and thought into acceptable versions of the same.

Any activity that makes people learn something new, feel good or at least less bad, to behave more like others is considered in some way therapeutic. If promoted by an individual who calls himself a therapist, the pleasant and helpful activity is called a treatment. Learning to dance, sing, play the piano, make baskets, or even improve one's abilities in sexual intercourse are all now considered legitimate, medically significant activities. I, too, share the value that it is good to learn to dance. But not knowing how to dance and singing off-key are hardly illnesses, and learning to improve these activities has nothing to do with medicine. One might indeed be happier having multiple orgasms rather than no orgasms at all, but one's health, mental or otherwise, is hardly at stake.

I end this chapter with a brief discussion of how society is being negatively affected by the widening use of the mental health profession to deal with moral issues, while simultaneously pretending that the moral issues are medical in nature.

There are many therapists who resolve or avoid the personal crisis created when their loyalties are divided between patients and the institutions that want the patient's behavior altered. Some of us watch in fear and loathing as trained behaviorists use electric shock, solitary confinement rooms, and other methods I call torture in bringing children into compliance with institutional demands. The use of mental hospitals to warehouse the unwanted known as schizophrenics has been described for years, but now we see tens of thousands of hopeless, abused teenagers being subjected to locked wards and powerful neuroleptics in the name of treatment and of curing their illness (Darnton 1989). Electric shocks and solitary confinement (time-out rooms) are routinely used to control unwanted actions. The arguments that justify these behaviors involve insisting that we are medical doctors and that our treatments work. Torture and paradigm-altering chemicals do work; but, stripped of the medical nonsense surrounding these behaviors, we see the psychotherapist as an agent of the state and not of the clients (Beit-Hallahmi 1974). The end cannot justify the means. Remember that it was medical doctors who "cured" the "Jewish disease" in Nazi Germany in the "hospitals" of Auschwitz and Buchenwald (Lifton 1986). We dare not go down that road again; yet, we may have begun.

Reports of overzealous, undertrained, and underpaid social workers removing children from homes based on rumors of abuse are beginning to surface and become common (*New York Times*, December 4, 1990). The trauma of such separation to the parents and children so accused cannot be overestimated. State- and city-sponsored social workers, as well as teachers and other administrative and medical personnel, diagnose unhappy children as mentally ill and demand that parents take them for costly treatment. If the parents refuse, then protective services may be called anonymously and the children be removed from their homes. In the name of helping children and their families, the Constitution is further destroyed. Once again in the name of medicine and mental health, professionals act as judge and jury for the state. Their actions benefit no one, especially a society based on constitutionally guaranteed rights to face one's accuser and to remain innocent until proven guilty by a jury of one's peers.

Still, other therapists take the opposite tack in resolving or avoiding crises created by conflicted loyalties. These therapists create still another serious problem for society at large. The therapists of whom I speak side totally with the individuals they support. They instead diagnose society or social groups as sick. Often such individuals call themselves "humanists" or "radical therapists." They declare society to be the cause of their patient's problems and treat these people from a vantage point outside of the sick society. For example, Mary Fridley (1989) quotes Debra Pearl, director of the East Side Center for Short-Term Psychotherapy, who claims to be a practitioner of "social therapy" as saying, "We decided a long time ago to create a therapeutic approach that was sufficiently independent of society to ensure that when we were helping people to change, we didn't end up adapting them to a racist, sexist, homophobic, and repressed society because of the institution we were part of." The therapist has now created a new series of illnesses to be cured: racism, sexism, and homophobia. People who do not like those of another race, or women, or men, or homosexuals are judged. The judgment is denied, hidden by pseudomedicine, and the offending group of individuals is called sick.

Once society is seen as victimizing its members and making them mentally ill, we have an endless number of patients and an infinite need for psychotherapy. Zilbergeld (1983) refers to the process as the "shrinking of America." Sykes (1992) points out that a leader of the codependency movement puts the number of "adult children of alcoholic" abusing and merely critical parents at more than 230 million—more than the total national adult population. Everyone is a victim, everyone is mentally ill, no one is responsible for his or her behavior, and we are all patients in search of treatment. A man late for work is the victim of "compulsive lateness syndrome," while those who spend more money at the shopping mall suffer from "compulsive shopping syndrome." (I recently discovered that I am not responsible for writing this book, as I suffer from Psychiatric Diagnosis Denial Syndrome).

According to the above it is not the individual seeking treatment who is sick, it is society that is afflicted. The individual's treatment helps him escape into a society of healthy people—those who like everyone regardless of race, sex, or sexual preference. But, which society is that? To what society has the now healthy individual adapted? Can a society be sick, or is the therapist using a metaphor to describe attitudes unwanted by her and wanted by some members of society? Does one make a society more morally pure by removing members from it and creating a new society? And when a new society is created, or the old one changed, are the professionals who are the agents of change practicing medicine, or are they practicing politics?

I believe that both the behaviorists working in hospitals and prisons enforcing institutional compliance and those treating a "sick" society by removing members from it are, in fact, playing politics. However, if we are to change our society and or enforce its laws, let both the conservatives and the progressives announce their intentions and work their changes through legitimate political processes. We must stop hiding such activities and their various unintended consequences behind a cloak of pseudomedicine and pseudoscience.

Let me now outline a possible solution to the professional quagmire described above. On a personal level, I am no longer in crisis or confusion regarding my professional work. I have created and operate within a paradigm that is psychological, social, and, I believe, consistent with philosophical humanistic morality. I do find myself in constant conflict and disagreement with many colleagues. However, the conflict is in awareness and represents the conflict between competing paradigms in a scientific revolution. I am increasingly developing skills that allow me to advance the paradigm begun by Szasz, Laing, and Sarbin and Mancuso, as well as many others to be discussed in the next chapter.

Chinese wisdom suggests that if one lives in interesting times one is cursed. The field of psychotherapy and its attendant professionals are living through interesting times. As I write, our field may fully fracture and disintegrate into warring camps of academics and practitioners, M.D.'s, Ph.D.'s, and M.S.W.'s. Psychotherapists now work for insurance companies trying to contain costs as regulators of the efforts of other psychotherapists. Unless our field finds a common working paradigm based on accepted scientific principles and explicated moral goals, the current crisis will multiply and become increasingly destructive to all concerned.

II

PHILOSOPHICAL AND
SCIENTIFIC CONSIDERATIONS

2
DEFINITIONS AND PROBLEMS

Let me begin to define *psycho"therapy"* and its simile, *psychoeducation.* Psycho"therapy" retains the traditional word psychotherapy, altered by quotation marks that denote its metaphorical medical meaning. Psychoeducation comes closer to expressing what it is that psychotherapists do, when what they do is effective and represents the efforts of individuals working in voluntary cooperation. In this chapter, I will not only define psycho"therapy" but also begin describing the philosophical and scientific underpinnings of the process and concepts being defined. I hope to begin to provide the reader with the paradigm or model that has freed my thinking from the pseudomedical terminology that has created professional crises for me since I left graduate training more than two decades ago.

DEFINITION: PSYCHO"THERAPY" AND PSYCHOEDUCATION

Psycho"therapy" (psychoeducation) is a process in which one person, the therapist, helps those with whom he or she works to voluntarily experience a paradigm shift or create and carry out a personal scientific revolution. A paradigm involves both the individual's theory or model of the world and the skills utilized by the individual to act on that world. In a paradigm shift or scientific revolution, both the meaning of the world and the skills possessed by the individual change, permitting the individual to live differently than before in a world that has different phenomenological meaning than previously. The paradigms of various individuals, the theory and skills that comprise personality, allow those individuals to describe, explain, predict, and control both themselves and their world in order that human adaptation may be achieved. Human adaptation is achieved when individuals can live as they choose by satisfying the variety of human needs and solving the problems attendant on need satisfaction. As a result of a paradigm shift, the individual can better satisfy needs, more easily solve a wider range of problems, and achieve a more adequate adaptation.

The efforts of the therapist help others create paradigms that operate more according to the modes and morals appreciated and valued by practicing scientists. Such paradigms seek to operate empirically, that is, individuals are more likely to make their own observations and draw their own conclusions as to the nature of the problems they confront. Second, as scientists, these individuals create explanations for their observations that are more likely to be tentative and probabilistic in nature. The personal beliefs of each individual can be more easily discussed and debated. These paradigms are more capable of assimilating new information and accommodating themselves more easily to contradictory information. An increase in empiricism and theoretical understanding leads to resolutions of personal crises and far fewer unintended consequences in the individual's life. The scientific method has no peer when it comes to learning about the world in which one lives.

Individuals' theories of themselves and their world provide the meaning of that world and are comprised of the cognitive and affective evaluations of the various situations that comprise their personal environments. Therapy can be restated to be a process that allows individuals to think, feel, and act in such a way as to choose for themselves the best way to live. Psycho"therapy" helps people reevaluate their past, perceive their present with more veridicality, and more accurately anticipate their futures in terms of their present and past experiences.

Psychoeducation is an intense human interaction between two or more human beings, each of whom engages the other through the medium of an existing personal paradigm. These individuals are seen as essential equals and are described as having, within variations, the same psychological processes and the same human goals that define adaptation. Psycho"therapy" is always a noncoercive process, freely contracted between the parties that have chosen to work together. Moreover, psycho"therapy" is a means to an end and not an end in and of itself. Neither the therapist nor the process of therapy is to be the end goal representing a patient's successful adaptation. Therapy has as its goal a change in a patient's capacities to create and achieve the goals that represent human adaptation.

The individual as patient is replaced with the individual as developing scientist in the process of psycho"therapy" or psychoeducation. However, *scientist* is a very general term. Scientists function in a variety of specific paradigms. One of the paradigms the psycho"therapist" seeks to help others develop is the "individual as scientific psychologist." The improvement in the ability of an individual to be a psychologist permits an increase in both self-understanding and the understanding of others. The ability to explain, predict, and control oneself and others improves mutual understanding and interpersonal relationships.

Still other metaphors can describe individual functioning. Psycho"therapy" seeks to help individuals develop these capacities as well. Individuals must also be sociologists in order to understand how gender roles, race relations, social class, and familial interactions determine one's developing paradigm. Each individual must also determine social policy as part of his or her role in human interactions and therefore play the role of politician as well (Tetlock 1992). An individual must understand the physical and chemical world in which he or she lives to some extent and thus must be physicist and chemist. Increasingly important to life in our modern world is an understanding of one's own biological processes, demanding of each of us to be a scientific biologist as well. Each of us must understand the role we play in society's economic structure and must have some understanding as an economist as well. Marx was clearly Freud's equal in explaining much of human motivation. Each individual can understand the present and make accurate predictions of the future only if he or she understands the historical context in which he or she lives. Thus each individual must also be a historian (Butt 1990), not only of his or her own personal past but of his or her larger social context as well.

Science, politics, economics, and the like make life capable of sustaining itself by allowing human beings to organize, feed, and shelter themselves as well as heal themselves when they are ill or wounded. But it is art and, to an extent, entertainment that make life fully worth living. I will argue below that each individual also seeks to be a creative artist as a central feature of his or her adaptation. I will also argue that art and science, at their best, have more similarities than differences and spring from the same human adaptational struggles. To live creatively means more than just painting, writing, composing music, or the like. Creative parenting, teaching, cooking, athletics, and, yes, doing psycho"therapy" are enhanced when individuals add their own unique visions and skills to these and every other enterprise. There is still one more metaphor to be introduced, and that is the individual as mythologist. I will leave the discussion of this all-embracing human role for a later chapter.

One of the central goals of psycho"therapy" is to help others separate their scientific descriptions and explanations from their moral (and other types of) judgments. The process of psychoeducation not only allows the individual an increase in scientific understanding and skill but also inevitably and simultaneously fosters ethically based lifestyles and improved moral judgments as well. Psycho"therapy," as with all life processes, is concerned with success and failure in adaptation. Polanyi (1967) writes that success and failure in adaptation are necessarily critical. Moral judgments and ethical evaluations must provide the justification for all scientific, sociological, psychological, economic, political, and artistic actions. The goals of all psychological and social processes are organized by their perceived moral worth but are not reduced to those judgments. The goal of therapy is to improve the scientific methods of various individuals and to help them establish themselves as their own spiritual and moral philosopher—our final metaphor of the individual.

The definition of psychoeducation contains a number of philosophical and scientific assumptions, as well as a host of descriptions and moral judgments. What is the relationship of description to judgment? What is the relationship of any human activity and morality? What is the relationship of science, philosophy, and psycho"therapy"? What is science, and with what justification do I assume all individuals are scientists? What is the relationship of the psychological to the biological and the cultural in comprehending in human behavior? What are the political, economical, and moral implications of psycho"therapy"? These and other related questions will concern the rest of this chapter and the next.

Philosophical Issues Related to the Definition of Psycho"therapy" and Psychoeducation

In the last chapter, it was suggested that many of the serious problems created by the medical model involved the confusion of medical description with moral judgments. I suggested that is just one instance of a nearly universal process wherein people confuse moral judgments with factual descriptions. Individuals keep trying to satisfy their needs for moral worth with their needs to understand themselves and others in the world. Most of the people coming for therapy are suffering from crises created in exactly the same way. In order to avoid falling victim to the same mistake, I should like to first discuss the differences between description and judgment and then explicate the moral assumptions inherent in my definition of psycho"therapy." In this way, scientific concepts and ethical and moral considerations can be disentangled one from another, coordinated logically, and used more effectively and appropriately.

DESCRIPTION

How does one define "description"? Webster's first definition reads, "an act of describing," followed by "discourse intended to give a mental image of something experienced." In short, to describe something is to relate one's phenomenological or conscious experience of a thing or process. Objects are described in terms of their perceptual characteristics: feel, weight, color, shape, sound, taste, and smell. Processes are experienced in terms of movement, change, or some other transformation. Placement, context, and relationship all become part of the descriptive process. Tolman (1932) suggests that we know an object by the sum of its *discriminanda* and *manipulanda*.

Descriptions can be represented to others as pictures, as movements, by words, or by other symbols. The communication of one's conscious phenomenological experience rarely captures the fullness of what is subjectively felt. Ultimately our descriptions are based on personal felt qualities; the best we can hope for is that those to whom we transmit our descriptions feel or experience them in some way similar to our own. Because descriptions are based ultimately in subjective experience, they are always prone to distortions and biases as they become communications.

That descriptions are subjective and prone to bias and distortion does not mean that shared experience is impossible. Science still speaks of discovering the truth of things in its effort. We still speak of reality as well as subjectivity in day-to-day discourse. Michael Polanyi (1958) states that all knowledge involves personal knowing, but that science bases its existence on the assumption that things exist independent of their being cognized by the human knower. It is the assumption that things exist independent of our descriptions that allows us the ability to validate our experiences consensually. Descriptions, which form the basis of our knowing the world, are subject to the validations of other experiencers of our shared world.

Science, as we will see below, sets up procedures to regulate the process by which shared descriptions validate the experiences of the individual. Science bases its validity on the sharing of observation and description and refers to this process as empiricism. Consensually validated descriptions establish what are known as facts. Science tries to create a body of factual knowledge with which to begin explaining, predicting, and controlling the world. By demanding consistency in the symbols used to communicate felt experience, as well as describing in detail the procedures and conditions involved in making descriptions, science hopes to increase agreement as to the nature of the facts.

What are the facts of psychology? If we describe our experience of other people, we can speak only of the behaviors we observe, the physical appearance of the others, and the communicated symbols used by them to express their own phenomenological felt experience. If we describe our own psychological processes, we make facts of what we see, hear, smell, taste, and touch as well as what we think and feel in terms of biological needs and emotions. Our own subjective processes can be known only to ourselves, but in this book it will be taken as fact that similar processes exist in every human being. (In Chapter 4 I discuss the relationship between individual phenomenological experience and third-person description of the experiencing individual.)

JUDGMENT

Webster's defines judgment as "a formal utterance of an authoritative opinion." Such opinions compare the relative (or absolute) worth of things described. Judgments tell us what any set of facts is worth. They define how objects, processes, and the like, which can be described, are valued by those making the description. "Good" or "bad," "worthy" or "worthless," "better" or "worse," "beautiful" or "ugly" are all common judgments. No matter how much description and fact are used to justify judgments, they are always still opinions and stand or fall on the basis of the authority making them.

Specific judgments concerning the behavior or psychological processes of individuals are moral in nature. Morality establishes, in someone's opinion, the worthiness and goodness of behavior. Such judgments (as with all judgments) rest with the authority of those making them. Judgments, moral and otherwise, cannot be consensually validated. Judgments are never facts, no matter how authoritative the opinion of those communicating them. However consensually validated by the description of what a person does, no matter how we determine the facts of behavior—once a judgment is made, we are in the realm of moral philosophy and not descriptive psychological science.

For example, a man shoots and kills a dozen people in the act of committing a bank robbery. No matter how we agree that he and his actions are wrongful and bad, the badness is merely our opinion and is accepted on faith of our authority to utter the claim. The claims of moral authority can be accepted no other way except on the faith that the authority is justified in making the judgment. If every person in the world agreed that it was bad for our perpetrator to rob a bank and kill twelve people, the agreement is based on authority's opinion and faith in that opinion.

Judging and Describing

The processes of moral judgment are as universal as attempts to describe, explain, predict, and control. Actions have consequence. Things happen to us. Sometimes the things that happen to us are the consequences of the actions of others. Often, our actions are the cause of the things that happen to others. The events that happen to us and the actions that produce consequences are experienced not merely cognitively, but affectively as well. In the next chapter, I will argue that the meaning of an event is never merely perceptual or intellectual, but is emotionally felt as well. Affect is the result of the same bioevolutionary forces that produced cognition. We evaluate a situation, and emotion or other affects result. Some of these evaluations can be called pleasurable, others painful. On the simplest level, those consequences that hurt form the basis of the judgment "bad"; those consequences that feel good form the basis of the judgment "good" (Kagan 1984).

As cognition become more complex, as the developing being increases the range of events that can be described, so too does the basis of pain and pleasure increase and grow in complexity. The physical pleasures and pains of childhood broaden with the emergence of social awareness to include fear, shame, guilt, loss, grief, happiness, joy, love, and a host of other felt meaning states called emotions. Although culture does shape the emotional expressions, as well as the cognitive interpretations from which emotions spring, certain events in every culture create pleasure and pain that form the basis of judgments of good and bad.

Actions or events that increase the viability of the species, health, wealth, social cooperation, personal autonomy, and creativity usually produce positive affects, while those that decrease longevity, health, wealth, closeness, cooperation, autonomy, and creativity are experienced as painful. Those actions producing positive emotions will be declared to be good, while those producing painful emotions will be judged as bad. While specific actions and consequences can produce different emotions in different contexts and cultures, to the degree that the facts feel pleasurable and painful, they will be ultimately judged good and bad.

At the risk of extreme redundancy, let me again state that if we describe an individual's behavior and the thoughts and emotions which determine that behavior, and if we then describe the thoughts and emotions of those affected by that behavior, we remain in the area of psychological science. But the moment we determine that any action, emotion, or thought is "bad," "destructive," "irrational," "psychotic," "good," "creative," "logical," or "healthy," then we have left science for the field of moral philosophy.

The last paragraphs begin to make clear the link between description and judgments. Judgments are based on the description of actions and events and their experienced consequences. Behaviors become justified by the judgments made about them, while the judgments are justified by the consequences of the behaviors they judge. Behaviors most judged to be moral and justified are those deemed most necessary to survival, growth, increases in pleasant affect, such as love, happiness, and joy, and so on. One might say that humankind's collective morality is the justification of collective behavioral necessity.

Descriptions allow us entry into reality, permit us recognition of our adaptive needs and the means to satisfy those needs. We can protect ourselves, our children, and posterity to the degree that we can explain, predict, and control ourselves and the world around us. Judgments prioritize our efforts. Judgments create hierarchies of importance, they direct us as to the order in which to satisfy our needs, when to satisfy our needs, when our children's, and when to endure the hardships of self-neglect in order to satisfy the needs of posterity. We need to be scientists, and we need to be moral philosophers.

From this perspective we might expect that human beings would keep their judgments and descriptions both disentangled and appropriately coordinated. It would make sense to maximize our capacities both to describe the world and to form moral judgments based on those descriptions. What is and what should be would be clearly delineated in human consciousness. Given the description of a behavior and its consequences, one might also imagine that there would be every effort to create uniform judgments about that behavior. Given a judgment of a behavior, we would be able to justify the severity of the judgment from the consequences of the behavior as they exist in consensually validated facts.

But we have seen in Chapter 1 that modern psychiatry fuses most judgments with their descriptive underpinnings. Judgments of people are used as descriptions, the judgments are denied, and in effect no real descriptions exist. The psychotherapist is judging but without knowing that he does so. He becomes unable to describe because that is what he believes he is doing as he is judging. Science and moral philosophy both suffer.

Why does this happen? More important, is psychiatrically dominated psychotherapy the only field in which this occurs? I believe that the conditions in which science and moral philosophy are kept disentangled yet coordinated, where one can justify both description and judgment with the other, are virtually nonexistent. Science often takes the impossible stance that it deals with facts and makes no judgments, while religion often behaves as if judgment were its only function. Let us turn to some of the reasons why judgments and descriptions become severed, how one begins to be used as if it were the other, and what are the consequences that flow from this fusion.

The Confusion of Description and Judgment

An action may have both short-term and long-term consequences. Short-term consequences may be felt as pleasurable, while long-term consequences may be experienced as pain. Drugs may cause immediate happiness but long-term agony. Short-term consequences may be painful, but in the long term, these same behaviors may produce much pleasure. The pain of attending college may lead to higher salaries and a life lived with many more pleasures than if college were not attended. Individuals who see only short-term consequences may have great disagreements with the judgments of those who also can predict the long-term consequences. Such disagreements define every parent-child relationship to some degree.

The human race may collectively engage in behavior that can produce catastrophic consequences a century or more in advance. Moreover, a pattern of behavior may have pleasurable consequences for an individual who claims the behavior is good, but pain for the other who judges it as bad. Behavior of one individual may be destructive to the group upon whose functioning rests the long-term survival of the offending individual. When parents disagree with children, when adults cannot agree as to long-term consequences, and when the individual disagrees with the group, a moral authority must emerge and find a way to reconcile conflicting judgments.

When an authority judges the behavior of children or of adults as bad along some set of dimensions, both the authority and those agreeing with authority's judgment are accepting on faith the wisdom and fairness of those making the judgments. It is implicitly assumed that these judgments are necessary because of the predicted consequences of the behavior in question. However, a question immediately must be asked about the relationship of the moral authority and the morally faithful. What if the authority is no wiser or no fairer than those who are either the faithful or the judged? What if the moral authority sets forth rules that merely benefit authority? Under such conditions authority would be loath to make explicit the basis of its judgments and might be equally loath to have the faithful question the underlying facts of its judgment.

When authority is confronted with a challenge to its wisdom or fairness, it can either admit to ignorance or unfairness and lose the basis of its moral authority or act to prevent the discovery that its authority is arbitrary and without descriptive justification. Often authority acts to obscure the relationship between its moral judgments and the descriptions upon which they are based. Authority declares itself to be inherently knowledgeable as to what is right and wrong and simultaneously declares the faithful to be inherently ignorant as to right and wrong. At the moment of such a declaration, the ties between descriptions of consequence and judgments of authority are severed. As long as authority rules by decree and the faithful accept the inherent wisdom of authority, no one asks for the connection between descriptive facts and the judgments that both justify and are justified by them.

Similarly, the faithful might accept the judgment that they are inherently unable to make moral judgment and might then seek to sever the connections between judgments and descriptions. The faithful endow the authority with an enormous power and numerous rights and privileges, but they also demand that authority take responsibility for their (the faithful's) decisions and judgments. Authority demands of the faithful their loyalty and compliance to authority's judgment and implicitly accepts the responsibilities and burdens that the freedom to judge brings. However, because the relationship of judgment and description is severed, the basis of judgment turns from a justification based on description, explanation, and prediction to one based solely on authority and personal prerogatives.

The logical process of severing description from judgment usually occurs as follows. Let us take the sentence, "John finished his math exam fifteen minutes earlier than the rest of the class." Step one is to stop describing John's behavior and form a judgment instead. "John finished his math exam quickly." Next we shift the adverb "quickly," which defines our judgment of "taking the math test," to a judgment of John by making the adverb into an adjective: "John is quick in math." We might generalize our judgment and say, "John is intelligent." The process becomes complete when we say, "John is quick in math (or he finished early) because he is intelligent (or quick)."

We started with a descriptive factual observation: John finished his test ahead of the others. We end up with a complete tautology in which positive judgments "quick" and "intelligent" now explain the observation that produced the judgment in the first place. What have we achieved by the destruction of both grammar and logic? We have an explanation that can cover John's behavior across a wide number of situations without asking anything concerning the context of the behavior. Was John in the wrong class? Was the test unfair to the other students? What is the role of the school, as it might relate to John's education? The explanation of John's behavior magically emanates from John, and we like John better because of his fine personal attributes.

Let me provide one example from psychiatry, although in a later chapter I will recreate this argument with a number of DSM III diagnoses. Mary states, "Space ships are controlling my behavior." We do not understand why Mary says such a thing. Perhaps Mary feels guilty and powerless, and creating such a myth frees her from such feelings. We say "Mary says 'strange,' 'bizarre,' and 'psychotic' things." This is followed by "Mary is strange, bizarre, and psychotic." Why does Mary talk of spaceships? Because she is psychotic. We have judged her and believe we have described and explained her behavior. We even have justification to control Mary and never once ask what conditions of Mary's life might have led to such desperate behavior.

As description begins to disappear and moral judgments reappear, there are necessary attendant changes in economic, political, and social structures. Social structure become more vertical as the superior authority ascends above the morally inferior faithful. Power flows from the bottom to the top, as does economic wealth. Decrees and judgments flow from the top to the bottom. As this imbalance grows worse, more and more authority is required to maintain the increasingly vertical hierarchy. People are described less and judged more to maintain authority and its hold over the hierarchy. One begins to hear authority speak of the restive faithful as disobedient, defiant and in need of discipline and control. Children who so rebel become "oppositional defiant disorders" according to the authority of psychiatric psychotherapists.

What are some of the justifications shared by both authority and the faithful to create and maintain a vertical hierarchy? Almost universally there have been appeals to the supernatural to make ultimate judgments. The king rules by divine right, and at his side is the cleric who speaks directly for the higher power. The shared belief in a social hierarchy created by God marked the Middle Ages, which, as Fromm (1950) points out, was one of the last times in history that the impoverished were contented with their place at the bottom of the social hierarchy.

In our time, God is still involved to endow authority with innate wisdom and goodness, but often other factors are also in evidence. State security and nationalistic concerns have largely replaced religion as authority's most powerful justification . In the case of psychiatry, the appeal to scientism (self-proclaimed worth of scientific authority) and higher education give the doctor the authority to make judgments and sever their connection from factual justifications.

Many factors control the stability of a vertical hierarchy based on judgments. First, all of the participants must get some needs met, even if these needs are unarticulated. The authority enjoys power and privilege, the faithful freedom from the responsibilities of growth and decision making. The authority must prove to have some real wisdom; group coherence must be maintained to some degree; day-to-day life must include some gratifications for the faithful. No hierarchy can be maintained once the faithful lose complete faith in authority. Authority without legitimacy is authority no longer (Fukuyama 1992).

However, much of the maintenance of a vertical hierarchy comes from the fact that people at all levels of the system lose the ability to describe themselves, their lives, and the social system of which they are a part. Judgments are internalized and need no further descriptive justification. Often people will become terrified to move either up or down in the system. They see those above them as godlike, omnipotent, and omniscient, while those below them are seen as dirty, stupid, evil, inferior, and psychotic.

One of the outcomes of a vertical system is the creation of suprahuman and subhuman beings. Often there are no human beings, but individuals loved by God and those hated, those with true perfect knowledge and those moronic and idiotic, and so on. Human beings can create vertical hierarchies in which some individuals make no mistakes and some make only mistakes. Any descriptive difference between people can then be judged to place them higher or lower in the hierarchy. Race, sex, age, religion, national origins, and the like are severed from their descriptions and become indications of moral superiority or inferiority. Any and all individual differences become hierarchically approved judgments. Vertical hierarchies often move from authoritarian to totalitarian. How and what people think or feel can be judged (as well as what they do) and placed in hierarchical order. With increased dehumanization of the faithful and increased deification of authority, abuses of power become ever more visible and brutal. There can be no debates or discussions between levels in the hierarchy. Psychological, social, political, and economic discussions are inimical to labels such as lazy, unintelligent, or mentally ill. Social control and the maintenance of discipline become increasingly important to those in authority.

In such hierarchies, the professor, the teacher, the scientist, and the artist become hated and feared figures. Science usually succumbs before art, as artists have traditionally found a variety of metaphors with which to describe their world that authority finds difficult to interpret. The poet, the painter, and the composer continue to describe, but in more metaphorical, abstract, and indirect fashion. In our century, we have seen the devastating effect of vertical hierarchies in Hitler's Nazism and Stalin's perversion of socialism. Both created rigid hierarchies that ultimately destroyed the political, scientific, and economic structures from which they sprang. I will return to the psychological and social consequences when moral labels replace their descriptive justifications. But for now, it is time for me to state my own scientific and moral position, one I believe will avoid the vertical hierarchy with its destructive effects and allow me to defend scientifically and morally my definition of psycho"therapy."

EXPERIENCE VS. BEHAVIOR IN HUMANISTIC
PHILOSOPHY

An issue related specifically to the practice of psycho"therapy" requires discussion at this juncture, and that is the difference between thought, emotion, and overt behavior and their relations to moral judgment. Sigmund Freud was led to the tenets of psychoanalysis by his discovery that the gross symptoms of mental illness were related to an individual's attempt to control sexual (and often other) impulses and feelings. Individuals seemed to fear that if they felt sexual feelings, these would take control of their behavior with disastrous social consequences.

Freud originally came to the conclusion that these sexual feelings or thoughts were related to actual seductions that had taken place during the young person's childhood (Masson 1985). In our own era we would have called these events sexual abuse and pedophilia. However, for reasons not to be conjectured about, Freud later changed his opinion and "discovered" the Oedipus and Electra complexes to explain the mental illness in question. The child had not really been seduced, argued Freud, but feared the consequences of innate sexual longings for his or her parents and siblings.

The child, Freud is suggesting, is reacting to fantasy and biologically determined wishes with the same fear and intensity as if these feelings were the result of actual events and behaviors. I agree with Masson (1985) and Fromm (1980), as well as others, that Freud made a terrible error in blaming the child for imagining an event that had really happened. Psychoanalysis was turned from a potentially revolutionary activity that supported the victims of abuse and injustice into a conservative endeavor that blamed the victim and supported the victimizer.

However, Freud realized that the cure for the problem came in the free ventilation, expression, and acceptance of the sexual feelings and the memories surrounding them. In short, regardless of who was to blame for these feelings (no small issue, as we will see later in this book), the feelings and thoughts surrounding them were to be accepted by the psychoanalyst and never to be judged by them. Freud was making a clear distinction between experience and the thing experienced.

If we examine the society that Freud operated within, we see that, in the moral hierarchy of Christian religion, sexual thoughts and feelings were as sinful as actual sexual behavior. When Catholicism was in power and where it still was the dominant religious paradigm, individuals guilty of sinful experience (thought and feeling) could confess to their priests and be given absolution. Martin Luther believed that it was confession that made the church corruptibly powerful, and in his new Protestant faith priests no longer heard confessions.

However, Luther and Calvin, who followed Luther, still retained the philosophy that thought, feelings, and behavior were equally sinful if they dealt with certain issues. Freud's Vienna was a Protestant city during the Victorian era. From many pulpits in the land, children were harangued by preachers who described the pits of Hell and eternal damnation that followed impure thoughts. It was this context that explains Freud's great moral stand. During the analytic session, thought and feeling are encouraged, rewarded, and held to be morally right and not sinful.

I believe that the separation of thought and feeling from overt behavior is morally correct because it is psychologically necessary. If, as humanists, we believe people must be free to choose their actions and accept the consequences that flow from them, then they must understand the basis of their choices and be free to reason as to their consequences before they act upon them. Psycho"therapy" always (and psychotherapy usually) holds that what people say about their thoughts and feelings should not be met with criticism. While I will discuss the psychological necessity of free speech and thought later, I simply state that the morality of psycho"therapy" allows that human experience, perceptions, thought, and affect are not subject to moral control.

3

SCIENCE AND HUMANISM

Lawrence Kohlberg (1984) both excited and infuriated the intellectual community when he traced the development of moral understanding in children from a Piagetian constructionist position. Kohlberg suggested that morality develops in three stages, each of which reflects the rules of cognitive organization that determine thinking at that stage. Young children during the sensory motor and early preoperational stage are hedonists. They define good and bad solely in terms of the pleasure or pain that immediately follows an action. Pleasing a parent, who in turn pleases the child, becomes part of this hedonism as the children become aware that other people exist and react to their behavior.

With the emergence of middle childhood and concrete operations, the morality of hedonism gives way to the "morality of authority" or conventional morality. Children have now internalized a set of rules. They understand that good behavior is that which follows the rules; bad behavior deviates from the rules. However, though goodness and badness are now understood in terms of rules, the rules are not understood in terms of the consequences that flow implicitly from the rules themselves. The rules are defined by authority and are good (or bad) because authority states they are so. Thus the rules are moral because the politician, the teacher, the cleric, and the parent say they are moral.

The child's reward and punishment in following the rules of authority are found in the consequences of authority's statements that to follow the rules is to be a good child. To deviate from the rules is to be a bad child. The rules themselves are not to be questioned, nor does the child ask for whom the rules are made. If the authority says the rules are good, they are good. No further discussion can take place. Kohlberg believed that most human beings remain rooted in conventional morality, seeking to be called good by authority and avoid being called bad by the same. (The medical model of psychiatry, with its implicit reliance on authority and diagnoses, clearly operates at this level of moral development.)

Finally, suggests Kohlberg, there is the emergence of formal operations, which lead to a "postconventional morality" or a morality based on "self-accepted principles." Children are now old enough to use logic and ask about the relationship of means and end, where their behavior is the means and the ends are the consequences of their actions. Good and bad are now based on the individuals' own perceptions of how they have affected others. The rules are followed because the individuals accept the necessity of the rules from the perspective of their own authority.

Kohlberg believed that once children understood that their behavior affected others, which in turn would determine how others affected them, they would naturally seek to develop relationships that were fair, based on mutually agreed-upon contracts and evolved along consistent democratic principles. In short, Kohlberg believed that morality had to be based on principles emerging from individuals who saw themselves as their own moral authority (a principle accepted by psycho"therapy").

There are two criticisms that, I believe, can be levied at Kohlberg. The first is that, as does Piaget, he sees morality almost exclusively as developing from intellectual growth and does not fully take into account the role that affect plays in the emergence of moral understanding. The second criticism, and the only one I will deal with at this juncture, is that Kohlberg sees moral development as basically pushed by internal maturational forces and does not pay enough attention to the social context in which this development takes place.

In Chapter 5 I present a theory of personality, one of whose cardinal principles is that behavior cannot ever be understood unless one understands the internal rules of development of that behavior and the rules governing the social context of behavior. I argue in the next chapter that psychological development is simultaneously shaped by internal biological demands and by the social situations in which the psychological must function.

Therefore, I believe that hedonistic, conventional, and postconventional modes of morality not only grow out of the developing individual's changing rules of thought organization and perceptions of reality but reflect, as well, a type of interpersonal structural organization that selectively reinforces different types of moral understanding. Hedonism both produces and is reinforced by social anarchy; conventional morality shapes and is reinforced by a vertical social structure that depends on moral judgments and authority's power, while a morality of self-accepted principles fosters and flourishes in humanistically conceived and democratic structure.

In the last chapter, I described how people become good and bad and how they stay that way in vertical structures. I agree with Kohlberg that human development determines that we pass through the stages of hedonism and authority-based morality, but that if adults remain at such a level, a fixation has occurred in their development. Only the development of both scientific thinking capable of description and a conscious faith in democratic living can guide the emergence of postconventional morality.

I. Bernard Cohen (1985) suggests that the rise of the scientific method was one of the most powerful forces for democracy in human history. The idea that each person could understand the world for himself or herself led to the increased notion that the same individual could learn to make moral choices. It must be remembered that the scientific revolution grew out of the Enlightenment and a number of religious and political revolutions that weakened centralized religious and political authority. The growth of science paralleled the growth of individualism and coincided with the French and American revolutions, which established the principles of participatory democracy and the growth of philosophical humanism. A free scientist and a free artist were now held, in some measure, to be the new authority in a new type of society.

The definition of psycho"therapy" is predicated on the notion that the individual as scientist and as philosophical humanist best flourishes in and adds to a participatory democracy. I agree with John Dewey (1929), one of the currently forgotten sages of our century, that development should foster the growth of empirical scientific skills as well as a respect for and love of democratic institutions. Following Dewey, I believe that the psycho"therapist" must anchor himself in two fixed notions: The best means of understanding the world is the scientific; the best way of living together is democratic. Finally I agree that scientific attitudes foster the growth of humanistic democracy just as democracy values the independent style of learning, problem solving, and creativity that marks the scientific endeavor at its best.

Let me turn to the specific process in which I have invested my faith: science and moral humanism. I cannot state with certainty that these principles represent a morality whose long-term consequences will benefit future generations. Doestoevsky has stated that without a God (or heaven) any behavior becomes lawful. Many religious leaders would agree that only divine guidance can assure both the survival of the species and the happiness that human beings seek to experience.

I believe, however, that the world is turned on its head and that only when human beings are raised to be their own moral philosophers and base their philosophy on the best of secular wisdom will the human race have a chance at successful living. More important for the topic at hand, only when "therapy" is based on and fosters a genuine psychological science and its goals and methods are justified by a morality that emerges from a human understanding at its fullest, only when both our science and our morality are clearly stated and followed in principle, then and only then will our field stop both its suppression of the individual and its participation in the destruction of the society in which it operates.

WHAT IS SCIENCE?

The primary metaphor of this book is that of the individual as scientist. It is time to discuss briefly the activity of the scientist from a psychological perspective. Science is a psychological activity, and psychology is the science that deals with the psychology of the scientist as well as other individuals who might become scientists. Laing (1967b) calls psychology the "prince of sciences." As with all human activities, science has a historical development, and the scientist has a personal history reflecting individual development. Science and scientific behavior are to be understood in political, economic, sociological, and religious contexts as well.

In recent years, strong attempts have been made to define science from a philosophical logical position. The logical positivists suggested that science deal only with observables and that scientific theory be limited to those statements capable of being proven with observable empirical data. Positivism, especially as it influenced psychology, reached its zenith with Bridgman (1927) and the concept of operationism. All concepts were to be defined purely in terms of the operations used to measure them. Skinner's radical behaviorism remained closest to Bridgman's and to positivistic demands when, for example, he would define hunger as "hours of food deprivation."

Positivism failed on logical grounds when it was discovered that many scientific statements could not be proven but remained scientific in the eyes of those utilizing them. For example, astronomy generates many hypotheses that cannot be directly tested and proven. The psychology generated by positivism required that the field ignore human consciousness, phenomenological experience, thought, emotions, and other critical psychological concepts. Human beings were reduced to the status of robots as simple environmental stimuli elicited responses from them or as reinforced behaviors were emitted from these machinelike beings.

Positivism gave way to the work of Karl Popper (1945, 1961), who argued that statements are scientific only if they are falsifiable. Once again a vigorous debate ensued (see Hacking 1981) as to whether or not a single logical criterion can define so broad a set of activities as science. It was soon pointed out that the statement, "All scientific statements are falsifiable," is itself unfalsifiable. Feyerabend (1988) argued vociferously that to rely on the aspect of logic or one methodology could only strangle the creativity inherent in the scientific process. More recently, Shanes (1992) and Puhakka (1992) have suggested that both positivism and Popper's falsifiability deal only with the justification of scientific activity while ignoring the crucial aspect of scientific discovery.

Other criteria are used to define and delineate scientific activity. One oft-cited criterion of true science is objectivity. The objective scientist is expected to be a detached observer of phenomena who never allows any personal biases to influence his or her judgments. In addition, the scientist is a supremely logical individual whose unbiased observations are complemented by what Popper (1945) calls the *rationality principle*. It is as if, suggests Bronowski (1963: 33), the sciences have attempted to "divide the world into ourselves (scientists) on one side of the screen as spectator, and everything else as a spectacle on the other side, which we are remotely observing." I would add that on one side of the screen are the rational beings and on the other beings of varying degrees of irrationality.

Why have all these attempts at defining science failed? Do they contain any truth? Do they shed light on the scientific process, or is this process unknowable and beyond our ability to describe? What accounts for science's success (which is not in doubt) if not its adherence to some principles of discovery? These questions are crucial and require some answer if I am to continue with both my metaphor of the individual as scientist and my need to establish a definition of scientific psychology capable of generating a process called psycho"therapy."

To help resolve the questions concerning a definition of science, let us examine a revolution in the philosophy of science that emerged with the work of Thomas Kuhn (1970), Michael Polanyi (1958, 1966, 1967, 1969), and Merton (1968). These individuals, as well as others, reflected dissatisfaction with the philosophical establishment that argued for a strictly logical definition of science. As early as the 1910s and 1920s physicists (Heisenberg, Bohr) came to realize that the act of observing a phenomenon both changes the phenomenon and, in part, determines the nature of what is being observed. Phenomenologists such as Husserl (1962) pointed out that reality is experienced reality. One cannot ignore the experiencer's participation in the encounter with that which becomes experienced reality.

When physics foundered on the issues raised by quantum mechanics, it turned to psychology for answers as to how the observer affects and is affected by the observed. Psychology was of little use to the new physics, as it was being conceptually bankrupted by the same philosophy of science that had become useless to physics. Both psychology and the philosophy of science were busy trying to fashion a myth and an ideology to allow them to rise above their subject matter. Both fields were creating a vertical hierarchy in which scientists—detached, logical, rational, and supremely intelligent—could be better than everyone else.

Thus the positivists and Popperians had much to say about the nature of science; but as Merton, Kuhn, Polanyi, Feyerabend and more recently Gergen (1985, 1988, 1991), Harré (1986), Rorty (1979), and Sampson (1983, 1985) have pointed out, one could understand only science within its sociological, psychological, economic, political, and historical contexts. Just as, in Chapter 1, I argued that the therapist and patient must be joined by common description and judged by the same criteria, so too I argue that the distinction between scientist and nonscientist, psycho"therapist" and patient must be one of degree and development, not of kind or type.

Kuhn (1970) argues that the standard textbooks of any science provide a kind of propaganda about that science. I suggest that part of that propaganda is the presentation of a myth that places the scientist above nonscientists and in psychology places the scientific psychologist above nonscientific psychologists. Kuhn argues that basic textbooks attempt to protect the scientific paradigm that dominates the field while it recruits developing scientists to its precepts. I argue that textbooks also protect the moral prerogatives of their authors while they seek to convert young readers into true believers in their moral outlook.

Let me provide an example from my academic involvement in psychology to elucidate the above. Any standard introductory text presents the psychologist as a scientist and psychology as a science in its first chapter. (As of this writing, most of the current texts are managed and homogenized mirror images of one another.) A psychologist scientist learns by making direct empirical observations. He collates and statistically analyzes these data, forms theoretical conclusions about the relationships of the observations, and then logically deduces testable hypotheses from his data. Experiments abound that permit him to verify or refute his hypotheses and the theories from which these were drawn. The virtues of this method are extolled, and the ethics binding the psychologist in his research efforts are made clear to the student.

One searches in the index for the chapter concerned with learning. Perusal of the chapter allows one to discover that learning occurs according to the principles of operant and respondent conditioning. The research that demonstrates the validity of these principles involves rats, pigeons, dogs, cats, and an occasional gorilla and chimpanzee. There is an ideology contained in this presentation. The psychologist learns through scientific methodology, the rest of humanity through mindless conditioning.

A careful study of the rest of the index of the volume reveals hundreds of such hierarchical concepts. A reading of the chapter on thinking suggests that artificial intelligence and computer analysis can demonstrate how people think. Psychologists follow their interests, passions, and morals in thinking about the world; their subjects are merely programmed. Rollo May (1991) points out that in a typical text the rules of memory are given as primacy and recency, and these rules involve memorizing nonsense syllables. May wonders how much of our textbook material and the presentation of the psychology instructor is nonsense.

In order to create a philosophy of science, we must begin by jettisoning our ideologies and ground science in its history, sociology, and psychology. We require a philosophy of science but must create a human grounding, which is exactly what Kuhn and Polanyi suggest. I think many would agree with me that psychology is not yet a full science. Kuhn suggests that a mature science is dominated by one paradigm. Psychology can demonstrate no such maturity. (See Chapter 5 for a fuller discussion of this topic.) Are psychologists conditioned as are rats, pigeons, and students? Or do students ever learn by employing the scientific method that others have achieved? Lakatos (quoted in Hacking 1981) states, "Philosophy of science without history is empty, history of science without philosophy of science is blind" (107). Once this grounding is complete we can then ask what human activities and processes are common to science and scientists that explain their success.

All scientists are human and all humans are (or can become) scientists. Each human being is a separate individual, who shares with the rest of humanity a historical and social context without whose understanding the individual's psychology can make no sense. Scientific activity is one form of knowing the world (the artistic and the religious being others world) that makes sense only in its proper context and with a proper analysis of its psychological components. I list here what I believe are the six components of scientific activity, and I describe the development more fully in Chapter 6, where I discuss the individual's successes and failures to develop into an effective scientist psychologist.

1. Science is empirical. All individuals, at least as infants, delight in exploring the world through their senses. Adaptation demands some understanding of how the world and its people exist if survival is to be maintained. A scientist is an individual who maintains a reliance on direct contact with some aspects of the physical world. The nonscientist, which includes the scientist when failing to be a scientist, satisfies the desire to understand by relying on authority to reveal necessary information.

2. Scientists are as objective as they can be despite their awareness that they see others and the world from their own unique perspective. Polanyi (1958: 30) states, "Any attempt to rigorously eliminate our human perspective from this picture of the world must lead to absurdity." What scientists do is constantly to try to take into account both their biases and the limits of their observations. There is something to be described that exists independently of their cognitive affective framework, but that something can never be fully known in and of itself. By decentering, deconstructing, and analyzing the process of observation, scientists engage in a never-ending battle to achieve something approaching objectivity.

3. As human beings develop they learn to reason about the world with rules of logic that change over time. According to Piaget (1950, 1952, 1957, 1975), infants know the world only through sensations and the motoric contacts they make with it. Younger children begin to discover a logic in the world and internalize this discovery, forming the basis of adult logic. Because they fail to achieve an adult understanding of the rules that govern the world, children's logic is termed

preoperational. School-age children utilize concrete operations. They are able to understand the rules that govern the relationships of the concrete objects that surround them. By adolescence children begin to use operations to understand the thinking with which they organize the world and thus achieve formal operations. A study of science reveals that scientists rely on formal operations when explaining the results of their perception.

Scientists are no more rational than anyone else. They utilize formal operations in analyzing the data of their observations, as well as in analyzing the processes they use to make their observations. Formal operations permit people to reason about reason, to think about thinking, and to confront, to a degree, the biases and level of logic contained in their psychological constructs. Only recently has history created conditions for the wholesale human development of formal operations. Science and social democracy have created the conditions to reward individuals for using formal operational logic.

4. Human beings never just perceive their world or think about it; they find meaning in their intellectual activities because of the arousal of emotions and other affective processes. Scientists are as emotionally involved in their activities as any other human beings and would be useless to themselves and others if they were not. All human thought is organized by and directed toward human emotions. Let me quote Bertrand Russell on mathematics and Albert Einstein on science to make my point.

Russell: "Mathematics, rightly viewed possesses not only truth, but supreme beauty, a beauty cold and austere, like that of sculpture without appeal to any part of our weaker nature, without the gorgeous trappings of painting or music, yet sublimely pure and capable of a stern perfection such as only the greatest art can show" (quoted in Stander 1988).

Einstein: "The most beautiful and most profound emotion we can experience is the sensation of the mystical. It is the power of all true science. He to whom the emotion is a stranger, who can no longer wonder and stand rapt in awe, is as good as dead. To know what is impenetrable to us really exists, manifesting itself as the highest wisdom and the most radiant beauty which our dull faculties can comprehend only in their most primitive forms, the feeling is at the center of true religiousness" (quoted in Barnett 1957: 105).

Scientists belong to that group of people Hofstadter (1963) calls "intellectuals." Their development has allowed them not only to utilize formal operations but also to enjoy, become passionate about, and take nurturant pleasure in utilizing intellectual and cognitive skills. Ideas are enjoyed simply as ideas. Polanyi (1958: 27) writes, "No sincere assertion of fact is essentially unaccompanied by feelings of intellectual satisfaction, or a pervasive desire and a sense of personal responsibility." Scientists are interested in their work and their ideas and committed to their procedures by the universal emotions that make any and all activities meaningful.

5. Scientists feel, and because of this truth they are as morally committed as any other human beings. The myth of scientific objectivity and moral neutrality is just that, a myth. Scientists are neutral to the degree that, once they have established faith in the worthwhileness of studying this or that, they describe and explain the object of their interests as free of judgments as they can be. (This of course assumes that they know the difference between a term that is descriptive and one that is judgmental.) Ultimately science is justified by morality, its methods are invested with moral faith, its interests morally chosen. But once scientists make the moral judgment that it is good to know, they then detach their judgments from the processes of knowing.

When science ignores the reality and necessity of its moral enterprise, much human misery ensues. I have detailed the pretense of objectivity and moral neutrality in the pseudoscience of psychiatry and clinical psychology in the last chapter. Bronowski (1963: 142) writes "Science has created evil by amplifying the tools of war while scientists have taken no moral stance on their use or production. Scientists did not create or maintain war but they have changed it." As scientists pretend aloofness, "They have engaged in acting the mysterious stranger, the powerful voice without emotion, the expert, *the god*" (emphasis mine).

As I suggest (and began to detail earlier), human misery grows exponentially in a vertical hierarchy where authority ideologically detaches itself from history, psychology, and sociology and engages in politics as if it were godlike. It is a common moral stance, in which people play god and treat others as if they were machines, puppets, or slaves. Unfortunately, it is just as common for people to play the puppet and seek out others to play their god (Fromm 1947). Modern science often plays god, while the public plays the willing puppet. How often I hear a scientific discovery referred to as "a miracle." This is nowhere more frequent than in the areas of psychiatry and mental illness.

6. Science allows dissent and fosters debate that allows good ideas to push out the bad. Popper is thus correct when he suggests that falsifiability is a criterion of science. However, the falsification of an

idea must take place in a context where it makes sense. Ideas need not be thrown out while they are still useful and will not be as long as people experience them as useful. As the context of science is social, it is necessary to allow social consensus, not merely a logical principle, to create the conditions of falsifiability.

However, when scientists play god, debate ceases. The gods know the truth, and it is eternal truth not to be trampled upon. We must now turn to the type of that social organization of science that fosters debate and determines which ideas are to be falsified. When one examines science as it operates in its most effective form, one discovers that it operates democratically, fairly, firmly, and responsibly and is guided by a humanist philosophy. I close this chapter by briefly discussing my faith in a humanistic philosophy, especially as it is demanded in a psychiatric science.

HUMANISM

When science operates as it should, it operates humanistically . Like all human activity, science must operate according to a set of rules. These rules are believed to be good because following them leads to consequences also judged to be good. Each scientist, in following a set of shared rules, must thereby submit himself to an authority. Who is that authority to be? Polanyi (1969: 75) writes, "Science is judged by the participating scientists involved in a discipline. There can be no higher authority. Their job is to keep out trash while allowing and supporting dissent. They must be conservative and revolutionary."

Polanyi is describing a democratic organization of individuals who freely submit to joint authority in order to set standards for its members. The organization is assured to be made up of equals, all of whom agree to share responsibility for the operation and goals of the scientific group in question. These individuals agree to disagree. They also agree to disagree in such a way as to preserve the dignity of their membership. The standard set by these individuals is assumed to represent the best efforts of each of its members as intelligent and moral human beings.

Humanistic philosophy asks several interlocking questions: What sets human beings apart from the animal kingdom? What represents the best that a human being can be? What are the means by which every human being can be helped to be the best that he or she can be? Humanism assumes that every human life is worth preserving and respecting and helping to develop even if (and especially when) that human being is not living up to the best that he or she can be. Humanism asks, "What are the necessary and sufficient psychological, social, economic, and political conditions to assure that each human being will live up to his or her fullest potential and achieve full humanness?"

Certain concepts run to the heart of humanism. One is that human beings become conscious of themselves, the world around them, their past, their present, and their limited future. Human beings learn of their mortality. With human consciousness, an awareness emerges concerning a human capacity to intend and make choices. With knowledge of death those choices become personally important to each individual. The capacity to choose is accompanied by an understanding of the consequences created by one's choices. The capacity to choose defines one's freedom and liberties. Understanding of consequences defines one's responsibilities. We are most human when we exercise our liberties and assume responsibilities for our choices.

The social conditions in which we live can foster our humanness or hinder its development. We can be deprived of our liberties, that is, our right to choose those behaviors that we believe will fulfill our greatest potential. Social conditions may try to teach us that our responsibilities can be lifted from us while we retain our freedom of choice. When we are oppressed or overindulged, we either lose or give up our ability to choose and assume our rightful responsibilities. In either case our humanness is compromised. At the moment we lose or give up our right to choose, we become puppets, slaves, machines, robots, or some other dehumanized object.

Just as we can be victimized by others, so too can we be the oppressor of others. We can burden others with our responsibilities and use force or other means to prevent others from making their own free choices. Individuals may at any time, especially if they do not understand the necessary relationship of freedom and responsibility, seek to increase their personal freedom while reducing their personal responsibilities. To achieve such an arrangement involves the dehumanization of another and simultaneously of ourselves.

Individuals so dehumanized may come to dehumanize themselves. Whether in the act of kindness or cruelty, individuals deprived of liberty may not develop the necessary personal skills to make choices and bear up under the consequences flowing from such choices. These individuals may seek further victimization either by having other individuals make choices for them or by oppressing others as they burden others with the consequences of their own actions. Victims thus become victimizers of self and of others.

Just as social conditions can dehumanize people, so too can social conditions foster the development of individual humanness. Individuals can help others develop the capacity to make choices, deal with their responsibilities, and understand the relationship between real freedom and responsibility. Individuals may help others set and agree to those standards that represent the best that a human being can be. They can seek ways to help those individuals develop the skills necessary to achieve their moral goals. It is ultimately the job of parents, teachers, and psycho"therapists" to do all of the above.

It is an assumption of this book that I consider freedom and responsibility to be developmental issues just as I do the cognitive and emotional processes that both justify and are justified by the moral concepts to which they relate. As children are considered unable to evaluate and cope with their world, they are neither accorded the freedom nor expected to live up to the responsibilities of adults. It is clear that if children are to assume full adult status, they must be treated in such a way that they have the skills and understanding to be fully free and fully responsible.

Parents, teachers, and psycho"therapists" can oppress those for whom they care either by prohibiting freedom or failing to demonstrate and demand how responsibilities are to be achieved. Children and others so victimized may become the oppressors of others or learn to oppress themselves. They may seek to remain part of a vertical hierarchy in which they deify those above themselves and dehumanize those below. They may either force others to do their bidding or depend upon others to do things they fear they cannot do for themselves. They may never learn to set those personal standards whose goals represent the best that they might become as human beings.

There are other categories of individuals whom we excuse from responsibility because they lack the skills to exercise their choices. The ill, the destitute, and the oppressed are such individuals. The response of the community to such individuals is critical if they are to become fully human. Such people can be treated with sympathy, understanding, and dignity and simultaneously with firmness of resolve while they recover the abilities that will permit full human participation.

The victims of oppression or life's unfairness can also be dehumanized by the very processes that are designed to help them. Often assumptions are made that those unable to function according to the standards of the community are inherently inferior and cannot be helped to grow. Such individuals are stigmatized by the very people who claim to help and end up as wards of the state or other institutions that in the name of kindness foster helplessness and inadequacy. How often I have seen individuals on welfare or social security disability engage in endless years of psychotherapy. One can hear therapists openly discuss how this state of endless dependency is the best that the individual can do, for without this constant support the individual will fall to the bottom of the social economic and political ladder. There seems to be no insight that the assignment of the individual to a fixed place in a social hierarchy is the very factor that keeps the individual from growing.

When individuals refuse to follow humanistic procedures and insist on denying others their freedom, their behavior may be judged criminal. Authority may have to deny such individuals their freedom until they assume responsibility for their actions. In a humanistic, fair, and just democracy, the denial of human freedom is a grave responsibility to the participating citizenry. No freedoms are withdrawn from an individual until due process is followed, which includes careful deliberation, a trial by the citizenry, and reasoned judgments by those chosen to make such judgments.

What to do with those considered guilty of violating their social responsibilities remains one of the most difficult of problems in any humanistic society. Does one seek to punish wrongdoers or to rehabilitate them? What is the most effective way of reducing crime and restoring social conditions that promote humanistic morality? How do we weigh the rights of the criminal with those of the criminal's victim? Is punishment the way to promote morality, or is it merely revenge taken on the criminal? Is revenge right or wrong on the part of authority? Do we as a society hold each and every individual to the same set of standards and apply our laws justly and fairly?

THE PARADOX

How one answers the above questions depends upon whether one describes or judges the behaviors in question. When one attempts to describe the psychological and social reasons for behavior, one ends up with an explanation for the behavior. When one judges the behavior, one comes up with an assertion of fault, blame, and an indictment and verdict concerning the behavior. To describe and explain or to judge and blame involves two incompatible psychological states of mind. One can describe and explain or one can judge; one cannot do both simultaneously. One can move from one state of consciousness to the other but cannot hold the two states at the same moment.

As I have argued, both states of consciousness are necessary. Without descriptions and explanations no science is possible. No empathy, sympathy, and other psychological states with which we identify with the people we describe are possible either. Without judgment, there can be no ordering of behavior according to good or bad, no standards set, no commitment possible to a direction or a goal. But while we are describing and explaining we may need to be judging, and while we are judging we may require descriptions and explanations. Here then is part of the paradox: We constantly must describe and constantly must judge and cannot do both constantly.

When we lose sight of our judgments, our description of behaviors implies judgment. To understand all is to forgive all, or at least to imply that the behavior being described is acceptable. To judge is to imply description. The psychiatric judgments already described amply demonstrate that. The most we can do to resolve this paradox is to develop a state of consciousness in which one moves back and forth between description and judgment until one is no longer able to do so. At some point we become committed to those behaviors (or things) we feel are good and become opposed to those behaviors (and things) we consider bad. At the point of commitment we will at least have some idea what the descriptive justifications of our judgments are. (This problem is discussed further in Part III, which deals with psycho"therapeutic" techniques.)

But our paradox has still other manifestations. As a psychologist scientist I often become convinced that my patients have no choice but to behave as they do. Between what they have learned and what they are ignorant of they must see and feel about the world exactly as they do and in effect choose behavior from a repertoire representing no choice at all. I have seen children who have never known kindness, love, or compassion. These children watched adults behave brutally, settling all arguments and disputes with insults and violence. How can these children, as victims of such a system, behave other than as the adults who represent their social world? If a child grows up in a vertical hierarchy maintained by force, how can he behave otherwise?

When I see children in such a system I feel sorry for their victimization. But if these children have no choice but to grow up into victimizers themselves, then how can I judge them when they victimize the next generation of children? If my scientific theory of development is deterministic, then how can I judge anyone? Am I now forced into a position of universal forgiveness and total moral relativism? And if I accept such a position am I not casting myself and my fellow human beings into a nonhumanistic position, insisting that we are all victims, robots, programmed machines, and puppets?

This then is the paradox that I now live with. I believe as a scientist that human behavior is determined and that our choices are always limited both by what we know and what we do not know. However, I must hold myself and my fellow human beings responsible for what they do, because to do otherwise is to believe in nothing. It is to believe that we are not human and to give up hope that change is possible in how we now behave toward ourselves and each other. To accept puppethood for humanity is to accept nihilism and to place oneself at the whim of each human being. Science and morality collapse unless we maintain ourselves on both sides of the paradox as best we are able.

The psychological question must then be asked: Can we develop a psychological model of human beings capable both of being scientifically deterministic and of seeing people as able, to some degree, to grow and control the environments that shaped them? Can we develop a theory that is empirically correct and allows human beings to see themselves as able to make choices, plan, create new ideas, and transcend their historical pasts? Can a psychological theory contain an explanation of the human capacity for moral belief and choice and still be scientific? I believe such a theory can be constructed, and it is to that task I now turn.

4

BIOLOGY, PSYCHOLOGY, AND SOCIOLOGY

In the preceding two chapters I attempted to define psycho"therapy." I also tried to explicate its roots as a science and its justifications and goals in moralistic humanism. I defined psycho"therapy" as a social interaction between people that attempts to change the psychological orientation of one of the participants. In order to describe the process of psycho"therapy" we must utilize a theory of human personality that not only is comprised of psychologically meaningful processes but also is capable of permitting an individual to change, grow, and become a more effective psychologist scientist and moral philosopher. Mahoney (1991) points out that a theory of therapy must include a theory of "human change processes."

Many of the difficulties described in Chapter 1 derive from a failure of many practitioners to define and justify their work as psychological in nature. We see instead the human subject of psychotherapy cast either as a biological being driven by hormones and neurochemical twitches or as a passive victim of unfair social forces. These attempts to describe human problems in living as biological or social are reductionistic and violate the psychological nature of the human being involved in therapy. Holzkamp (1992) calls most theories of psychology "one-sided."

Such theories do not allow that human beings have the possibilities for shaping and altering their conditions. Only psychological processes such as thinking and feeling permit liberty and responsibility to exist in some meaningful fashion. Consciousness, intentionality, choice, and the ability to make predictions are some of the necessary psychological processes and capacities that transform a human being into a creature with needs for understanding, love, dignity, creativity, spirituality, and moral grounding.

The medical model exists, in part, because so many practitioners use either a psychoanalytic or a behavioristic model of personality to guide their work. Psychoanalysis permits a view of human beings as pushed by biological urges, while behaviorism conceptualizes humanity as complex robots controlled by external stimuli. Many system and family therapists utilize theories that are complex forms of behaviorism: The individual is at the mercy of social and familial forces, rather than being in mutual interaction with a social environment.

In *Cognition and Affect* (1986) I outlined a model of personality that would allow the psychologist and the therapist to conceptualize the people they work with as psychological beings capable of the same achievements as themselves. I pointed out that both Freud and Skinner (and their various followers) could not utilize their own theories to explain how each or the other could create a theory of personality. I suggested that both violated their subjects by not dealing with those processes that permit the scientific, philosophical, and artistically creative activities that are so central to human endeavors.

In the next chapter I outline the specific criteria I believe that any psychological theory must utilize if it is to be useful in the process of psycho"therapy." This chapter will remain in the realm of philosophy by attempting to define and justify psychology as a science of the psychological. Moreover, I will seek to define parameters of psychology that will allow for the ultimate discovery of universal laws applicable to explain the behavior of all human beings. I will also attempt to define the psychological processes that grow from biological processes and are shaped by social processes in the course of human adaptive struggles.

THE MIND-BODY PROBLEM

At the base of so many reductionisms apparent in behaviorism, psychoanalysis, and the medical model lies a failure to resolve the mind-body problem from a scientific vantage point. Scientific theory is predicated on a materialistic set of explanations that avoid spiritual or other types of dualism. As Dennett (1991) so ably points out, many therapists deny the Cartesian dualism of mind and body but do not resolve the dualism sufficiently to avoid creating dualisms of their own. Freud describes a biological organism inhabited by id, ego, and superego while his followers describe beings tormented by "pathological introjects" and the like. Skinner simply ignores psychological processes in describing a being incapable of anything except complicated versions of the knee jerk.

The medical model pretends that human beings are nothing but the neurological workings of their brain, but it must create ghostlike pathogens to explain mentally ill behavior. For example, in explaining obsessive compulsive disorder (OCD), a recent paper states that "parasitic ideas" take control of the OCD sufferer's intellect. Thus we have ideas with a life of their own, mind stuff, somehow circulating in the brain or mind of an individual. These parasitic ideas make decisions alien to the thinking of the person who has created them. Whenever one says that the mind or personality becomes a thing that can, in and of itself, become sick, a dualism has been created.

Patients will often express the fear, "I am losing my mind," as if their psychological processes can be lost in the same way as their wallets or keys. In these and so many other ways we conceive of ourselves as a duality, a mind that inhabits a body. The mind controls the body, the body can affect the mind, but still both remain separate. If the mind inhabits the body, at what point does it interconnect? What is the stuff of mind? In Descartes's duality, mind was equated with soul, and the source of the soul was God and Heaven. The mind soul connected to the body at the pineal gland. Descartes never did solve the problem of how extensionless immaterial stuff connected with and controlled physical stuff with extension, but that problem must be solved if we are to create a science of psychology.

Let me digress for a moment to continue a discussion that will sharpen the problem of dualistic theories of human beings. We see the concept of dualism dominating human affairs for as long as recorded history. Plato, whose philosophy shaped much of the intellectual development of Western culture, divided the universe into a world of corporeal substance and one of ideas. Most religions see the universe as comprised of a physical place and a place of spirituality. The latter involves gods or a god inhabiting a sphere of reality entirely different from the one inhabited by our living beings.

As a scientific materialist, I hold the belief that human beings create the dualism inherent in religions and philosophies and not the other way around. I take my belief on faith, recognizing that many colleagues and most of my fellow citizens believe quite otherwise. For them it is the world of the gods or other supernatural phenomena that precede and encompass the world of everyday reality. If these others are correct, then the only psychological question worth asking is why a small persistent minority of people refuses to believe in the supernatural world. For me, the interesting question is why a majority of human beings insists on a supernatural world with its separation of mind, soul, and body. How can I create a mechanistic and materialistic psychological science that both explains humanity's spiritual needs and respects those needs and beliefs as well?

Why have human beings bifurcated their universe (and themselves) and insisted on maintaining such a division? If we examine the descriptions of the spiritual realm, we see that it is endowed with permanence, perfect goodness, complete justice, and total moral authority. A benevolent and just God can deliver to any individual all the fairness that one can wish for, if not in this life, then in the next. If one's soul (or mind) comes from the gods, then not only is one's consciousness immortal, but the creation of such consciousness by the gods endows psychological life with an inherent meaning and purpose. Pain and suffering can always be justified; there are no accidents; and no matter how horrendous one's own behavior, the possibility of forgiveness always exists. By joining with the gods we become better than those who do not, and we can therefore and most important achieve certainty in our knowledge (Dewey 1929).

Certainty banishes doubt, and materialist scientists must live in doubt. For those who speak for and listen to the gods, truth is spelled with a capital "T." The ideas of the godless are intolerable and certainly wrong. Once we create a social hierarchy with a spirit world on top, those who speak for the gods can easily dismiss the demands of those who do not. The ease with which kings ruled with divine right or slave owners disposed of their "mindless, soulless" slaves fills human history.

As discussed earlier, one of the biggest dangers inherent in duality is that those who are "superior" do not have to explain their actions to those who are "inferior." Superiority and inferiority are inherent to one's place in the vertical hierarchy. Science demands descriptions in nonjudgmental terms. The abilities of the scientist to describe are developed and not inferred as part of a dualistic universe. It is this developmental principle to which we now turn, for it allows us to bridge the gap between those who behave wisely and morally and those who do not. The development of individual skills and knowledge separates the psycho"therapist" and those who seek his assistance. The development of individuals (and of species) allows us to utilize a hierarchy, but to base it on nondualistic, nonjudgmental, scientifically described principles. Let us turn then to the concept of development that ties biology to psychology, allows us to create a usable psychology, and in turn ties psychology to sociology.

PHYLOGENESIS AND PSYCHOLOGY: PSYCHOPHYLOGENESIS

Psychological factors emerge (in part) from the biological, according to the rules of evolution. We cannot understand the development of the human being unless we place it in context, as one developing species among many. Individual human development cannot be understood without recourse to a human history that is both collective and personal. The biological human being cannot be separated from the history of our total species. This raises the possibility that life forms other than our own also have a psychology; if so, we will be forced to dispense with one more set of preciously held dualisms.

In the present theory of psychology, it is the concept of consciousness that defines that which is most human. However, as Dennett (1991) points out, consciousness is rarely defined. The assumption is made that what each of us calls being conscious is assumed to be what all of us call being conscious. Dennett calls this the error of the first person plural. It is further assumed that this undefined consciousness is unique and common only to human beings. In his most important book (the reader is urged to assimilate Dennett's ideas), Dennett creates a developmental schema of consciousness in keeping with evolution of the human species and development of the human individual.

It is clear from Dennett's discussion that consciousness is a many-layered phenomenon and exists even when the individual is unable to describe what he or she clearly knows. Polanyi (1958) articulates a very similar idea when he suggests that we all know more than we can say. I will define what I believe to be the basic unit of consciousness. However, in the developmental definition of consciousness, it is clear that much, if not all, of the animal kingdom also possesses consciousness.

I submit that it is consciousness that is the basic unit of psychology. With the development of increased forms of consciousness, attention, memory, anticipation, intentionality, perception, emotions, thought, and all other psychological processes come into existence, a process referred to by Holzkamp (1992) as psychophylogenesis. However, animals with less-complex brains are capable of less-complex forms of consciousness and fewer psychological processes. The behavior of human beings cannot be reduced to that of the amoebas, but each human being shares that which is in common with our protozoan progenitors. Let me now define consciousness.

Consciousness is (the least degree of) meaningful experience capable of stimulating purposeful activity. I will need to discuss some of the terms in my definition before turning to the developmental issues related to my definition. A paramecium (or any single-cell organism) is stimulated with an electric probe. The paramecium is not touched hard enough to be moved by the force of the probe. The paramecium moves away from the probe once the electric current is applied to it. At the point at which the paramecium moves, I will make the assumption that it felt the electric charge, that its feeling was painful, and that pain belongs to a class of experiences known as affective. The feelings produced by the probe were therefore meaningful to the paramecium. Finally, that the paramecium moved to reduce the pain produced by the electric probe means that the movement was purposeful. It can therefore be said that the paramecium was conscious of the electric probe. Consciousness is created by the very nature of nervous tissue, which defines what is called the Animal Kingdom.

The paramecium is not capable of being conscious of what created the current or of who directed it to its body. It is probably not conscious of having a body. It is not conscious of choosing the direction or speed of its flight, of recording the history of the event, of anticipating its reoccurrence, of communicating its experience to other paramecia, or of being conscious of pain. It lacks what can be termed reflective consciousness. Because it cannot be conscious of being conscious, it lacks what human beings usually speak of when they say they are conscious of an event. The paramecium is conscious but cannot process the information provided by the probe to any greater complexity than its simple nerve net will allow. The paramecium does possess what can be called prereflective consciousness.

Human beings have the capacity to respond consciously to an electric probe in the same simple terms as the paramecium. A person touches a hot surface and almost immediately pulls his hand away. We are told in introductory psychology that such a response to a stimulus is reflexive and that reflexes are without consciousness. The reflex is mediated by the spinal cord, and by the time the information reaches the cortex we have already pulled our hand from the hot stove. But a reflex fits my definition of consciousness. We are conscious of the hot stove and purposefully pulled back our hand. As time passes, additional processing takes place and we become conscious of having been conscious of the stove. Prereflective consciousness is an element of reflective consciousness.

A human reflex and a paramecium's response represent a basic evolutionary adaptation to felt dangers. The human capacity to become aware of being conscious and to store the memory of the hot stove and thus learn not to touch it again are added capacities that have emerged through the developmental evolutionary process. Evolution of complex creatures adds complexity to information processing. Organisms become conscious of more in their environment and conscious of themselves being conscious.

With increased complexity comes encephalization and a division of labor in sensory apparatuses. Eyes, ears, and the senses of smell and taste are added to touch, and thus there is a broadened consciousness of the world around the experiencing organism. With a mammal such as a cat, there is a huge increase in the processing of information and thus in consciousness over that of the paramecium. My cat stares at a squirrel and begins stalking the smaller beast. There is no doubt in my consciousness that he is aware of and purposefully directed toward the squirrel. He is conscious of the squirrel.

We, as human beings, can be conscious of the world just as the cat. I have often driven my car to work and had no memory of the drive. I do remember being conscious of the lecture I was to deliver when I got to my college. I must have been very conscious of driving the car, the road I was on as well as the cars moving in complex patterns all about me. I successfully and safely reached my destination, which would be impossible without conscious control of my vehicle. I was, however, not conscious of being conscious of driving my car.

Being conscious of events and processes and not being conscious of our consciousness of these events and processes pervade human life. For example, we are awakened by an alarm clock. When did we first become conscious of the alarm? The immediate answer would be to say we are conscious of the alarm once we awaken. However, must we not have been conscious of the alarm to have been awakened by it? Once we are awake we are conscious of being conscious of the alarm. Wakefulness involves increased cortical activity, broadened sensory input, and thus an increase in consciousness over our sleep state.

As we walk, talk, play the piano, or write a tract such as this, we are "conscious" of our activities. But we are not similarly conscious of how we will or organize these activities. To try to articulate how one plays the piano is to destroy the capacity to play in any coherent fashion. We must be conscious of walking, talking, or writing, as these are purposeful activities. Our consciousness, however, as we write contains consciousness of consciousness concerning only the product of our writing. We are conscious of the writing process but not conscious of being conscious. Polanyi (1958) calls these nonverbal aspects of consciousness the "tacit" dimensions of mental life.

My definition of consciousness demands that the experience of whatever it was that was experienced be meaningful. Let us briefly examine the meaning of "meaningful." Consciousness begins with the perception of a stimulus of some sort. Perception is a cognitive activity. It permits, by use of sense organs, some evaluation or appraisal capacity of aspects of the environment in which the organism lives. Paramecia have simple appraisal abilities; human beings have complex capacities to appraise their environment. In addition to perception, adult human beings can also think about their perceptions of their environment. Thought is also a cognitive activity. Part of the meaningfulness of any experience is therefore cognitive.

However perception or other cognitive appraisals of the environment must also produce an affective response in order for the experience to be meaningful and capable of producing purposeful activity. The simpler the appraisal apparatus of a creature, the simpler the affective component of meaningfulness. In human beings, especially after a prolonged individual development, cognitive appraisals are vast and so are the felt, affective qualities that are part of the conscious experience. Both this development and the range of emotion comprising the bulk of human affect will be discussed in a later chapter.

Meaningful experience produces purposeful activity. The purpose in human activity is directed toward changing the meaning experienced in various life situations. When one acts toward a situation, one seeks to alter or maintain those aspects of the situation that in turn alter or maintain the affective response to that situation. In general, an organism acts to maintain or increase pleasant affects and reduce, terminate, or avoid unpleasant affects. An action continues in its purpose as long as the cognitive affective experience of the situation demands it to continue.

A single example on a human level will demonstrate the above. I see a dog approaching me on the street. I note (rapidly and without much additional processing than perceptual) that its ears and tail are down, its fangs are exposed, and the dog is growling. Such a cognition is immediately enriched by the emotion of fear. My consciousness of the dog is now meaningful, and I begin to act purposefully. Until the point at which I evaluate and feel safe from the dog, my chosen behaviors to change the meaning of my experience will continue.

We know from the study of evolution that simple perceptual and affective responses preceded higher-level thinking and linguistic evolution. A paramecium has a single nerve net capable of responding with feeling to a limited range of environmental stimulation. A human being can collect and cognitively analyze vast amounts of information capable of being felt emotionally. My examples of the paramecium and of myself and the dog differ only in the degree of consciousness and in the range of responses I can make in comparison to the paramecium and the dog. But the responses of both are purposeful and arise from meaningful experience. The paramecium, dogs, cats, and I myself are separated by the degree of development and little else.

Consciousness exists as a successful adaptational tool. Human consciousness exists for the same purposes as the paramecium's. It grows out of the evolutionary struggle for adaptive success. Consciousness exists in order that human beings may describe, plan, predict, and control the environment in which they live, in order to adapt. Each human being is, as is every other life form, a scientist in its environment, with differing capacities to process information, feel affect, and act upon the felt qualities provided by the information. *Human scientific capacity is the human form of consciousness.* George Herbert Mead writes, "The scientific method is after all, the evolutionary process grown self conscious" (quoted in Mahoney 1991).

Human consciousness is directed *purposefully toward something* (even if in adult human beings it is directed purposefully toward itself). We are conscious about things and processes. Consciousness takes an object external to itself (even if the object is itself). We are directed toward the sources of food, sexual gratification, places of safety, and spiritual and creative activity as well. Psychology is the study of consciousness. It is the study of how we appraise our world, how and what we feel as a result of appraisal, and how we purposefully act toward the world as a result of our meaningful experience of it.

The study of psychology cannot be reduced to the study of the brain and the perceptual organs and motor apparatus that support consciousness and purposeful activity. Consciousness cannot take place without biological apparatuses but cannot be explained by them either. Consciousness is what transpires between the living biological organism and the world it meaningfully experiences and acts upon. Neurological activity takes no object even though it makes meaningful awareness of the object possible. When I run from a dog or write on this page, both the dog and the page are necessary to understand the psychology of my behavior. No amount of neurological understanding can encompass what occurs between people and the other objects with which they interact.

The study of comparative psychology allows us to document the psychological changes brought about by the increasing complexity of various organisms' consciousness. The study of human psychological development allows us to understand the changes in the consciousness of our own species. Because ontogeny (to a degree) recapitulates phylogeny, we find many areas of agreement in the changes in human consciousness and phylogenetic changes in animal consciousness. All creatures have a psychology, but with development their psychology becomes more complex and more difficult to understand.

I will not spend more time documenting the changes in psychology brought about by either phylogenetic or species development at the present except to note one trend. With increased development and evolutionary complexity, consciousness moves from a more or less purely reflexive phenomenon to a more active, anticipatory, and motoric one. Mahoney (1985) calls this motoric quality the *feed forward* quality of complex consciousness. With improved memory (the capacity to experience meaningfully various events), organisms begin to prepare for the possible reoccurrence of those events. Human consciousness exists in a preparatory state ready to respond and process some information sources differently than others. An outgrowth of the capacity to predict and differentially respond to possible future events is the inherently constructive quality of such consciousness.

When an organism begins to anticipate future events, it must construct a scenario of possible outcomes. At choice points the organism must commit itself to some alternatives rather than others. The construction of the scenarios that comprise possible alternative future realities is based on past experiences and present perceptions. But because these constructed scenarios exist only in a yet-to-occur real future, all but one of them, at best, are wrong to some degree. Once an organism commits itself to a scenario, the chance exists that it is committing itself to the wrong one.

To improve its predictive ability, an organism must study its environment and discover regularities of behavior in those aspects of the environment with which it must interact. The discovery of regularities allows an increase in construction of correct future scenarios. Ultimately, if an organism understands regularities in behavior, it may be able to influence events, still further improving future predictions and thus still further improving adaptive success. Each new discovery of the regularities of behavior in the objects and creatures surrounding it, as well as each new constructed future scenario, represents an increase in the organism's consciousness.

Once again we see that the search for regularities and the construction of a theory of future events are not limited to human beings. Watch an animal, such as a hunting cat, begin to chase another animal that it wants for lunch. The cat leaps from cover after stalking its prey, which may be a squirrel. The squirrel begins to run from the cat and zigzags to elude the oncoming predator. The cat must commit itself to a number of possibilities created by the squirrel's evasive action. The degree to which the cat has constructed a theory of squirrel behavior and the degree to which at the last moment the cat guesses right about which way the squirrel may leap is the degree to which the cat eats or goes hungry. Every animal is a theory of its environment.

Humanity's search for regularities and the need to construct explanations to predict the future are merely a more complex form of what is found in the cat. Our awareness of the world is greater than the cat's and our capacity to search for regularities much broader, and our predictions cover much greater time periods than the cat's. But the process of controlling consciousness in order to make correct predictions is based on the same needs as the cat's. That need is the need to adapt to a world and help future generations be able to adapt as well.

Human beings have developed a variety of tools that permit a search for regularities of behavior and construction of future scenarios that are superior to any other life forms. Language is among the most important of these tools permitting symbolization of present, past, and future. Thought is perhaps the most powerful tool of all to increase adaptive capacity. Thought, suggests Piaget, is internalized behavior. When thought is represented by words, numbers, and other appropriate symbols, a significant increase in consciousness takes place. As thought is purposeful behavior, its stimulation by meaningful experience represents a special kind of consciousness. It is this consciousness that human beings recognize as their own.

Human thought, suggests Piaget (1952), develops in stages that are also the product of evolutionary struggle. I will detail Piaget's theory more fully in a later chapter, but the present discussion requires his introduction. The human infant becomes increasingly conscious of the sights, sounds, smells, tastes, and feel of its environment. The stimulation and demands of the environment are responded to by increasingly sophisticated skills with which to manipulate the environment. As development progresses, behavior becomes internalized and becomes what Piaget calls operations.

With full maturity we see the activity of self-examination and creative manipulation of existing operational structures. It is this capacity of increased consciousness that permits the evolution of the most powerful adaptational theories and strategies. It is with full human consciousness that our species has begun to take control of the evolutionary process itself. Scientific activity may be viewed from an evolutionary perspective in which scientific theories emerge and compete for dominance in the same way that species of animals or other life forms do. See Mahoney (1991) for an excellent discussion of the concept of evolutionary epistemology.

The human capacity to think about thinking allows us to create theories about our theories. The philosophy of science discussed in the last chapter is in itself an evolutionary development designed to improve our capacity to create adaptive theories. As we will see in a later chapter, Freud called the capacity to criticize one's own theories and skills *insight*. One of the goals of psycho"therapy" is to help others develop insight so that they may evaluate the paradigms with which they adapt to their world.

The conflicts between religions and scientific theories can be viewed from evolutionary developmental principles. Each competing set of ideas embodies a set of beliefs and prescribes a set of skills that are based on long-term predictions that concern human growth and survival. As discussed in Chapter 2, competing moral systems are based on implicit beliefs concerning human adaptation, and morals are justified by those predictive constructions that, in the face of ignorance concerning the future, promise adaptive success.

The evolutionary emergence of consciousness of consciousness creates a new set of needs that go beyond the simple need of survival. Only creatures who have awareness of their own consciousness will develop these needs. With self-consciousness comes self-criticism. By later childhood there emerge a consciousness and a critical need to evaluate the consciousness of others. The need to give and receive positive moral evaluations grows organically from this new complex form of conscious experience. We see in human beings a shared conscious experience.

In the last paragraph I moved from the emergence of psychological phenomena to that of sociological phenomena. As evolution produces more animals with extremely complex forms of consciousness, it also produces animals with longer periods of immaturity. This immaturity is made necessary by the needs of a developing individual to learn a wide variety of skills required in differing environmental surroundings. Human beings have adapted to frozen tundras, dense tropical jungles, and vast hot deserts, as well as huge cities of their own creation.

The long dependency of childhood, with its complex apprenticeships, demands both social cooperation and a division of labor. The survival and growth of a human infant require that others lay aside their individual struggles and competitiveness and work together for the common good of those social units upon which individual survival and growth depend. The family unit exists in one form or another in all human societies. Larger social units comprising various forms of cooperative activity also exist, such as communities, towns, cities, and countries. The necessity for social cooperation can therefore be cast in terms of evolutionary demands and development.

The use of Darwinian and evolutionary theory to explain and justify society and social policy began in earnest in nineteenth-century Great Britain. Carl Degler (1991) writes that Social Darwinism dominated nineteenth-century thought, particularly as it justified and shaped industrial and capitalistic growth. Survival of the fittest was seen in terms of individual competition as to who could accumulate vast wealth. It also justified punitive policies toward the "inherently inferior": the poor, women, and various races. From a more modern understanding of evolutionary theory, it is clear that Social Darwinism neglected to take into account the degree to which cooperation between and within species is as common and necessary to survival of a species as is competition.

At the level of mammalian development we see increasing instances of family life and of cooperation between adults of a species. Lions hunt in prides, while cattle, deer, and other species live in protective herds. Primates all show a need for social involvement that in some ways rivals human society. As we examine more complex life forms, we see increasing consciousness of the need for social cooperation as well as the emergence of specific emotions that promote social bonding and cohesion.

Two issues emerge with increased dependency of the young on the mature members of a species. The young have more and more to learn from the mature members, who must figure out how much social cooperation and cohesion must be taught to the young, as well as which competitive skills must be allowed to flourish. When seen from the developmental perspective, the morality of social groups is exactly the attempt to balance individual expression of skills with individual conformity to group demands. It appears to me that achieving the balance between individuality and conformity has been the most difficult for human beings to achieve. It is the area where our ignorance is greatest and our social struggle most intense.

We seem our most ambivalent when we sponsor and reward individuality and simultaneously punish it. Our reliance on spiritual and supernatural direction to achieve a balance is perhaps greatest when it comes to this area of ignorance and necessity. The rules of cooperation are literally written in stone in Western society, and the stone is a gift from the world of the supernatural. Societies rise and fall as they move from noncooperative anarchy to tightly controlled authoritarian vertical hierarchies suppressing all individual expression. In both anarchy and despotism, we see either too much individualism or too little, too much competition or too little.

Raymond Cattell (1987) has attempted to create a set of moral principles based on evolutionary theory that he calls *Beyondism*. He points out that whenever groups show too much or too little competitiveness, the skills necessary for adaptation both within and between groups suffer. World War I depleted or destroyed the best of the social gene pool in Europe and opened the way for the excesses of Hitler, Stalin, and World War II. We have seen in our era how excessive totalitarian control in the Soviet Union led to a collapse of individual initiatives in economic and political life. I will suggest below that the dependencies demanded of the so-called mentally ill in our present welfare state are helping to sap the creative and individualistic energies of our own culture.

Degler (1991) points out that the collapse of Social Darwinism was followed by a denial of evolutionary theory and the rise (by mid-twentieth century) of what might be called the purely sociological view of human beings. In this new viewpoint, human beings were assumed to be biologically equal, with all individual differences the result of social advantages and disadvantages. The extreme environmentalism of Skinner and others had ensconced itself as the dominant philosophy of psychology, especially in the university system of our country. The theory of society as the sole creator of human behavior dominated the university system as a whole. The social-force theory determined the philosophy of the country's political policy as well as "wars on poverty" and other social welfare programs. The utopian belief emerged that if society could eradicate poverty a new and perfect dawn would rise in our world.

The present volume is part of a new emerging trend that tries to understand human behavior as determined by the forces of evolution and by social determinants. Biological complexity gives rise to psychological awareness, which in turn gives rise to sociological necessities and organization. However, we must still further develop the evolutionary principle if we are to avoid creating other unintentional dualities.

I have already argued that psychological principles cannot be reduced to their biological underpinnings. I have also demanded that we do not interpret psychological factors solely in terms of sociological or environmental factors. I do not wish, however, to run the risk of creating a theory in which psychological laws can explain sociological phenomena. I also wish to avoid suggesting that psychological realities do not affect their biological underpinnings. I therefore state a principle of *reciprocal developmental interactionism*. This principle can be articulated as follows: Simple structures shape, in part, the more complex structures they give rise to. Simple structures then undergo reconstruction by the more complex structures they have created.

Neurological complexity gives rise to a new order of phenomena known as consciousness. With still more complexity, consciousness gives rise to consciousness of consciousness. Consciousness cannot be reduced to or predicted from the function of neurons or collections of neurons. There is, however, a demand made of neurological organization because of the functioning of consciousness and other psychological phenomena. With increased consciousness there emerges a need for social interaction and cohesiveness. The psychological demands of the adapting individual will be found to shape every level of social organization. For example, without the problems inherent in meeting a child's needs, there would be no need for family.

However, with complex social structures, with increased differentiation into social hierarchies, there emerges a downward demand made on the psychological consciousness of the individual. It is this downward pressure that creates a whole set of social and psychological needs such as the need to be good and moral. A whole new set of needs now exists, which includes the need to live with and among people. Living with others will then shape the individual's psychological and biological being.

Psychological needs associated with consciousness are irreducible to physiological factors. At any given moment an individual can be evaluated neurobiologically, biopsychologically, psychologically, psychosocially, and sociologically. Each level of organization contains its own rules and determining laws. Each organization is worthy of its own science. Each level of organization reciprocally interacts with each other level, even as one level cannot be reduced to or absorbed by the other. From a logical point of view one cannot understand a human being unless one understands the laws of each level as well as the principle of upward and downward reciprocity of all three.

As a psychologist, I must understand the laws of consciousness and the needs that arise from consciousness, especially consciousness of consciousness. I must understand that human consciousness exists in both a biological and a social context. I cannot ignore either how human biological needs influence conscious functioning, or how psychological functioning influences an individual's biological functioning. In addition, I cannot ignore the social factors that shape human consciousness (and biological functioning), just as I must be aware of how biological needs and psychological consciousness make demands upon sociological organization. My primary focus is human consciousness, but I cannot understand that consciousness independent of its biological and social contexts.

How do we create a developmental theory that is capable of generating laws true to an irreducible psychology that is nonetheless understood in its biological and sociological contexts? In recent years we have seen the emergence of a paradigm—embodied most clearly in the work of Jean Piaget, Michael Mahoney, Richard Lazarus, myself and many others—that might be called cognitive constructivism. Constructivism allows us to create a paradigm of paradigms. Constructivism permits us to create psychological concepts conscious of themselves. Such psychological concepts can be traced from both their biological roots and the sociological forces that arise from them. It finally allows us to examine the manner in which sociology influences these same psychological concepts.

Constructionism permits a view of maturing human beings as capable of making increasingly complex choices as a result of developing an increasingly complex consciousness of themselves and their world. As a result, these individuals become increasingly capable of enjoying liberty and being held morally responsible as well. Constructionism permits us to conceptualize human beings as being creative and capable of producing sciences and religions that are both dualistic and nondualistic. Constructionism allows us to see a child and an adult as separated only in the evolution and development of the personal paradigms that comprise their personalities. Patient and therapist differ as to their perspective, world views, and the skills they possess to explain, predict, and control the world in which they both live.

Constructionism suggests that all creatures are "theories of their environment," with human beings creating the most complex theories. These theories will be referred to as a *paradigm*, after Kuhn's model of scientific functioning. Each individual has a theory of reality experienced phenomenologically as a perceptual cognitive affective truth. Although each individual experiences the truth of his or her phenomenology, that truth may always contain error.

Error in humanly constructed experience comes from three sources: (1) the working of our brain, nervous system, and perceptual apparatuses; (2) our psychological needs and the demands of consciousness; and (3) the demands of the social environment to believe what others (often authority) tell us is true and real. Whenever we behave toward the world according to faulty paradigms, there are unintended consequences. Adaptation demands of each of us that our paradigms undergo constant revision in which our search for the truth improves, however difficult the truth may be to achieve. What is called mental illness is nothing more than a variety of paradigms deemed faulty by some authority, as well as the unintended consequences flowing from the issue of such paradigms.

Finally, there is a scientific method that meets the demands of scientists if they are to study and modify human consciousness and its role in adaptation. Dennett (1991) calls this method *heterophenomenology*. Therapists will recognize that with certain modifications, this method is the basis of much of their work and is congruent with many aspects of psychoanalysis and psychoanalytically oriented psychotherapy. I briefly present Dennett's method in order to close this chapter and return to it in Part III, which will describe psycho"therapy."

Dennett argues that traditional phenomenology forces us to accept first-person-singular accounts of reality, which closes any access to the methods of description used by the individual in question. Heterophenomenology demands that we begin with third-person descriptions of the individual, as we would in all other sciences. We therefore describe in as great detail as possible the neurological, historical, and environmental conditions of the individual from the outside as we describe in detail the behavior of the individual. We then take phenomenological reports from individuals concerning our pertinent prechosen variables.

We treat the phenomenological reports of the individuals as a "text" that is to be correlated with the information we have compiled from our third-person vantage point. We utilize what Dennett calls the "intentional stance" (36). He stated, "We must treat the [verbalizer of his own experiences] as an agent . . . indeed a rational agent who harbors beliefs, desires and other mental states that exhibit intentionality or 'aboutness' and whose action can be explained (or predicted) on the basis of the context of those states." The heterophenomenologist, who now has access to both the individual's phenomenological experiences and the third-person observations that relate to those experiences, "neither challenges nor accepts as entirely true the assertion of the subject; rather, maintains a constructive, sympathetic neutrality in the hopes of compiling a definitive description of the world according to the subject." I have finished explicating the philosophical underpinnings of psycho"therapy" and can now turn to developing a theory of personality capable of directing the enterprise of psycho"therapy."

III

ELEMENTS OF A
THEORY OF PSYCHOLOGY

5

FROM PHILOSOPHY TO PSYCHOLOGY

Our field of psychotherapy is at a crossroads in its development. All of the participants are aware, in one way or another, of the enormous changes now taking place. I experience these changes with two simultaneously opposing dialectics. On the one hand, I see the biologisms of the medical model increasingly controlling the field and threatening to become monolithic in their dictation of diagnosis and treatment. I watch, with a small group of vocal others (e.g., Kovacs 1988), as this model threatens to devour not only the field of psychotherapy but perhaps society itself. Many of us fear a brave new world in which all atypical human strivings and human tragedy are trivialized as illnesses and then controlled by the use of powerful drugs, perhaps drugs ultimately derived from the human brain's own biochemistry.

On the other hand, there has never been a more exciting, life-enhancing, and hopeful epoch in relation to my intellectual life as a scientific psychologist. The theories of psychoanalysis and behaviorism, so sympathetic to the medical model, are simultaneously disintegrating and fragmenting (Omer and London 1988), as well as being reborn and reintegrated with a wide variety of intellectual currents. Some of these trends include the notions of *social and cognitive constructionism*: Berger and Luckmann (1966), Gergen (1985, 1988, 1991), Howard (1985, 1991) Harré (1984, 1986, 1991, 1992), Mahoney (1980, 1985, 1991), Sampson (1981, 1983, 1985, 1989), and Shotter (1991); *hermeneutics*: Ibanez (1991), Spence (1982, 1987), and Strenger (1991); and *feminism*: Chodorow (1978), Feldman (1992), Benjamin (1988), Gilligan (1982), Hare-Mustin and Maracek (1988), Lerman (1986), Scarr (1985), and Reynolds (1992).

The works mentioned provide the framework for a more humanized and contextualized psychology that has the potential for revolutionizing the field of psychotherapy. These trends can, if framed properly, turn the currently dismal nature of earning a living in the field of psychotherapy into an exciting and invigorating experience for all concerned. In this chapter, I turn to some of the elements or criteria that can comprise a theory of human functioning capable of supporting the type of therapy defined earlier and to be described in more detail later in the book. In the next chapter, I outline a dynamic theory of personality that has become the basis of my own professional work.

HUMAN SCIENCE

I believe that the first criterion of any theory of psycho"therapy" and human functioning must be that both the theory and the techniques belong to a human science. Giorgi (1970) and more recently Helme (1992) have made the case that mainstream psychology has been influenced by the natural sciences throughout its development this century. The natural sciences cannot properly describe that which is most basic to human functioning: human consciousness and human experiencing. The natural sciences place human experience as secondary to and dependent upon either environmental stimulation or biological and neurological activities. Although a human science would recognize the importance of environment and biology to human experience, it would begin its description of human functioning with consciousness itself. Consciousness would be the central and irreducible element in the psychology of human functioning.

As a result of placing human psychology with the natural sciences, human experience was either reduced in importance or lost altogether. The nature of psychology's dehumanization is documented in a long list of works that include those of Chein (1972), Braginsky and Braginsky (1974), Frankl (1969), Fromm (1980), May (1967), Reiff (1966), Sarason (1981), Bevan (1991), Bandura (1989), Sampson (1985), and Simon (1986). Kelly (1955) pointed to a particularly troublesome aspect of psychology's failure to deal with human consciousness: "Psychologists rarely credit the human subjects in their experiments with scientific aspirations." Neither Freud nor Skinner could utilize his own theory or that of the other to explain how each had created either psychoanalysis or radical behaviorism.

Psychology created a moral hierarchy in which researchers, therapists, and other scientists did work in order "to improve the prediction and control of certain human phenomena." This work was done with subjects and patients "propelled by inexorable drives welling up within them" (Kelly 1955) or exhibiting behavior "elicited" and "emitted" by environmental stimulation. Lost were those human qualities that permit choices to be made and responsibility to be taken for those choices. Lost, too, were those same attributes that allow human beings to experience their world, to discover what there might be to discover, and then to create those scientific and moral visions that best describe the human enterprise.

PHENOMENOLOGY REDISCOVERED

We can begin creating a human psychology by turning first to the works of Edmund Husserl (1962), Don Idhe (1986), and more recently Neil Rossman (1991), among others. A human psychology must begin by confronting the nature of human consciousness. I have already (see Chapter 4) defined *consciousness* as the least degree of meaningful stimulation capable of producing purposeful activity.

Implicit in my definition is that there is something experienced whose existence is independent of that of the experiencer. This definition implies that it takes activity on the part of the experiencer to make that which is experienced psychologically meaningful and that we behave in response to that meaning.

Idhe (1986; 43) writes,

"Every experiencing has its reference or direction toward what is experienced, and contrarily, every experienced phenomenon refers to, or reflects a mode of experiencing to which it is present. This is the intentional or correlative a priori of experience taken phenomenologically. Husserl gave the two sides of this correlation names. For what is experienced, as experienced, he used the term "neoma" or "noematic correlate," and for the mode of experiencing, which is detected reflexively, he used the term "noesis" or "noetic correlate."

Therefore, although a world is assumed to exist independently of our experience or knowledge of it, the only way in which the world can be known is through an intentional act of the experiencer. The world is given its psychological existence through the processes of human consciousness. The world is not created by consciousness, but there is nothing psychologically meaningful without a human intention to make it so. Thus a stimulus becomes a noema through the processes of noesis. Without noema there is no noesis, without noesis there is no noema.

The above means, among other things, that psycho"therapy" begins with the experience of the patient and not with the conditions that are either antecedent to or correlative with experience. People behave toward the world as they experience it or are conscious of it, not as anyone else experiences it or believes he or she should or must experience it. Therefore, we cannot talk about environmental stimuli producing responses, or about realities in the environment affecting the patient without taking into account how the patient experiences those stimuli or environmental realities. Stimuli and reality are stimuli as experienced and reality as experienced and have no status independent of experiential processes.

If we speak of the neurological and biochemical processes that permit conscious experience to occur, we must remember that individuals do not experience their brains creating consciousness, even if they know that their brains do so. Phenomenologically, we all say, "I have a brain," rather than "I am a brain" or "My brain is me." Although we may respect the powers of the environment to affect behavior and the powers of our nervous systems to process environmental information, it is what we experience that determines our actions, and not the stimuli or nervous system that does so. Critics of phenomenology are often quoted as saying that the "I" in the sentence "I have a brain" is an illusion. I agree that the self that "I" refers to does not exist as Descartes would have us believe. We do not have a ghost in the machine. But I experience myself as an "I," as do my patients. Unless we respect and study the subjective processes of the human being, we are not studying the human being as human, but as some mechanical or biological facsimile of what we experience ourselves to be when we recognize that we are human.

Laing (1967b) points out that when a patient speaks of being a machine, of not feeling alive, of not existing as a whole person or as an "I," we can call him psychotic. Laing asks, by what logic do we as scientists cast the patient in these same terms? When Skinner writes of an individual emitting behaviors as a bulb emits light, is Skinner describing what he experienced as a living active purposeful being? I must insist that consciousness be central to our study and treatment of our patients.

CONSTRUCTIONISM

The junction point between the philosophy of the phenomenologist and psychology is contained in the ideas of the constructionists, including Jean Piaget (1952, 1954, 1973, 1975, 1981), Michael Polanyi (1958, 1966), Michael Mahoney (1980, 1985, 1991), George Kelly (1955), and others whose concerns are involved with human cognitive functioning. Certain assumptions, however, separate constructionists from other cognitive theorists. These assumptions, often tacit to any given constructionist in question, are friendly to the concepts that underlie phenomenological philosophy.

The central feature of cognitive constructionism is stated by Mahoney, whose seminal work (1991) is highly recommended to the reader interested in a fuller discussion of the present ideas than can be developed here. The central notion of contructionism relates to the philosophical concept of "noesis," which is that human beings are constantly "active and proactive" (Mahoney 1991: 100) in constructing their understanding of the world around them. Consciousness, which according to Piaget is comprised of operations, which are themselves internalized actions, is motoric in nature. Therefore, while human beings are ever reactive to their environment, they are also ever active in the process of understanding and relating to that environment.

We do not wait for the environment to act upon us but are constantly preparing to act in specific ways when it does. We do not simply see reality but construct reality in ways that foster and promote successful adaptations. We become ready (and are born ready) both to react to some environmental events and not to react to others. The influences on our constructive processes are many and contain elements of the biological, psychological, and social factors in which our lives are lived and embedded. It is the job of heterophenomenological psychology to discover how our constructions of reality define experience and how the biological and social influence our constructions. Here are some examples of constructionism. The world is experienced as a visual field that is smooth, stable, and seamless. Yet within every ongoing second our eyes shift, during which time we are functionally blind to environmental events (Bridgeman 1992). If we look at a sequence of rapidly shifting lights or a series of still pictures flashed before our eyes, we see one light moving or a smoothly evolving motion picture (phi phenomenon). Finally, if we examine a Necker Cube (Figure 5.1), we see not a two-dimensional drawing but a three-dimensional cube that shifts its forward surface depending on how we perceive it. It is clear from these and many other "gestalt" experiments that there is not a one-to-one relationship between our perceptual experiences and the physical world in which we live. Our experience or conscious awareness of the world is created by the interaction of the environment and individual effort, and it is that which is constructed that determines our behavior in the world in which we live. Just as I experience myself as a person (self is constructed), so too I react to the projected still pictures moving through a motion-picture projector as real motion. Reality is constructed and not given to us by the passive processes involved, for example, in photography.

It is important to discuss the differences between the psychological construction of reality and the psychological fabrication of reality. Husserl's agenda for phenomenology was expressed in the statement, "To the object or things themselves." The scientific constructionist's notion is the same. We live in a real world and must solve real problems and satisfy real needs in order to adapt to that world. The ideas of constructionism are not solipsistic.

Figure 5.1
A Necker Cube

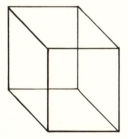

There is a reality, but it is as experienced—and experience is entirely constructed by the individual.

The notion of mental illness, especially those psychological experiences judged to be psychotic, involve not the construction of reality but the reconstruction or fabrication of reality. What constructionism makes possible is an understanding of the relationships between the construction of reality and the fabrication of reality. Once we accept that all our ideas of reality (all the truths and scientific laws of nature that we accept as true) are those that have been discovered by applying psychological rules of "seeing" the world, then we must also accept the notion that constructionist activity is capable of being influenced by many factors that can change the nature of what is discovered to be true and lawful about the world in which we live. Constructionism thus states that there is truth and there are laws governing reality, but these laws are never known except as they are given psychological life by human beings. Under such a formulation, truth becomes far less absolute and reality far more subject to those creative processes used by human beings for reasons other than the discovery of reality. What is real may be experienced quite differently by different people in different cultures at different times in history. What is real to one person is fabrication to another.

What is experienced as most real to any of us is that which we experience as real through the basic perceptual processes of sight, hearing, smell, taste, and touch. What we experience as real is still constructed and therefore is capable of being influenced by those processes that favor fabrication. At any given time and place, groups of people decide what is real, truthful, and lawful. These individuals become upset especially with those who claim to experience the world perceptually in ways that the majority would judge to be fabrications. Such fabrications are called psychosis, madness, or even divine revelations, but they are always of concern to those whose basic perceptions of reality have been challenged.

We, as yet, have little understanding of the processes of construction—both those that "take us to the things themselves" and those that take us away from the things themselves. I assume that both are the result of millions of years of evolution and are controlled by tacit processes influenced by biological, psychological, and social events. I assume that all of the processes that control the construction of experience serve adaptation, which will be defined in the next chapter. What we must focus on are how these tacit processes influence their end product, which is what we feel and experience to be real. For it is what we feel to be real that is the bedrock upon which all adaptive behavior takes place.

Finally, we can briefly examine one more assumption central to constructionism. The final goal of human constructionism is to predict the future. Our adaptions are always made in relation to what will or might happen. Kelly (1955) describes the fundamental operation of human experiencing as prediction of the future. We seek to find patterns in past and present experience that allow us either to replicate or to avoid these patterns in the near or distant future. With this assumption, let me now turn to a discussion of psychological processes or elements of consciousness: the cognitive and affective processes.

COGNITIVE PROCESSES

Any theory of human functioning will have to come to grips with the full range of human intellectual processes. The function of our cognitive processes is to allow the individual to describe, explain, predict, and, where possible, exercise control over himself, others, and the physical world in which he lives. It is the success of these processes for which the tools of adaptation exist. Cognitive processes include perception, memory, thinking, judgment, and a variety of anticipatory processes, including the capacity to make predictions. Perceptions of the present are made simultaneously in the context of memories of the past and in the light of anticipation of the future.

I agree with Kelly that our cognitive constructs describe a fundamental operation that involves predicting the future. We live facing forward in time even as the past and present form the context of prediction of the future. Similarly, I have discussed how traditional psychology has long recognized the reactive aspects of cognitive functioning. What is stressed in the present context is the active motoric nature of cognitive activity. Even memory, long held to be a repository of historical information, is increasingly recognized to be a motoric process in which the past is arranged and rearranged, as necessary, for present functioning and future predictions. Spence (1982) has suggested that memory presents narrative rather than historical truth. I will, where necessary, return to descriptions of cognitive processes, realizing that the present discussion is the merest introduction to the topic. Cognitive activity and the motoric abilities and skill of the individual form a cohesive structure that I have called a personal scientific paradigm. With development, this paradigm can reflect on itself, and it is through this active reflection on the basic adaptive processes that an individual's sense of self emerges. But the cognitive processes alone do not a living paradigm make, and it is necessary to turn to the other basic element of human consciousness, which is affect.

AFFECTIVE PROCESSES

Human consciousness is never just cognitive, but is fully informed by affective processes. Affect is defined by Piaget (1981) as any process that organizes and motivates human activity.

I will briefly consider a variety of affective processes in the present context, which includes the drives, the emotions, and a variety of unnamed affective processes that accompany the basic cognitive processes just discussed. Traditional psychology has long ignored the emotions or has conceptualized them as interfering with the smooth functioning of the cognitive processes. But just as there has been a cognitive revolution in recent years, so too have the emotions been resurrected as a legitimate topic of psychological inquiry. The work of Izard (1977, 1979, 1984), Kagan (1984a, 1984b), Zajonc (1980, 1984), Frijda (1986, 1988), Mandler (1984), Plutchik (1977, 1980), Mahoney (1991), Simon (1986), and especially Lazarus (1968, 1982, 1984, 1991) have been in the forefront of this revolution. The works listed above, along with a plethora of others, suggest that human behavior cannot be understood on the basis of cognitive activity alone.

First, I will discuss the emotions, the most important of the affective processes. The emotions, just as with our cognitive processes, are the result of bioevolutionary development and are as critical for our survival as the cognitive processes. The emotions develop along with the cognitive processes and have the function of organizing and directing cognition. I utilize Izard's (1977: 48) definition of the emotions in the present theory: "Emotions are complex processes with neurophysiological, neuromuscular and phenomenological aspects." Further,

> There is in each emotion a pattern of electrochemical activity in the nervous system, particularly in the cortex, the hypothalamus, the basal ganglia, the limbic system, and the facial and trigeminal nerves. At the neuromuscular level, emotion is primarily facial activity and facial patterning and secondarily it is bodily (postural, gestural, visceral, glandular and vocal response). At the phenomenological level, emotion is essentially motivating experience and or experience that is of immediate meaning and significance for the person. (49)

Emotions are aroused when an individual cognitively evaluates a situation. This may mean a perceptual appraisal of a situation, the remembering of one, or the anticipation of a situation. The arousal of the emotion makes the situation real to the individual and provides the cognitive evaluation with its felt qualities. Therefore, the meaning of an evaluated situation is to be found in its cognitive and emotional components. The emotional aspects of meaning can vary greatly in intensity, although emotion is found to some degree in all experienced evaluations of situations.

Once the meaning of a situation is experienced by the individual, the individual's motivation toward that situation can be understood. We are meaning-seeking and meaning-responsive creatures. We are motivated toward or away from situations in order to maintain, increase, decrease, terminate, or avoid our emotionally based phenomenologically experienced meanings to situations. Our main motivational system can be understood as attempts to maintain and/or alter the cognitive emotional meanings found in the situations that comprise our lives.

The primary function of the emotions is motivational, but the emotions are expressed in such a way (facially and gesturally) as to signal others as to the meanings their actions have for us and what our responses to these actions are likely to be. If one individual evaluates the actions of another as threatening, then fear and/or anger is likely to be the result. The signaling of the other that one is angry or afraid has the potential effect of changing the behavior perceived to be threatening. A signal of fear may lead to a cessation of hostilities, or a signal of anger may produce fear and withdrawal instead of continued threat.

Psychology and psychotherapy have just begun to understand the nature of human interactions steeped in the simultaneous experience and expressions of emotion. Zajonc (1984) calls such interactions "hot" and has even suggested that emotions are primary to and not dependent on cognitive appraisals for their elicitation. Although I still agree with Lazarus (1991) that emotions are dependent on some form of cognitive arousal (perhaps only a very brief perceptual evaluation of a situation), I do believe that it is necessary for psychotherapists to have a working model of the emotions, as both motivational and social signals, in understanding human interactions.

Izard (1977) has suggested that there are ten discrete primary emotions; Plutchik (1980) suggests that there are eight. I agree with Kagan (1984) that there are probably as many emotions as there are situations and interpretations of these situations that arouse emotions. However, to discuss the topic, we will have to create abstract names for the emotions and focus on certain specifics of these categories in trying to understand human behavior. Psychotherapists have traditionally placed emphasis on shame, guilt, and anxiety. Fear and terror are overlooked in creating the unwanted behaviors judged to be pathological.

Also important to the understanding of human adaptive responses are the emotions experienced as pleasant or pleasurable. Surprise, interest, curiosity, joy, love, and pride are as necessary to our understanding of the functioning of personal paradigms as are those emotions that function as pain and from which individuals seek to escape. All of these emotions need to be understood in terms of both their motivational and their interpersonal effects.

Less important than emotions, but still vital, are the roles played by the biological drives such as hunger and thirst and other homeostatically based needs. The drives operate in much the same way as the emotions, in that they organize the cognitive and motoric skills of the individual by changing the meaning of situations that comprise a human life. The world looks different to us when we are hungry, sexually aroused, or tired; and we act to change or maintain the meaning of the situations that now relate to those new appraisals.

There are also affects that are inherent in perceptual and cognitive activities for which there are no names. How do we know the difference between an apple perceived to be real and an apple created by an act of imagining? How can we tell the difference between percept and image? The answer is that it feels different to imagine than it does to perceive. These feelings are affective and form the basis of our experienced reality. We know reality because we experience various situations as real. We become certain that the apple is real when we see it as real. Certainty is an affect just as much as it is a cognition.

When a patient hallucinates, he experiences an image as real. This image produces the same feeling of certainty as when he perceives the object. Oftentimes the individual may lack the total experience of certainty and be unsure as to whether he is experiencing an image or a percept. This phenomenological experience is often followed by the most intense forms of anxiety possible. We often will remember an event and be uncertain as to the reality of the event. Are we remembering a real event or a dream? What makes the phenomenological difference in our conclusion is the degree to which we feel certain as to the nature of the memory. What is important in this discussion is that reality is experienced, as such, both cognitively and affectively and we are just beginning to recognize this fact as we seek to understand human behavior.

SOCIAL CONTEXTUALIZATION

The last two sections focused on the criteria necessary for the understanding of the noetic side of the phenomenological correlate. This section discusses the necessity of conceptualizing the noemic side of the phenomenological correlate. Our cognitive and emotional processes begin with the various situations of our lives. Although it is clear that the physical and social environment can be known only through our constructions, we do assume that the environment exists independent of our experience of it. The heterophenomenologist seeks to correlate various conscious experiences with various environmental situations, which requires that the environment be differentiated along some set of descriptive parameters.

There is an assumption inherent in the above discussion. A heterophenomenologist believes that certain environmental events have consistent effects in shaping the noetic processes of different individuals. Individuals do not construct or fabricate experience in some random fashion according to some capricious set of personal standards. If we do not assume a primary role for the environment in shaping conscious experience and instead focus exclusively on the processes of noesis, then we can never develop nomothetic laws of a psychological science. We will fall prey to solipsism and a kind of total subjectivism that makes science impossible.

Much of psychology decontextualizes the individual, just as so much of psychology denies the constructive elements in human conscious experience. Therapists must include both the rules by which human beings construct and fabricate experience and the actual events and situations that are correlated with those rules. Therapists will often describe patients' fabrications (hallucination and delusions) without describing the context in which they occurred. The therapist's descriptions create the impression that the patients began hallucinating simply because the patients were pursuing a whim.

What are the "normal" human responses to the type of violence, sexual abuse, degradation, and debasement regularly discovered in the lives of our patients? Might not the therapists themselves reconstruct reality and make it more palatable if they had experiences similar to those of their patients. Although no two individuals deal with reality in the same exact way, we must assume that certain realities produce commonalities in human response to them.

Human beings experience an enormous array of differing environmental, economic, social, political, and biological events. How then do we begin to categorize environmental events, that we may then look for regularities in human noetic process? Obviously, a thorough interpretation is impossible, but we can focus on various patterns of social interaction that have a profound effect in the shaping of human interpretive processes. Human relationship can be organized in three basic interrelated ways: anarchic, authoritarian/totalitarian, and democratic/humanistic.

Throughout the rest of this book, I focus on what I believe to be the economic, political, and social forces shaping human paradigmatic functioning. As I do so, I also try to adopt a language that is relevant for human experience, in that it deals with color, vividness, sound, touch, and temperature and otherwise describes the perceived behavior of real people, dealing with real situations and displaying real characteristic human behaviors. I do not discuss "stimuli," "responses," "average expectable environments" (Hartmann 1958), or any other terms that reduce and avoid human phenomenological experiences.

Human relationships can be described in a variety of ways. Relationships can be anarchistic, that is, anomic, chaotic, and sporadic, and based on interactions in which the participants act without shared conscious rules, defined roles, status, and mutual obligations. People can either ignore each other or come together for brief transactions based either on mutual need or on the needs of one or the other. Relationships can exist as chance meetings, be fleeting, and lead to separations. Such a social organization may be seen as the end of civilization or as utopian, for those who fear the role of authority in human affairs.

To the degree that human beings must cooperate in order to survive or otherwise adapt, anarchistic organization cannot exist. Anarchy, seen historically, gives way to more formalized social interactions. Most common is the authoritarian relationship, in which group activities and goals are decided by a few and then transmitted to the rest of the group. Allocation of resources is made by authority with little or no group participation, except submission to authoritarian decree. In Chapter 2, I discuss the roles played by those in power and the enforcement of obedience in such structures. When authority tries to control the very thinking and feeling of group members, one can then speak of totalitarianism.

A third type of organization, the second type that is formally organized, is the democratic. In a democracy, decisions are made by an authority that rules because of a prior decision of the governed. Authority is given its power, with the consent of the governed, in a formalized procedure known as voting. Authority in a democracy is more broadly based than in an authoritarian system, with wide participation of the members of the group under consideration.

Much of the consciousness and development of individuals is shaped by their experiences of belonging to one type or another of social grouping. What people think and feel about themselves, what skills they develop and, in general, the type of personal paradigms they form, can be understood not only by the qualities of social interactions but the languages used to describe experiences in these differing social organizations. When individuals enter psycho"therapy," they come with expectations formed in previous relationships.

People expect to have a certain power or freedom, or no power and freedom at all. They see themselves in terms of the skills they possess and in terms of the social roles they played in a prior social organization with its perceived status and social worth. They have learned to judge themselves or describe themselves and may or may not know the difference between the two.

What an individual finds in "therapy" may either confirm or deny all previous social experience. As most relationships are structured toward the authoritarian-totalitarian, the experience of the humanism-democracy inherent in psycho"therapy" provides a new set of experiences, which in turn demands new behavioral patterns. I return to this issue in Chapter 7, which deals with individual differences in modes of adaptation, as provided by the three types of social organization under consideration.

COGNITIVE AFFECTIVE DEVELOPMENT

The next criterion for a theory of human functioning must involve how human consciousness changes, as a function of age and accumulated experience. Our mode of experience, our noesis, undergoes constant changes as a result of biological development and the interaction with noema. Piaget, among others, has suggested that our mode of cognitive appraisals changes along four developmental stages: sensorimotor, preoperational, concrete operational, and formal operational. As these cognitive changes take place, the individual evaluates his/her world differently, creates newer and more complex constructions, and, as a result, begins to experience not only different emotions in the same situations but new emotions as well.

I have suggested elsewhere (Simon 1986) that those patterns of behavior and modes of experience that are labeled pathological and especially irrational are, in fact, describable as either sensorimotor or preoperational forms of thinking and perceiving. They are judged pathological because they fail to meet social and chronological expectations of operational thinking. I will propose some reasons why an individual might utilize preoperations, rather than expected formal operations, in the next chapter.

Bruner (1966), Rotman (1977), and others have pointed out that Piaget's stage theory is really an epistemology and not a true psychology. A true psychology allows for dynamics and motivations that are virtually lacking in Piaget's formulations. The closest Piaget comes to creating a theory of motivation and integrating it into his descriptions of cognitive functioning is in his concept of disequilibrium. Disequilibrium exists when an individual attempts to assimilate something from the environment and must accommodate existing skills to complete the assimilation. Until the accommodations are complete, the individual is in disequilibrium.

We can see Piaget's stages as providing the basis of differing modes of experiencing of one's life situations. While the sequence of emergence might be shaped by biology, each stage remains a part of an individual's permanent mode of intellectual skills and each serves a useful function in relation to adaptation in varying situations. Each mode of functioning is particularly well mated and valued by different types of social and political organization that may exist as human beings cooperate in the struggle to adapt. I have already suggested that preoperational thinking and authoritarian social structures function well together, as do operational and democratic structures.

I briefly describe here some of the characteristics of Piaget's developmental stages and the ways in which they might be useful in adaptation, particularly as they relate to the social structures in which they best function. Basic moment-to-moment perceptual evaluation is and remains sensorimotor. Our discoveries of the world are perceptual and motoric (Puhakka 1992; Shanes 1992). We explore and physically relate to the people and objects of our world through the sense and physical operations connected and coordinated with the sensory impressions. Basic empirical discovery and survival skills, the stuff of practical intelligence—what Freud called the reality principle—are all based on sensorimotor and preoperational intelligence. The joys of eating, bathing, sleeping, and sex remain rooted in our sensorimotor involvement, with the physical social world around us.

Sensorimotor intelligence, however, does not allow for evaluations of past or future probabilities. Judgments of goodness or badness must exist in terms of pure hedonism or, as Freud suggested, according to the pleasure principle: If it feels good, it is good; if it feels bad (or not good), it is bad. Sensorimotor evaluations do not permit individuals to decenter from the immediate perceptual field in which they perceive reality or to delay actions that arise from emotional reactions resulting from perceptual experience. Sensorimotor intelligence is not, in and of itself, adequate to insure human survival on an individual basis or to foster the cooperative behavior necessary for group action.

Preoperational intelligence permits an expanded appreciation of the world around the child. Continued high levels of egocentrism create an anthropomorphic relatedness to the objects and events being appraised. The inanimate world is alive with human qualities, and events take place with human purposiveness. Judgments of good and bad are made, and the lack of seriation present in these judgments makes them absolute. Therefore, "good" becomes "best" and "bad" becomes "worst." Time and place remain here and now, making here "every place" and now "forever."

The capacity for reality testing improves with the great increase in motor skills that mark this period. The child's thinking now binds her or him to her or his social structure and allows the political structure to seem not only right but the best and necessary. Obedience to rules, seen as absolute, insures loyalty to the group as well as to authority. The individual perceives herself to be embedded in the group, which is embedded in a lively world and universe. All aspects of the world are mutually aware of and respectful to one another. Right and wrong are clearly drawn. Life is full of purpose. One is guaranteed survival and justice, if one follows authority and authority's rule. I believe there is no better form of evaluation and social structure than this, when a group is hunter-gatherer competing with the rest of the animal kingdom for survival under harsh physical environmental conditions.

The merits of preoperational thinking in adaptations are accompanied by problems that require for their solution the evolutionary experience of operational structures. Preoperational thinking still does not permit adequate planning for the future. Hypotheticodeductive thinking is still lacking. The inability to go beyond the immediate perceptual situation does not allow for the decentering that permits alternative solutions to become manifest. There is no capacity to reflect on one's own cognitive and emotional experiences and no ability to find errors in logic or to question either one's motives or future course of action. Finally, there is not a real capacity to question the wisdom of authority's actions in terms of predicted consequences (by separating judgment and description).

The emergence of formal operations permits the development of genuine hypotheses concerning a probabilistic future. It allows for critical self-examination of one's own thinking (called by Freud insight) and the critical evaluations of the motives and logic of others. It permits the individual to separate and distance himself or herself from the immediate perceptual field and to rove through time and space in a decentered fashion. Einstein was able to ask what the universe would look like if one moved through space riding the crest of a wave of light. (Such "mind experiments" began four hundred years earlier when Copernicus asked himself how the solar system would look if he stood on the sun rather than on the earth where he lived.)

The emergence of formal operations creates problems just as it solves them. One moves from moral absolutism to moral relativism. One can create principles to judge behavior but detach them from the practical, felt realities provided by sensorimotor and preoperational thinking. Formal operations permit the emergence of what I call the "future principle" (Simon 1986), which allows the individual to set up long-term goals that structure life and give it purpose. But the future principle can become detached from the reality principle and create a mode of experience in which an individual lives disconnected from the here and now.

In general, formal operations can become autonomous from the emotions and earlier forms of thinking, creating a hierarchy in which individuals think but do not feel. They create bold visions for the future on principles of right and wrong that are detached from the practical, moment-to-moment needs that make up people's lives. Rossman (1991) calls this process the separation of consciousness. When ideological visions do not include practical consequences, then the conditions are right for individuals to set in motion horrors such as we have seen in Hitler's Germany and Stalin's Russia and in a long list of other human tragedies.

6

HUMAN ADAPTATION

Adaptation is the concept that defines the goals of human behavior and hence the descriptive criteria justified by moral judgments. The evolution of human intellectual and affective processes has been shaped by and in the struggle to adapt. The adaptive process makes sense of both individual and group patterns of behavior. Defining adaptation is therefore the primary goal of this chapter. However, adaptation must be defined in human terms, not just in terms of the usual biological criterion of successful adaptation, namely, procreation.

If we successfully define adaptation and place the concept in its human configuration, then our second goal is to define the nature of developmental changes as they relate to the goals of adaptation. I will argue that when we meet a patient for the first time, we meet an individual whose behavior can best be understood as the end state of his adaptational struggles up until that moment. We are seeing an individual of biological organization developing consciousness as he or she interacts with a physical and, more important, a social environment.

Psycho"therapy" is a process that attempts to alter the nature and direction of an individual's adaptive mode of being in the world. Only by being able to state what human changes processes are and how they occur can our therapeutic techniques have any meaning. A heterophenomenological theory of human functioning must make explicit whether or not human behavior can be changed and what interventions can be demonstrated as both necessary and sufficient to exact that change. Finally, we must also make explicit whether or not the activities that we design to influence changes in human behavior meet the stated moral criteria inherent in humanistic democratic social relationships.

THE STRUCTURE OF INDIVIDUAL ADAPTIVE
PARADIGMS

I begin this discussion of adaptation with a graphic description of the elements in a human paradigm and some of the dynamics that flow from its structure. Figure 6.1 describes the structure of personal paradigms in terms of the elements described in the last chapter. Experience begins with an individual in a situation, social or physical, that is appraised by the individual. (I am using a modification of the model developed by Richard Lazarus [1991] whose work is also required reading by students of psycho"therapy.") The appraisal of the situation represents the cognitive experiencing of that situation. The appraisal is part of the noesis that creates noema and is made necessary and possible by noema.

The initial appraisal of a situation is usually perceptual and, as development continues, also involves memory of past similar situations. Simultaneously, the perception of the present is evaluated, not only for the qualities present but also for how these qualities bode for the future. As an individual perceives the present he is comparing the qualities of the situation with past experiences in order to anticipate and predict its potential. The primary cognitive appraisal, referred to as PCA, is shown in Figure 6.1.

The PCA is followed immediately by an emotional response that, along with the PCA, provides the meaning of the situation for the individual. The emotional response is organismic. It involves a physiological reaction that readies the individual for action toward the situation, a facial expression that signals the potential nature of the action to be taken, and an experiential quality that defines meaning itself. Although each emotion has its own neurophysiological configuration and facial expression, it is labeled by the individual in the context of the situation that helped bring it into existence.

The experienced meaning of a situation defines the motivation toward that situation. The motivation has no existence on any other level except the experienced meaning of the situation. One important additional element in emotional arousal involves the individual's cognitive evaluation of the skills he or she possesses to deal with the demands of a situation as he or she experiences them. The motivated consequences of an individual's response to a situation, which utilize the action and motoric skills of the individual, are guided by what Lazarus calls the secondary cognitive appraisals of the situation (SCA).

Actions taken in regard to the situation continue until the individual experiences a change in the meaning of the situation. The desired and perceived changes of events in the situation sought by the individual are the goals of the motivated actions. At the point at which the individual cognitively evaluates that changes have occurred in the situation, emotions aroused by PCA are resolved. This resolution signals an end of the action sequence with regard to the meaning experienced by the individual. I define needs as those cognitive

Figure 6.1
The Structure of a Personal Adaptive Paradigm

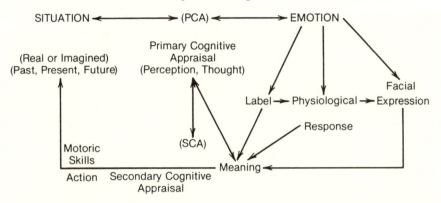

affective meanings that cannot be resolved until changes are made in the environment that signal an end to an action sequence. Threats to life and safety can lead to unresolvable fears when an individual cannot take action or is not able to engage the help of others in resolving his perception of danger. Hunger that cannot be fully satisfied may lead to preoccupation with food that will persist for as long as food is not fully available.

As development proceeds, the individual develops a repository of experience and begins both to predict the reoccurrence of situations and to make plans to engage those reoccurrences. Anticipations of the future always are rooted in past experiences but are hypothetical and involve imaginary construction of the events yet to happen. These activities are what has been referred to as *feed forward*. Under certain conditions, an individual may begin action sequences to avoid future situations. This avoidance may not permit him or her to experience the future event as it occurs, if and when it does occur. Thus, the past so colors the future that the future is seen as only a replica of the past. The anticipated event, when it does occur, is perceived as a replica of the past and thus the noemic qualities of that situation are never experienced by the individual as they potentially exist for noesis. Figure 6.2 shows the interrelationship of PCA and emotions as they simultaneously exist in past, present, and future experience.

As development continues the individual begins to evaluate his or her potential for achieving certain changes in experienced meaning. Although the dynamics of such development are complex and usually involve interaction with others (which will be discussed below), there emerges in the individual a generalized hypothesis of his or her probability of influencing future events. Julian Rotter (1966) called this expectancy *Locus of Control*, suggesting that those individuals who predict the success of their efforts to bring about change experience an internal locus of control, while those

Figure 6.2
Interaction of Cognitive Appraisals Related to Past, Present, and Future

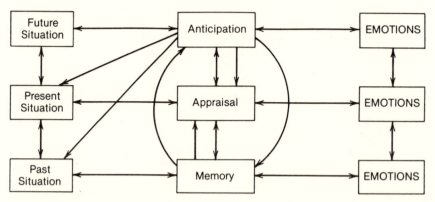

individuals who see future change as not influenced by their efforts experience an external locus of control.

Figure 6.3 suggests some of the complications that occur in sorting out just which emotions relate to which cognitive evaluations. Life does not proceed in so orderly a fashion as suggested by my figures. We may be called upon to evaluate a variety of situations either simultaneously or in short order. The situations we find ourselves evaluating are often not of our choosing or under our control as to flow and rate of experience. Moreover, some of our adaptations are long term, such as pursuing a degree or writing a book, while others may be of momentary duration, such as eating a snack or making a phone call.

Emotions aroused in one situation may color and affect the appraisals of other situations, while the struggle to achieve long-term goals can affect the perception of short-term goals. It is possible to develop permanent emotional moods that color all else. Such moods are the result of past events that are perceived by the individual to be still occurring or that he believes will reoccur no matter what efforts he makes to prevent them. An individual's locus of control creates permanent moods. Long-term moods are created by those existential realities, such as death and dying, that emerge in human consciousness with the intellectual development of formal operations. Finally, moods can develop or change as an individual develops the kind of long-range existential goals that organize and reorganize an individual's structuring of life situations.

Figure 6.4 represents a social interaction in which two individuals evaluate and emotionally react to the evaluations, emotional reactions, and motivated actions of the other. Each individual is motivated to assert and telegraph an action to the other based upon the emotional expressions and actions of the other. It is unfortunate that psychology has yet to develop a language of

Figure 6.3
Interaction of Simultaneously Aroused Cognitive-Affective Appraisals

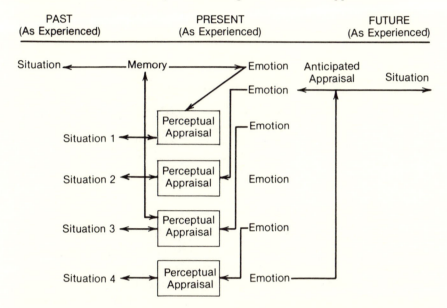

simultaneity that would permit us to describe the rapid feed forward and feed back taking place between two individuals. Psychology certainly lacks the ability to define the actions and reactions taking place in groups larger than two individuals.

There is no language to describe the phenomenological experience of the individual experiencing another experiencing him. Or, the experience of one individual experiencing another experiencing him experiencing the other. Or, the infinite regression of mutually experiencing individuals experiencing both themselves and the other experiencing both themselves and the others. Laing tried to describe the cognitive and emotional aspects of such mutual experience, but he ultimately resorted to a sort of poetry to do so (Laing 1967a). I will later suggest that only in art can we do justice to describing complex social interactions.

Figure 6.5 deals with another aspect of cognitive emotional appraisals that emerges with development. With the emergence of formal operation and reflective consciousness, the individual can appraise and react emotionally to his own developing paradigm. He can appraise his own thinking, emotions, emotional expressivity and the motoric skills with which he acts upon his world. With description comes explanation, as well as the emerging ability to predict his own reactions and control them. What we call self-control exists in its fullest state when an individual can act intellectually on her or his own personal adaptive paradigm.

Figure 6.4
Individual Adaptive Paradigms in Social Interaction

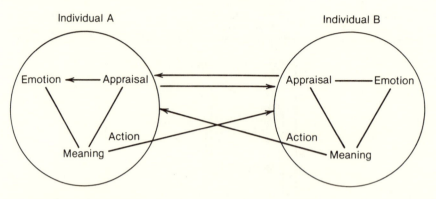

DEFINING ADAPTATION

Until this point I have been discussing a basic model to help us understand human psychological functioning from moment to moment. We function in relation to each situation we encounter in terms of our cognitive affective relationships to that situation. Our functioning can be understood in terms of our conscious experience of the world in which we live, where consciousness is comprised of our perceptual cognitive appraisals of the world and the emotions aroused by those appraisals. Consciousness, however, evolved as our main tool of adaptation. Perception, thought, memory, emotions, and motoric skills all exist as tools of adaptation. We live in order to adapt and because we do adapt.

Adaptation is one of those terms, like consciousness, that is universally used yet rarely defined. When a definition is attempted one discovers that the manner of its usage varies from one user to the next. The undefined difference in usage leads to many conceptual difficulties and intellectual conflicts. Lazarus (1991) is careful to define emotion but never defines adaptation. Mahoney (1991) does attempt a definition and in fact discusses a variety of definitions, but ends up defining *adaptative* in terms of the synonym *adjustment*, which goes undefined as well.

A definition of adaptation can be attempted in two separate yet coordinated ways. We can define adaptation both by the processes involved and by its goals. Successful adaptation or adjustment is our judgment of either the processes or the goals and as such has no part to play in its definition. The almost universal and invisible notion that adaptation implies success or something positive creates many of the difficulties in its discussions. We must not confuse our description with our judgment, our science with our morally held goals and values.

I first define adaptation in terms of its processes, then define the goals of adaptation, and finally the valued adaptations that are the goals of psycho"ther-

Figure 6.5
The Structure of Reflective Consciousness

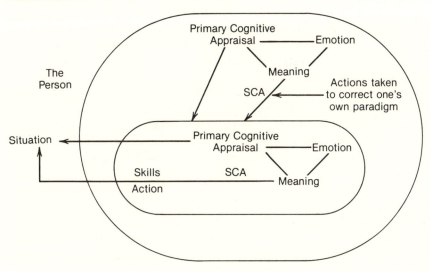

apy." We begin our definition with Piaget and to this end make use of the following schema.

Adaptation

Biological	Assimilation – – – – – – – –	Accommodation
Psychological (Modern) (Natural Science)	Needs – – – – – – – – – – –	Problems
Experiential (Postmodern)	Cognitive – – – – – – – – – Experience	Affective

Piaget defines adaptation in terms of its two subprocesses, assimilation and accommodation. Assimilation is an organism's successful attempt to *take in something from the environment or to achieve a specific goal* with its existing skills. As an organism interacts with each new situation, it attempts to use its preexisting knowledge and motor skill. All existing skills are the result of the development that took place in all previous attempts at adaptation.

When an organism cannot assimilate its goals with its existing skills in its encounter with a given environmental situation, it must accommodate or modify those skills so that assimilation can take place. Accommodations are those modifications in skills or knowledge made by an organism to fit the demands of the environmental situation. An adaptive act is over once assimilation takes place, but assimilation cannot take place unless (if necessary) the accommodation of skills takes place first. During the accommodative process new skills are learned, and such learning takes place only because of the adaptive demands made during the encounter with the environmental situation.

Assimilation and accommodation are terms derived from the biological struggle of all organisms to adapt. I believe that we can connect these terms to psychology by recognizing that in the act of assimilation we are trying to satisfy a need (or a want) and that when we accommodate we are struggling to solve problems attendant on need satisfaction. However, need satisfaction and problem solution are third-party descriptions that belong to the natural sciences. Needs and problems are experienced in both their satisfied and unsatisfied states by their cognitive affective representatives in consciousness.

What we think and what we feel as we interact with our physical and social environments define what we need and what problems must be solved. If we can accept these three levels of a definition of adaptation, we can go beyond Piaget's concept of disequilibrium and create a psychological and experiential phenomenological system of motivations as relates to human adaptation. We also have a definition of adaptation congruent with the demands of a heterophenomenological theory that begins with what human beings experience and tries to correlate experience with biological and environmental correlates of experience.

Before I go on to discuss the dynamics of adaptation and adaptation in terms of goals, a number of further issues must be discussed in terms of the process definition. First, it is clear that, just as assimilation demands accommodation, need satisfaction creates those problems that arise when the environmental situation will not yield up the goal that provides the satisfaction of needs. Need satisfaction usually cannot take place unless a variety of problems are solved. Accommodation takes place as the skills necessary for problem solving come into existence under the pressures of trying to satisfy needs. We must also discuss need satisfaction in terms of the phenomenological representation of needs, namely, the drive and the emotion. Although some needs arise out of biological disequilibrium (hunger, thirst, oxygen, sleep, elimination), our psychological needs are defined by specific emotional states. Every emotion is the experiential expression of a psychological need. If we examine Maslow's hierarchy of needs, we can see that the need for security is represented by fear; the need for love by loneliness; the need for esteem by the experience of shame or guilt; and the need for self-actualization by a variety of emotional states such as despair and anxiety. Similarly, the satisfaction of such need would be experienced by emotional states as well: security, love, pride, and joy.

If the emotions represent our psychological needs, then so do they define our problems. We feel a problem exists the moment we have a need to satisfy or an emotion to act upon. Therefore problems create needs just as needs create problems. Once we reach the phenomenological level of analysis there is, in effect, no reason to differentiate between needs and problems. As both are represented by affect, they are one and the same. They are the very terms that define our consciously experienced meanings of the situations that make up our lives. Therefore, it is also true that needs satisfied, problems solved, are defined by changes in the individual's experienced meaning of the situation that is encountered.

If Jerome Kagan (1984a) is correct in assuming that there are as many specific emotions as there are felt reactions to appraised situations, then it is also true, as emotion defines our needs, that there are as many needs and problems as emotions. However; just as we label and group emotions in order to create a science of psychology, so too can we label and group the needs. It is this task to which I now turn.

HUMAN NEEDS

Let me begin my definition of *need* by contrasting it with *want*. Both needs and wants are experienced by the individual in terms of cognitive affective representatives. Both are aroused by or directed toward a goal, which can be an environmental object, a change in the environment, or a change in the status of the individual who needs and wants. Once a goal is achieved the need is satisfied, or in terms of cognitive affective representation, a drive has been *satiated* or an emotion *resolved*.

Want and need are experienced by an individual as desire for something. If wants are not satisfied, the emotions that represent them can be resolved by an alteration in the appraisal system that aroused the want emotion in the first place. However, needs, both the biological drives and certain emotionally based desires, will not be so resolved until some action secures the necessary goal. It is easier to understand a need when a drive is involved. The hunger drive requires food. If no food is available, the hunger becomes more intense; no matter how an individual may ignore the hunger or even banish it from conscious experience, the hunger remains unsatiated. Eventually unsatiated hunger, as with all homeostatic drives, leads to death.

Psychological needs, represented by emotions, function just like drives, with the difference that death does not ensue if these needs go unsatisfied or the emotions are unresolved. Needs are preemptive and seem to demand the attention of the individual. Once aroused they have the power to eventually coopt and direct all behavior, creating what in the medical model are called obsessions and compulsions. Some needs, like a desire to create, to improve oneself, or to achieve some ambition, may determine and organize behavior over the lifetime. Some needs are experienced so powerfully by individuals that they will actually die for the goals of resolution or commit suicide if they cannot achieve them.

It is impossible to determine in advance when an cognitive-emotional experience will be a need and when it will be a want. One must understand and accept that the difference is in the experience of the individual and is created by his or her history and life situations. I suggest that we define needs in the same way Skinner defines "reinforcer." A reinforcer is so named after the fact: If it leads to a repetition of the behavior that it follows, then it is a reinforcer. A need is a need if it is unresolvable without achievement of its satisfying goal, if it preempts other behaviors, and if it otherwise behaves like a drive.

We all have a tendency to declare certain cognitive-affective motivational states to be needs in others because they are experienced as needs in ourselves. Moreover, our utopian visions of human beings, our morally chosen end goals, will lead us to select certain motivations to be called needs. Thus, Maslow (1986) believes that love, esteem, and self-actualization are powerful human needs that must be satisfied if we are to be fully human. I suggest that love and esteem (pride) are certainly experienced as needs by many, but seem not to be needs at all by many others.

I agree with Maslow that living without love or dignity and ultimately failing to voice one's poetry and song of life have serious consequences, but these consequences are our moral judgments and expression of what we (Maslow and I and those who agree with our moral philosophy) have experienced we need to feel fully human. Thus, while in my work with patients I try to help them feel such emotions, experience them as needs, and then satisfy them, I recognize that I am being guided by my faith in the moral enterprise of humanism and not in an objective scientific description of something universally in existence.

Let me briefly discuss some cognitive-affective states and the needs they define, which often bear on my clinical work. The first set of needs or emotions relates to what I discuss later as attachment and separation-individuation. There are emotion-based needs that bond us to others. We need to communicate with others, feel we belong, feel we are loved and can love. Fear is an emotion that is often resolved by the ministration of others.

Similarly, human beings seem to need to be alone at times as well. Anthony Storr (1988) points out that creative needs are often impeded by the presence of others and that those judged creative are often individuals with very poor social relationships. The exercise of new skills is a powerful motive. Hartmann's (1958) concepts of the conflict-free ego sphere and the functional autonomy of ego relate to those emotions that define the inherent emotional pleasure in self-expression and mastery. McClelland (1953), White (1959), Erikson (1968), and others have all spoken to the importance of these needs, which allow human beings to achieve a constructed sense of independence and autonomy of self.

Related to the above (and overlapping with it) are the needs for moral worth. The need for recognition in the eyes of parents, at first the child's proof of continued care and survival, not only develops into emotions that define an attached or bonded relationship but also into those emotions that define the good and worthy self. Shame and guilt are unbearable expressions of worthlessness, while pride is as powerfully sought an emotional experience as any other.

Finally, there are needs that represent our basic scientific aspirations. The ability to describe our world and to explain the events in it and our relationship to them, the capacity to predict events, and (related to our discussion of mastery and autonomy) the feeling we can control these events are represented as powerful (but often overlooked) needs. Interest and curiosity are felt representations of our desire to describe and explain events. Anxiety, an emotion long held important by clinicians, emerges the moment we cannot describe or explain events that we have judged important to our adaptation. Anxiety motivates intense searching behavior and (see below the discussion on defenses) often desperate efforts at creating explanations for events and predicting their reoccurrences.

When we struggle to master our environment, we can experience frustration, which defines a thwarted goal achievement, as well as stress, which emerges whenever we perceive that our goals are beyond our controls and skills. Boredom is a powerful emotion that is, in a sense, the opposite of stress, in that it motivates us to seek problems to solve.

All of the emotions/needs mentioned in this section define for us our adaptive struggles and success in adaptation. Some of these needs are shared with other species, and some are peculiarly human, which allows us to define adaptation in human terms. I have not tried to describe all those needs that various authors consider most vital to understanding what makes human beings human. It is time now to discuss the dynamics of adaptation.

DYNAMICS OF ADAPTATION: INTRODUCTION

The discussion of the dynamics of the individual begins in this chapter and continues throughout the following chapters. I have already introduced most of the concepts necessary to begin describing the adaptive process. If we return to Figure 6.1, we see that at any given moment each individual is in interaction with a situation in which adaptation is taking place. The cognitive evaluation or appraisal of the situation and emotional reaction to the situation define not only the meaning of the situation to the individual but also the nature of the needs (wants, desires, etc.) and problems that relate to the situation. (Our needs and problems are therefore also the meaning of the situation seen in terms of adaptation.)

Our affective responses represent both the problems and the solutions to those problems. Does the situation provide food, water, or a comfortable room where biological needs can be satisfied? Does the situation represent a source of danger requiring fight or flight, or is the situation a sought-after sanctuary from which danger can be avoided? Based on these appraisals and affective responses, each individual takes whatever action seems called for from an existing repertoire of adaptive behaviors. The goal of adaptation is to serve the self-interest of the individual as he or she experiences it.

To the knowledgeable psychologist, it might appear that I am describing the process of operant conditioning. But behaviorism merely speaks about the repetition of successful or reinforced behaviors. Behaviors that are repeated, however, change in the efficiency with which they operate. The increase in the operating efficiency of these behaviors, which have thus far been referred to as skills, leads to an increase in the range of situations the individual is willing to engage adaptively. As we interact with an increased number of situations and successfully satisfy the problems encountered there, assimilation and accommodations are taking place. The constant interaction with the environment leads to, along with biological motivations, changes in perception, cognition, and our whole set of adaptive skills.

Thumbnail descriptions of the stages suggested by Piaget are relevant at this juncture. We change not only because of our experience but by the way we have succeeded in engaging and altering our experiences. Whenever we succeed in satisfying a need (resolving an emotion or satisfying a drive) and solving the problems attendant on need satisfaction (again this means resolving an emotion), we have changed both the bases of how we experience and the skills we possess to act upon the situations that provide us our experiences. Satisfying needs and solving problems change both the intellectual and motoric skills with which the next arousal of needs and the next experienced set of problems will be faced. Both the skills that provide appraisals of situations and determine the choices of need satisfaction and mode of problem solving and the hands-on motoric actions that manipulate the world of real objects and people are crucial to human development. Both must be included in our assessments of development and our judgments of successful and failed adaptations.

Part of what we experience takes place when we succeed in satisfying our needs and in solving problems. Part of what we also learn is that we can fail to satisfy our needs and/or to solve problems. We learn to feel and deal with those emotions that represent failure. Sometimes we go hungry, and sometimes we remain afraid. Sometimes we go unloved or remain ashamed, guilty, unfulfilled, or lonely and do so in a wide variety of situations. Inherent in our learning process is the inevitable presence of appraisals critical of our (or others') efforts at adaptation. There is no way we can avoid failed adaptation and therefore no way we can avoid learning and making judgments that differentiate between success and failure in adaptation.

Animals possessing prereflective consciousness learn failure as well but do not reflect on and become aware of success and failure in so focused a way as do human beings. They certainly lack the language to define critical terms of judgment as they try to understand and generalize the causes of success and failure in adaptation. They certainly do not make generalized efforts to correct maladaptive behaviors and to plan to avoid them altogether. They never dream about creating perfection in adaptations and taking ideas of perfection as legitimate goals for their life efforts. Human beings do all of these things, and these critical activities figure centrally in comprehending human behavior.

As human beings develop, therefore, the meaning of a situation is not just described but also judged. The emotions aroused toward the situations are not only those created by description but also those that relate to judgment about the adaptive demands of the situation and judgment about the success and failure in achieving adaptation. A hungry animal that fails to capture its prey is left motivated by the intensifying hunger that first motivated its hunt. A hungry human hunter not only is left with his hunger but is now motivated by those emotions that have been aroused by the question, "Who or what is at fault for my still being hungry?"

What is judged changes with development. The younger the child, the more judgments are applied directly toward the felt consequences of the actions and not the actions themselves. With the emergence of preoperational thinking the actions of the child exist not merely as tacit means toward ends, but as the object of newly developing internalized operations.

The child becomes increasingly aware of the relationship between his or her actions and the consequences produced. These actions themselves may be judged as good or bad. An important point to be made is that for the preoperational child actions, consequences, and the motives that generate actions are seen as indivisible, as a single unit, and therefore are judged together as good or bad. In the preoperational child a painful consequence of an action can lead not only to "I did a bad thing," but also to "I am bad." Piaget referred to the logic growing out of such an appraisal-judgment as immanent justice. The child believes, "If I have done a bad thing (or I am bad) then I must be punished." However, it is also true for the child, "If I am punished (that is any painful event takes place) then I must be bad (or have done a bad thing)." A child who finds himself or herself in constant pain may well conclude that he or she is totally and permanently bad. Harry Stack Sullivan (1953) refers to the child's conclusion that he or she is irredeemably bad as a "malevolent transformation."

With the emergence of operational appraisals the child can now judge his or her own thinking and emotions, that is, the operation of consciousness itself or the totality of his or her adaptive paradigm according to various standards. If the child possesses an articulated definition of logic, he or she becomes capable of taking corrective action after questioning his or her own modes of solving problems and utilizing forms of logic. He or she can correct the grammar and structure of a written essay or other cognitive creations. Standards become articulated as to the worth of music, art, debates, and the like, and the individual becomes capable of mature criticism.

However, if an individual thinks he or she is bad in essence, then the essence of one's paradigm and the constructed sense of self become judged as inadequate. "I am wrong, or crazy, or evil" can be an ongoing and permanent part of every appraisal of every situation that makes up the individual's life. The past is recalled in terms dictated by the individual's perceived deficit of self, and the future is predicted through the same lens. When moral criteria become detached from specific adaptive criteria and the individual judges himself or herself as less than he or she "should be," then a never-ending adaptive struggle can begin that preempts all others. The dynamics of an adaptive struggle that begins with some malevolent transformation of self will be discussed in later chapters, as it is these struggles that often comprise the work of psycho"therapy."

I must make clear at this point that there must be standards by which we judge our behaviors and thoughts. These standards, however, must remain articulated and justified by criteria that define successful or failed adaptations. Psycho"therapy" must have as one of its goals a change in the logic and motor skills of those who seek treatment. Often psychotherapists (and increasingly teachers and others who work with children in other capacities) believe that if they flatter patients or excuse a patient's failures in adaptation by appealing to the victimization of the patient, then self-esteem will improve. I believe that only with each new skill and each new experience in need satisfaction and problem solving can an individual's pride and self-esteem legitimately increase.

The nature of an individual's adaptational struggle changes with development. The needs of a newborn are not the same needs of an adult in whom cognitive affective development has taken place in regard to a wide variety of life situations. The struggle of an infant for food gives way to a struggle to learn to walk and speaking followed by a struggle to deal with parents, teachers, and possibly a mate. The struggles on the playing field give way to struggles on a battlefield or perhaps in a corporation or bureaucracy. The fifteen-year-old fears that no one will love him or her; the fifty-year-old struggles with the fear of death. Comprehending basic language is replaced by a need to comprehend chemistry and gives way to comprehending the meaning of life, the purpose of suffering, and the nature of morality.

I am not minimizing adolescents' anxiety concerning social acceptance in the face of their parents' anxiety about their children's future. The suffering and struggle are as real to one age group as they are to the other. The adaptive demands are equal on each, given the fact that the parents have long since mastered the children's problems concerning social acceptance and in doing so have developed the skills to be parents. Often children look at the power and freedom of adults and become envious of such power without realizing the responsibilities that go with such freedom. Adults easily forget the pain of learning algebra as they struggle with the responsibilities of paying their monthly bills.

Adaptation is a lifelong process, and the mastering of the skills of one age brings awareness and skills that must once again accommodate to the demands of ever new, ever more complex adaptations. With increased understanding we see more of life's beauties but also more of life's horrors. Only an adult who has mastered many tasks can experience the stagnation of middle age or the despair of old age, as the aged individual judges his or her own life to be unfulfilled (Erikson 1968).

A special note must be made of situations in which an individual must deal with irresolvable pains. There are a number of categories of psychological experience that define irresolvable pain. Any need that goes unsatisfied is defined experientially by an emotion that is irresolvable. Anxiety is unresolved if an individual cannot get access to the information she or he experiences as necessary to continue adaptations. Guilt continues if its resolution is dependent on the forgiveness of another that is not forthcoming. Continued contempt and disgust by important social relationships lead to unresolved shame. Constant threat produces irresolvable fear or even terror. Problems that cannot be solved may be marked by ongoing pressure, stress, and frustration. Inability to decide between various alternative goals can place one in irresolvable conflict.

Although psychotherapy literature often seems to avoid the issue, life is often tragic. We must suffer, as Shakespeare has written, "the slings and arrows of outrageous fortune." Diseases, natural disasters, accidents, and crimes of all sorts can happen to any of us or our loved ones at any moment. Such events are beyond our explanation, prediction, and control and present us with all manner of irresolvable psychological and physical pains.

Pain is also created by moral judgments that cannot be corrected. The crimes, accidents, and diseases that can happen are also judged morally. Not only can we not understand why we were victimized, but we may also have to live with the pain created when we stare at misfortune and say, "It's not fair." Often we begin saying "It's not fair" in early childhood and do not stop our moral protests until we are dead.

Pain can be lived with if certain conditions are met. The first condition exists if we recognize that we have a need that is unmet, a problem to solve, or a misfortune to contend with and then employ some cognitive-philosophical conceptualization to accept and live with the pain. Statements such as, "Into every life some pain must come," allow the pain a place in the life situation. They make the pain inevitable and in a sense an ordinary occurrence. Comparing one's pain to that of someone with even more pain ("I cried because I had no shoes until I met a man who had no feet") often allows the pain to be acceptable.

The second way in which pain is made acceptable is if it is justifiable. The emergence of the reality principle allows an individual to forgo pleasures if he can comprehend that as necessary in permitting life to continue. Psychoanalysis has long recognized that self-control develops once an individual can recognize the adaptive consequences of satisfying or not satisfying a need. With the emergence of the future principle, individuals can develop life goals that permit the acceptance of long periods of deprivation and unsatisfied needs. If an individual cannot philosophically accept the presence of a pain and cannot justify such pain as necessary, then the individual may turn to defense mechanisms as a solution.

Unconsciousness

Let me begin the discussion with some terms related to various aspects of consciousness. We have one way or another discussed all of the material before, but it is necessary to bring the trends of this topic together for additional clarity. Consciousness exists wherever an organism is able to respond with purpose toward a situation that is meaningfully experienced. The situation becomes meaningful as a result of some perceptual cognitive processing and the arousal of an affect. This definition, however, runs counter to what might be called the commonsense definition of consciousness, which requires that an individual be able to reflect upon and communicate to others or himself about his experience.

Rossman (1991) would place my definition of consciousness in the category he calls prereflective consciousness. He would place the commonsense usage of consciousness in the category he refers to as reflective consciousness. The emergence of reflective consciousness brings into existence the constructed self and leads to the common adult belief that consciousness is necessary for voluntary, purposeful adaptive actions to exist. This belief is fostered by the adult experience of the Cartesian self—that is, a self that is aware of all relevant sensory impressions and is the necessary actor if action is to take place.

As with so many "naive" impressions of our world, science teaches us that what we experience as real may not be real on further analysis. The earth appears flat to us, the sky a round dome above us, while the sun moves from one horizon to another while we remain still. Day-to-day survival continues quite well even if we never learn that how we experience our world can be altered by a further analysis and the application of formal operations. So, too, it is necessary for us to experience ourselves as actors and objects in the day-to-day flow of our lives.

But further analysis is necessary if we are to understand other aspects of our own functioning. Most of our adaptive functioning is beyond those experiences that form the Cartesian self. We hear our alarm clock ring or our baby cry while we appear to be fast asleep. We walk, speak, play sports, or write without reflecting on the tacit processes that make those activities possible. In fact, almost all of our reactions to things that threaten us are well under way before we are able to reflect on either what has happened to us or how we chose those appropriate voluntary responses to deal with the threat. To understand all of these activities one must define more broadly what is meant by reflective consciousness.

If we examine our prereflective consciousness, we see that our tacit behaviors are of two types. One type, represented by those skills that allow us to ride a bicycle or see a Necker Cube as solid, is forever hidden from reflective consciousness. These basic developmental processes have their origins in early evolution and require their unreflected status if they are to function correctly. The second type of tacit processes is represented by higher-order, better organized behaviors that function as tools to some adaptive end. Often those behaviors came into existence as the objects of conscious experience but are now so routinized and automatic that they are taken for granted. These behaviors are not usually the object of reflective attention.

Wherever the skills of survival might benefit from the corrective function of reflective consciousness they remain available for conscious scrutiny. Eventually, development allows us to become reflectively conscious of our thought processes and emotions. We therefore become reflectively conscious of consciousness itself. However, psychoanalysis makes us aware that any object of reflective consciousness can join those tacit processes on which we cannot reflect. Rossman calls these once-available objects of reflective consciousness and the processes by which they cannot once again be reflected upon as nonconsciousness or unconsciousness.

What we must eventually understand is the process by which reflective consciousness is lost. How does that which has a potential for reflective consciousness lose the potential? Traditional psychoanalysis conceptualized the explanation for unconsciousness in a variety of ways. Consciousness was conceived of as having levels, in much the same way that a house or structure has levels. Reflective consciousness was referred to as consciousness proper, thus conforming to the commonsense definition. That which could be reflected upon but at any given moment was not being attended to was in the preconscious level. If a content of experience could not be made conscious, then it was in the unconscious.

What determined the difference between inhabiting the preconsciousness and the unconscious was the defense mechanisms, chief of which was the mechanism of repression. The defense mechanism repressed or otherwise consigned experiences to the unconscious if they were in some way painful or threatening to the individual. Therefore, certain sexual feelings would be placed in the unconscious if they conflicted with society's prohibition of them or if society would threaten the individual with grievous harm if these feelings were expressed or acted upon. Environmental events of any kind could be repressed and banned from consciousness if they sufficiently threatened the individual.

I will not discuss the enormous conceptual problems created by the traditional analytic notion of the unconscious. These problems include dualities of all kinds. The theory creates a subterranean world of thoughts and feelings operating as it were in another sphere of human existence. As thoughts must have a actor to be thought, this solution produces a bifurcation of self or ego, creating two Cartesian selves or actors operating independently of one another. In recent years psychoanalysts such as George Klein (1976), Matthew Erdelyi (1985), and Roy Schafer (1976, 1980, 1983) have retained the idea of unconscious processes but abandoned the structures and dualisms inherent in analytic conceptualizations.

The present system offers an answer as to how certain psychological phenomena remain outside of reflective awareness. But the explanation lies in the manner in which the individual does not reflect on what is otherwise perfectly conscious. There are no places called the unconscious or energy systems blocking thoughts from emerging into consciousness or subterranean actors pressing thought into consciousness or into the unconscious. Describing consciousness from a "bottom-up" evolutionary point of view runs counter to our "top-down" dualistic Cartesian point of view. The benefits of the bottom up approach help avoid the problems inherent in the other approach.

Defense Mechanisms

Defense mechanisms are adaptive behaviors in which conscious experience is altered in some essential way. Defenses involve the denial and distortion of experienced reality or reality as experienced. In one way or another, defenses involve the reconstruction or fabrication of reality. They involve a phenomenological mode of experience in which the individual is taken away (so to speak) from the very same objects to which Husserl insisted scientific phenomenological experience should take him or her. Defenses exist at all developmental levels of experience and involve the alteration of any and all aspects of the personal adaptive paradigm. Both appraisals and emotions can be altered in defenses.

Defenses are adaptive for the individual who uses them. When individuals are confronted with situations that are experienced as failed adaptation, when needs remain unsatisfied and problems remain unsolved, when drives are not satiated or emotions resolved, then defenses create the experience of a successful adaptation. If one examines the consequences of the use of defenses as clinicians often do, then it is easy to see that from a third-person point of view defenses are very maladaptive. Defenses usually bring about an intensification of the very conditions that led to their usage. But from the experience of the user of defenses, these modes of adaptation bring about short-term reductions in anxiety, guilt, shame, loneliness, fear, and other emotions that define unmet needs and unsolved problems.

Defenses may create the experience that a problem that cannot be solved does not exist and thus no solution is necessary. The world is made to go away by altering the appraised experience of various situations presenting unsolvable problems. Dangers whose existence are denied can cause no fear. Anxiety is reduced by creative explanations and by developing faith that such explanations are absolutely true and inviolable. Where there were doubt and confusion there are now certainty and calm. Emotions such as loneliness can be reexperienced as a hunger for food and satiated by a hearty repast of foods associated with mother's love.

Any and all judgments can be redefined with a bit of inventiveness. A "hard-working" individual is judged as a "type A obsessive compulsive personality," while those judged to be "lazy" are merely "flexible" and "laid-back." A "bully" is "masterful," while a "living doormat" becomes a "saint." Horney (1950) was a master at describing how judgments, when used defensively, can idealize any weakness and turn it into an experience of strength. There is no act that one individual might consider too hideous even to have taken place that another individual might not take great pride in.

Defenses allow us to create justifications for those pains that come unbidden with life's tragedies and injustices. With defenses we can be immortal, the good never go unrewarded, and the bad never go unpunished. We can experience a world as it should be and not as it is. We can assimilate without having to accommodate and recreate an image of our constructed self that is lacking in flaws, needs, or any other condition that cannot otherwise be corrected. We can be perfect. We can be gods!

Let me briefly discuss defenses at the sensorimotor preoperational and operational levels of cognitive functioning. At the sensorimotor level individuals can withdraw from the world in sleep or alter perceptual experience with a variety of hallucinatory phenomena. Freud became interested in mental illness when he studied "hysterical" patients with Chariot in Paris. These patients (mostly women) had become functionally blind, deaf, paralyzed, or anesthetized even though it could be demonstrated that experience was taking place in other than reflective conscious modes.

In subsequent chapters, I argue that all hallucinations that have meaning are defensive alterations of perceptual experience. Seeing, hearing, and speaking to God allow a wide variety of terrors to be resolved and a host of serious problems to appear solved. In our present era we are particularly harsh in our judgments of those who alter basic perceptual experiences, even though we have no idea how these often impressive and creative achievements are managed. It is true that working with an individual who creates and hears voices can be emotionally draining. Therapists have all experienced their own "annihilation," as a patient states, "The voices say they are real and you are not. I believe them." We call people who use such defenses psychotic.

Most defenses operate by altering beliefs rather than perceptual experience. To this end, preoperational thinking allows for the freest creation of assimilative fantasies. To live in a world enlivened anthropomorphically and be able to appeal to the stars, the gods, or other forces to help us solve problems is propitious indeed. With preoperational thinking there are no accidents, and with thoughts endowed with magical powers those forces hostile to us can be begged, intimidated, or otherwise negotiated with. Most "neurotic" "irrational" thinking is preoperational. Preoperational thinking is usually in force when we first learn to be terrified of the world and is usually retained to deal with those same terrors.

Most religions satisfy their faithful by retaining and utilizing peroperationally created concepts and belief systems. However, an individual who uses the exact same logic to satisfy needs or to solve problems by belief in non–socially accepted forces is likely to be declared delusional and once again declared psychotic. The use of defenses allows the individual to experience as real what another believes to be fantasy, while reciprocally those things held to be truest by one are complete fantasy to the other.

Defenses also exist with operational thinking. Operational thought does not permit the fantastic manipulations achievable with preoperational thinking. With operational thinking there can be accidents, and logic forces us not only to accept our own mortality but also to contemplate the extermination of the species. When defenses are employed simultaneously with formal operations, they usually involve detaching the emotions from the experience of conclusions that threaten adaptation. Thus a military planner can discuss with mathematical precision "acceptable losses in a nuclear exchange that number 50 million dead and one hundred million injured."

The fabrication of reality goes on rather continuously by us human beings. Our religions, ideologies, delusions, myths, and theories are constantly invested with them. No discussion of reality can avoid the notion that we human beings alter reality to at least the same degree to which we discover it. Psychologists are often amazed by philosophical discussions of reality, science, and the justification of theory that do not take into account a discussion of the psychological defenses employed by the philosophers involved in the discussion.

7

INDIVIDUAL STYLES OF ADAPTATION

In this crucial chapter I discuss how various individuals develop, maintain, and change their unique modes of being in the world, arguing for two points necessary for my theory of psycho"therapy." The first point is that any dispassionate analysis of human behavior and development would find it to be highly unlikely that any two people could ever come to experience the world and adapt to it in exactly the same way. The second point is that our understanding of how human beings develop and adapt is incomplete and shrouded in an ignorance that dwarfs our as yet minimal efforts to comprehend our own human behavior.

I believe that any clinician who accepts these two points would be forced not only to see his or her patients in a very different light but to treat them in a different manner than is now dictated by perceptions determined by the medical model and existing clinical theories of behavior. The clinical-medical model creates two illusions for most current therapists. The first is that they can scientifically organize all human behavior into two categories: normal and abnormal. The second is that they understand how various biological defects or childhood traumas and deprivations create abnormalities, pathologies and disorders. In short, much human uniqueness is judged to be bad in some way, and the condemnation is experienced by the clinician as both descriptive and explanatory.

In my argument I also wish to avoid making the inverse of the clinician's error. In asserting the position that we have as yet no scientific basis for organizing human adaptive paradigms into meaningful categories, I do not want to advocate a moral position that uniqueness represents, in itself, something necessarily good. I am arguing that the clinical position fails to see human beings as unique because most forms of adaptive uniqueness are judged before they are ever described or understood. Though I feel compelled to conclude that we cannot understand human behavior unless we perceive it in all its variations, I am not equally compelled to conclude that all of these variations are morally acceptable.

It is the clinician's error, as I have now dubbed it, that makes this particular chapter difficult to read and accept. Those aspects of my own training and my tendency to moralize and justify human uniqueness have made this a very difficult chapter to write. It is not easy to describe how human beings can use drugs, commit murder, or abandon their children as adaptive modes of being in the world and not to moralize about such behavior. It is equally difficult for many of the same clinicians to understand how any behavior becomes determined and inevitable if seen both historically and through the subjectivity of the individuals and not to take a moral position that seems to say, "To understand all is to forgive all."

Where then to begin in understanding the experience of human differences? Let us assume that three young men walking down a street are suddenly confronted by several snarling dogs. One young man immediately looks about for objects with which he can defend himself and simultaneously begins estimating a method of retreat if defense is not possible. The second young man drops to his knees and loudly prays to God to protect him from harm from the dogs. The third young man sucks his thumb and begins to hallucinate that he is elsewhere. He begins a conversation with people that only he experiences as being real.

If we apply the clinician's error to this scene we might well argue that the first man is adapting best to the situation and that the second is not adapting as well to reality but we can understand his motivations. The third individual has not adapted at all and should probably be diagnosed as schizophrenic. I suggest that we throw out all of our judgments and answer that, from the phenomenological experience of each individual, each is adapting as it makes sense for him to do so. If we make such an assumption, then we must ask why each young man sees fit to express his self-interest in the way he has. Why do all three react differently to the same situation?

To complicate the point further let me assume that we observe increasingly large numbers of individuals as they react to the same situation. We might observe more reactions that might be characterized as practical, prayerful, or pathological. I would assume that many more categories of response would emerge. However many discernible categories might finally exist in our descriptions, in the final analysis we would observe that no two individuals would adapt to the situation in the same style and manner. Quite apart from the issue of judging which mode and styles of adaptation are superior is the problem of explaining why so many differences exist.

By assuming that every response to the dogs is an adaptation, I can now begin to ask why there is so much variability in the modes and manners of doing so.

A simple way out of the quandary is to appeal to pure subjectivism for a solution. Each individual behaves in terms of his or her appraisal of and emotional response to the situation. However true this answer may be, it does not satisfy from an heterophenomenological point of view. To answer the heterophenomenologist I am forced to confront my ignorance and my prejudices and try to construct some explanation for why adaptive differences exist.

SOURCES OF VARIABILITY IN ADAPTIVE FUNCTION

Most therapists will assume three interconnected sources of variability in human adaptive responses: biological, psychological, and sociological. I believe that human variability is contributed to by all three, but only as each is contextualized by the other two and by all their interactions as contextualized historically. For the sake of pedagogy let me briefly tease out some of the biological and social factors that might be shaping an individual's moment-to-moment adaptive behavior. I stress that all of my conjecturing is theoretical. Finally, for reasons I will presently make clear, I will spend most of this chapter on the social and psychological contributors to human variability.

Biological Factors Shaping Adaptive Differences

In recent years it has again become possible to suggest that human beings are psychologically different from one another, because of biological, inherited differences. By mid-century and the subsequent decade or so, it had become anathema to suggest to a psychologist that human beings were biopsychologically different from one another. In 1959 I took a course on human growth and development with Kenneth Clark, who was a recognized scholar and revered institution at CCNY based on his writings and his contribution to the decisions of the Supreme Court in *Brown versus the Board of Education of Topeka, Kansas, 1954*. Clark's attitude was representative of that of most of my professors when he insisted often and passionately that John Locke was most correct in depicting the newborn human being as a *tabula rasa* or blank slate. All human differences were purely environmental and socially induced.

There are many reasons that clinicians have insisted on seeing all variability as coming from environmental sources. First, it violates one's sense of fairness that individuals might be born unable to compete for success in one or another of life's arenas. Second, therapists and educators perceive their desires to change the behavior of others as doomed from the outset if biology determines human behavior. Third was the realization that positive biological differences between groups such as the races or the sexes seemed always to lead to the creation of social hierarchies based on judgments of those differences. These social hierarchies then justified the most pernicious and discriminatory political, economic, and educational policies.

As scientists, however, we must insist that if we do find biological differences to exist between individuals or groups we note that such differences exist; then we must take care that we neither allow nor participate in social policies that dehumanize or denigrate any human being. Once we do note these differences, we are also bound to use them to help us understand differences in human adaptation, even if such differences contribute to what we believe is adaptive failure.

What biological differences might exist, and how do they contribute to differences in adaptive strategies or modes of conscious experience? In recent years researchers such as Thomas, Chess, and Birch (1968) have urged us to see that children are born with varying responses to basic environmental stimulation. A light or sound that might arouse the curiosity of one child might greatly upset another. Children seem to differ from one another as to things like pain and perceptual thresholds, intensity of emotional responsivity, and developmental speed of varying abilities. Such research adds to commonsense beliefs that certain inborn reactions allow some individuals to respond differentially to musical sounds, color, and so on and thus provide the bases for increased adaptation to music and art and the like. (For three years I worked at a music college where a moral hierarchy of major proportions existed. Musicians born with perfect pitch tormented those born with variable pitch.)

Jerome Kagan (1984) has done valuable research that suggests that inborn differences play a role as to how timid or bold a developing child might be. In the next chapters I shall suggest that many of my so-called schizophrenic patients have extreme emotional and perceptual sensitivities, making the use of certain protective defenses necessary from their phenomenological point of view. An emerging set of research data suggests that adaptive patterns are in part determined by inborn biological differences, which include cortical organization, neurotransmitters and levels of hormones, handedness, and sexuality.

In general, I believe the case can be made that human brains must be as anatomically and physiologically different from one another as human faces. Although some of these differences might be the result of random genetic variations and others might be the result of eons of adaptive struggles, they leave each individual experiencing the sights and sounds of the world uniquely. However any group or individual defines adaptive success or failure in any given situation, it is clear that each individual will be led, because of these (as yet uncharted and uncategorized) innate differences, to carry out the adaptive struggle as only that individual can and must. Which individuals develop skills, which use defenses, and in which situation any given individual will use one or the other will have some biological factor as part of the explanation of differences.

Environmental Factors Shaping Adaptive Differences

It would appear that the adaptive strategies of human beings are created and shaped as they encounter and engage the environments in which they must live.

To understand why in our example the three men reacted to the dogs as they did requires an understanding of not only how they came biologically equipped to respond to this world but also how that equipment was shaped, reinforced, punished, and fit into the varying physical and social environments in which these men had been embedded and enfolded since the moment of their conceptions. Not only is such information most often not known to us, it is also mostly unknowable. Yet, if we are to influence the consciousness of individuals, we must have some theory and information as to the shaping of their individual paradigms.

I will limit this brief discussion to a theory of how consciousness may be shaped as a result of interactions with other human beings, although it is clear that interactions with animals and the physical environment will also direct the development of our adaptive paradigms. It is relevant to note whether an individual lives in an urban, suburban, or rural area. We are shaped differently by interactions with landscapes designed by technology or by nature. Our paradigms are differentially affected if we live at times of peace or war, of famine or of plenty, in valleys or mountains, in forests or tundra, or in other settings too numerous to categorize. Here I concentrate on an aspect of human interactions that shapes the adaptive paradigm.

From the moment we are born we begin to make a most basic discovery: Sometimes we need and want to be with other people, and sometimes we neither need nor want to be with other people. How we satisfy the needs and solve the problems that involve both our coming together with others and separating from them create many of our adaptive differences. From the point of view of the psycho"therapist" the differences in strategy and skills developed during the earliest years of joining with and separating from people are the differences that require the most understanding. What therapists most often seek to understand and change are the conscious modes of being in the world shaped in the context of the consciousness of others.

I will assume that the role played in shaping individual differences by social interaction begins at birth. I will also assume that these differences are shaped in the course of the developing child's interaction with the primary caretakers and involve issues related to the establishment of attachment, separation, and individuation. In this regard, I will draw on the works of John Bowlby (1969, 1973, 1979, 1980, 1988), Mary Ainsworth (1985, 1989), L. A. Sroufe (1987), Margaret Mahler (1968), Heinz Kohut (1971, 1977), D. W. Winnicott (1965), Daniel Stern (1977), and Jessica Benjamin (1988) among others in both the academic and psychoanalytic communities. I will also try hard to avoid the clinician's error built into these discussions by describing the development of children who fail to form attachments as different rather than automatically calling these patterns traumatic and pathological.

I will also discuss development and the shaping of individual adaptive differences from the vantage point of the three types of social interactions discussed earlier, the anarchistic, authoritarian-totalitarian, and the democratic-humanistic. In this regard it seems to me clear that when one reads the literature on attachment and models of separation-individuation as espoused, for example, by Jessica Benjamin (1988), one is reading about preferred, idealistic patterns that are the prototypes of democratic-humanistic adult relationships. Although I completely share Benjamin's values, certain assumptions must be explicated about the preference.

The first is that little time is spent describing the development of children who fail to meet preferred standards except in negative judgmental terms dictated by the medical model. The second as yet unwarranted assumption is that there is a cause-and-effect relationship between failure in attachment and/or separation and specific forms of adult behavior (in pathology). Grunbaum (1984) has effectively demolished that argument, leaving us to fret over the fact that there is no evidence to support or to negate the analytic hypothesis that infant experiences in and of themselves are necessary and sufficient to determine specific patterns of adult behavior, pathological or otherwise. Kagan (1984) has similarly argued against this hypothesis. It appears, then, that as we discuss the topic of how infancy and social interactions may shape adaptive paradigm differences we must recognize that we are essentially ignorant on this issue, no matter how compelling the argument is in both commonsense and moral terms.

I will make a conservative hypothesis that the first social shaping of the individual's adaptive paradigm occurs in infancy and involves the manner and mode of the development of attachment and the manner and mode of separation-individuation. I will also assume that at any moment in an individual's development his or her style and skills of engaging others and maintaining separation are the product of all previous experiences as well as those begun in infancy. It is, however, distinctly possible that the conscious experience of social interactions occurring in infancy has a more powerful and enduring impact than those later in life in that they create assumptions about self and others that act as self-confirming and self-fulfilling prophecies.

Attachment assumes theoretical importance as a shaper of personal paradigms, in part because Bowlby (1979) and others have assumed that it is an adaptive device resulting from the evolutionary process. At birth the human baby requires extensive adult intervention in satisfying a wide variety of needs if it is to survive. Moreover, the baby comes equipped at birth or soon after with a variety of skills, such as crying, smiling, making and holding eye contact with adults, and preferring the shape of the human face to other patterns of stimuli, that seem to allow him or her to engage actively and develop ongoing relationships with his or her caretakers.

The infant's apparent desire to establish human relationships seems both instrumental, in that it assures adult continuance in need satisfaction, and also reflective of need for human contacts. It appears to be innately satisfying for human beings to relate to other human beings. If these hypotheses are correct, then the perceived availability of the caretaker for need satisfaction of both the biological and social needs of the infant represents a range of potential problems for the infant. How the infant solves these problems, the skills used, and the defenses employed might well create powerful tendencies to behave in similar ways whenever human contact is needed or interpersonal cooperation is demanded.

It is beyond the scope of this book to begin to exhaust the possibility of differences in adaptive strategies emerging from infancy. Clinicians are often most concerned with the differences produced in those who succeed and fail in establishing secure attachments with adult caretakers. Workers in the field refer to failed attachments as resulting from maternal separation and deprivation. I suggest that, from the infant's point of view and from a variety of social perspectives, anarchy in family and community relationships is parallel to maternal deprivation. Attachments do occur in authoritarian caretakers' relationship to children, but workers in the field might call such mothers rejecting and punitive. The ideal of attachment and separation called for by clinicians conforms to my notion of democratic-humanistic relationships. Each style of interaction creates differences in the emerging individual adaptive paradigm.

Let me briefly define attachment. As a result of maternal or caretaker availability, of having the caretaker satisfy basic biological needs over time, of experiencing success in one's efforts at altering and affecting caretaker behavior, and of experiencing his or her existence as being recognized (and perhaps pleasing to) the caretaker, the child develops an attachment to the caretaker. An attachment, suggests Ainsworth (1989), is a special type of emotional bond. Emotional bonds are defined by several criteria: (a) They are marked by long-term ties to another person, who becomes unique as an individual and "interchangeable with no other" (71). (b) Inexplicable and unplanned separations from the person with whom the bond exists lead to emotional distress, while (c) pleasure and even joy result from being reunited with that individual, and (d) permanent separation leads to grief and mourning (which I assume is the process by which emotional bonds are dissolved). Attachment is an emotional bond in which one experiences security and comfort from the relationship with the partner.

Attachment and its failure are hypothesized to be the prototypic relationship that influences not only how an individual will come together with others but also how an individual will learn to be on his or her own. Even as the developing child is forming an emotional bond with a caretaker, skills are developing in the child that will allow her or him to satisfy her or his own needs and increasingly solve her or his own problems. Eventually, the individual will be able to seek out and expand the range of her or his human relationships. The process of growing more independent of one's attachment is referred to as separation-individuation.

As children separate and try new skills, they inevitably reach a point at which they encounter difficulties too great for them to manage. They extend themselves in ways in which the adventure of separating becomes frightening. They might encounter what they perceive to be threat and danger. At these moments children turn toward those to whom they are attached for help in satisfying needs, solving problems, or being comforted in the face of fear-inducing situations. Children's willingness to risk change and continue development of skills allowing independence seems deeply affected by the nature of the support they experience in the attachment relationship.

A vast literature exists on the hypothesized difference between securely attached and poorly attached children as they develop. With intellectual development children internalize images of the source of perceived comfort, allowing them to control fear and soothe themselves without the caretaker being present. This internalization of a comforting presence affects the distance children will move comfortably from home. Kohut has referred to the internalized images of the caretaker as self-objects. One potent source of individual differences in adaptive paradigms might well rest with the fact that some individuals create while others do not create self-object images.

I will now contextualize the process of attachment and separation-individuation along the lines already discussed, the anarchistic, authoritarian, and democratic modes of social interaction. As Stern (1977), Benjamin (1988), and others point out, these early processes are part of a child's overall social contextualization. They do not proceed according to some ordained biological fashion free of social contexts. The shaping of the adaptive paradigm, as the child forms attachments, is what produces the differences in the paradigm. Let me briefly describe the shaping processes of each mode of social organization and some of the dynamics and styles of adaptive paradigms that seem to result.

Anarchy

All children, in one way or another, develop skills and defenses not only to master the needs of attachment but also to deal with the stresses, fears, and dangers attendant on separation. I am beginning with the processes and outcomes of anarchistic relationships for reasons that will become clear in a moment and will spend the bulk of my theory in dealing with the other two interactive styles.

We are beginning to see increasing numbers of children, brought to the mental health system with complaints by teachers, family members, and law enforcement officials, who have developed in what I have chosen to call anarchy. Parents maybe divorced, often fathers are absent from the home or not even known by the mothers. Mothers may be on drugs and not available in the most minimal ways for their children. These children may have spent time in a substantial number of foster homes and a variety of public agencies. Social workers and mental health personnel have passed through their lives in numbers too great for the children to remember them, let alone develop a relationship with any.

These children have often experienced sexual encounters and violence of a variety of types. One of the children I interviewed had watched her mother prostitute herself for drugs and on occasion had herself been offered to the customers. A little boy was taken by his mother's boyfriend, along with his younger brother, to what turned out to be a drug transaction. The drug deal went bad, and this little boy watched as his brother and the mother's boyfriend were shot to death. Often these children spend long unsupervised hours on streets where drugs, guns, and violence are commonplace, loyalty does not exist, and rules are established by those possessing the most power.

My experience with these children is often surreal and unreal. The modes of consciousness with which they appraise the world are so alien to my own that establishing a relationship becomes most difficult. My ability to engage them and create attachment processes is poor and knowing where to begin to set moral limits most difficult. The children often do not expect sympathy or understanding, and when these are offered they are experienced as weakness. As they have no real sense of property, these children do not understand the differentiation between mine, yours, and ours.

When I discuss the therapeutic processes of these children with colleagues I hear similar laments from them. There is difficulty both in making emotional contact and in setting limits. One plays games with them, which makes the hour pass quickly. There are no adults with whom to engage and set up a family therapy as adjunct to the individual process. Often there is a deep sorrow for these children as well as a growing sense of alarm that, as the number of them grows, so too will the most serious social problems and dislocations. Sympathy and pity are not the most productive of emotions with which to justify any relationship, and those relationships that depend solely upon these emotions often turn frustrating and angry in nature.

In the next decade or so, if the number of these children continues to grow, there will be massive social problems, which the mental health system will be called on to treat. At that point I can predict a host of new disorders will emerge, as well as new therapies that will involve drugs and behavioral techniques, both of which will be dictated by the needs for social controls as adjuncts to or instead of prisons. Therefore, I turn now to those more traditional contextualizations of human development, the authoritarian-totalitarian and the democratic-humanistic.

Authoritarian-Totalitarian Interactions

However much authoritarian parents are emotionally bonded to their children and love them, they experience themselves as inherently superior to their children. Like most of humanity (including most psychotherapists), they perceive the child as a defective adult. The job of parenting is to see to it that the child becomes the superior being that the adult has become. Children are usually perceived as passive, not able to know what they like, and often as gullible, innocent and naive. Often too, children are viewed as easily corrupted people who will be damaged irreparably if exposed too early to the world of the superior adult.

If children engage in behaviors that displease adults, it becomes the parental job to instruct them as to responsibilities. Effective adult power must be used to achieve these ends. Children must be reminded constantly of their moral failing and moral responsibility and must not demand or assert themselves beyond their true place in the family hierarchy. Parents are motivated by their positive moral quality. They are good, caring, and hard workers, while children are lazy, disobedient, disrespectful, and sloppy. Sometimes children are "filled with the devil," and it may be necessary to "beat the devil out of them." In order to get children to respect their superior elders, it may be necessary to hit or spank them, justifying this by saying "you need a good beating." Children who continue to resist adult power are willful and thoroughly ungrateful for all the good being done to them.

In totalitarian homes children have to be told what they feel as well as what to do. "Eat, you are hungry." "Go to bed, you are tired." If children express an emotion that is unacceptable to judging adults, they may be asked, "What has gotten into you lately?" "What kind of child are you?" "What's wrong with you?" "What's the matter with you?" or even, "Whose child are you?" Children are spoken to as if they are beings from another society or species. Clinicians are often concerned about the effects on development when caretakers experience their infants in this mode and discipline begins at birth rather than with separation-individuation.

Lying to children is extremely important so that they do not get upset or traumatized and parents can fulfill their needs to be good or even perfect parents. One of the most potent of these lies is, "There is nothing to be afraid of," followed by, "Why are you such a baby?" and, "Why can't you act more grown up?" When something does go wrong, adults don't ask what has happened but instead affix blame and find out who is at fault. There are no mistakes, only sins and moral transgressions.

Adults have the duty to see to it that children know their place. Adults have rights because they have responsibilities. Children often have responsibilities but cannot have rights because they are children. No one in these structures has needs. All needs are rights, and somebody has the responsibility to satisfy them. Often the individual with rights insists that it is somebody else's responsibility to meet their rights and fulfill their obligations to the rights of others. If a need is aroused and is expressed as an emotion, it is not the need or emotion of the one who feels it but instead it is the fault of someone else, who now has to take responsibility. "You made me feel angry, sad, guilty, ashamed. . . . "

Problems do not exist between people or as issues to be solved or resolved but rather as in people. People with problems have something wrong with them, and what is wrong needs correcting. "You (or I) need to change" means becoming not only different but a better person. All conflicts exist on a personal level, and those in power usually are able to ascribe blame for the conflicts to those who have less power. The leaders invariably have fewer problems than those who follow them. The real power in such structures is the power to assign blame and define who has or does not have problems or "something wrong with them."

As all human beings have a place in the hierarchy as defined by moral worth, those who insist on living elsewhere in the hierarchy are in effect trying to escape the metaphors that have defined their place. Thus a woman who is "a nice piece of ass" and a "good little homemaker" can become a "bitch with an attitude problem" if she tries to change her place in the moral hierarchy. Moreover, if she is disciplined by those in power for her "problem" she will not only "get what she deserved" but she also will have "brought this punishment down on herself." "She really asked for it, didn't she?" She may then be told, "I know what is good for you," and therefore, "I hurt you for your own good." We have been destroying people since civilization began, in order to "save them from themselves."

Democratic-Humanistic Interactions

In this system the parents recognize their authority in the life of their children and the content of both their power and their responsibilities vis-à-vis the children. There is a realization that the parents are motivated by their thoughts and feelings toward the children and that the children's behavior is motivated by their thoughts and feelings toward the parents. Moreover, the parents recognize which thoughts and feelings are theirs and which are the children's. The parents simultaneously realize that they can, at best, only guess what the thoughts and feelings of the children might be. As a result, parents use sentences that begin "I think" or "I feel" and never use sentences that begin "you think" or "you feel."

Although parents do judge their children's behavior, they are accepting of their children's thoughts and emotions. Not only do they not tell their children what to think, but they do not set up moral standards expressed as, "You should (not) think or feel." Parents want to make their children aware of the relationship between motives and action and therefore ask, "Do you think . . . ?" and "Do you feel . . . ?" If the child denies such thought and feelings or cannot articulate an answer the matter is dropped temporarily until the child finds it possible to articulate a response.

When children need discipline the parents use the above methods and provide the children with an explanation of procedures and why they are being applied. The parents understand either intuitively or reflectively that their children are both the experiencers and the observers of what they do to them. What the parents do is going to provide a model of behavior for their children to follow whenever the children are placed in a position of authority. Parents try to get the child to see that the consequences of their actions make the actions right or wrong. If the children cannot understand this relationship, then the parents provide consequences that the children can understand. Right and wrong are always clearly defined, and consequences result from the choices the children make. Finally, the parents understand that they will ask their children to do as they do and not as they say to do while doing otherwise.

Adaptive Paradigms and Social Interactions

I have only scratched the surface in my description of the modes of interaction that shape the differences in adaptive paradigms. I shall, even more briefly, discuss some of the differences that seem to emerge when individuals successfully adapt to either the authoritarian-totalitarian or the democratic-humanistic modes of interactions. I should add that most therapists are in one way or another the product of humanistic and democratic systems. It is in the democracies, born of the Enlightenment, that therapy has appeared and flourished. Most of the people we see and most of the world's population are shaped by authoritarian and totalitarian systems. In the next chapter I try to demonstrate that the most common forms of pathology are, in fact, the adaptations that result from authoritarian and totalitarian systems, with the most severe pathologies the result of totalitarian rejection and punishment of children's emotions, beginning at birth.

Paradigms shaped in the authoritarian mode of interaction foster the use of judgments acting as description. The individuals see others in terms that create moral hierarchies. They see themselves in the same way, and they rather continually gauge their worth in terms of the moral hierarchy. Those perceived as higher in the social stratification are admired, followed, and labeled with superlatives, while those lower on the hierarchy are deplored and ignored, while loyalty and obedience are demanded of them. People are seen as motivated by their "character traits," which are created by the judgment made about their behavior. People are thus nice, mean, heroic, cowardly, loyal, or treasonous. Tens of thousands of such terms can be used to describe character or personality.

I have already noted that the appraisals that utilize such judgments tend also to maintain these judgments by employing preoperational thinking. When people are placed in categories, these categories tend to be discrete and do not require or even allow seriated gradations of any sophistication. Once I am labeled nice or mean, normal or abnormal, I am totally nice, totally mean, totally normal, totally abnormal. No further measuring or counting need exist. I believe that the loyalties engendered in such a system require an action-oriented pattern of judgments that are supplied by preoperational thinking.

The democratic-humanistic mode of development fosters attention to details and behavior, creating a view that people are motivated by psychologically describable events such as thoughts and emotions. Often the mode of development leads to appraisals in which individuals can neither judge nor react and act rapidly toward situations. The capacity to describe and explain produces very different reactions to situations than when judgments are involved. Judgments are critical and demand action, which descriptions do not unless they are followed by critical evaluations.

If we contextualize these alternate modes of appraisal we can see that each has its benefits in different times and places. Where group solidarity and action are the modes of meeting common challenges, then authoritarian systems might well be superior. Where learning and understanding are required, where individuation is tolerable and time and space allow exploration of surroundings, then the democratic-humanistic mode must be superior. It would appear from our modern world and its politics that a huge conflict is now underway with large segments of the population struggling to decide which lifestyle is best for them and their children. My own biases are clear and I could not conceive of living in an authoritarian-totalitarian system.

Play and Work

I wish to introduce another topic at this juncture that I believe adds to the individual differences in human adaptive paradigms, and that is the amount of time the developing child spends in play or work. I define play as any activity, physical or psychological, that is engaged in for its own sake and has, at the moment of its occurrence, not anything to do with adaptation as its goal. Play involves activities that are ends in and of themselves. I define work as any physical or psychological activity that is directly related to adaptation, that is, the activity has as its goal the satisfaction of a need or the solving of a problem. These activities have goals external to the activities themselves; they are means to an end. Often play and work occur simultaneously, as in the case of activity that is rewarding in itself and yet seeks a goal involving adaptational ends.

Play is usually valued as an activity related to childhood, and work is valued as related to adulthood. Yet many adults engage in play, and children find much of their time struggling to survive, which by definition is hard work. Thus play needs to be understood in terms of developmental and interpersonal theory. An infant engages in a variety of activities because of the pleasures they bring physically or because of the interesting effects they produce in the environment. This is referred to as sensorimotor play. What we notice is that those activities that are pleasurable and produce interesting consequences are the same activities that have a survival and adaptive function in later development. They are activities that seem to have an evolutionarily created reward system that sees to it that children practice them until they develop levels of adequacy appropriate to adaptive demands.

With the emergence of preoperational thinking and the possible emergence of emotional bonding, the games of children are often those that will lead to the development of skills that are socially valued and promote social relationships. Playing "house," "doctor," "cops and robbers," "space wars," and a host of imaginary "as if" games allows rehearsal of future social activities. These games promote prosocial activities as they are valued by society and involve the working out of sharing, competition, status relationships, and moral standards.

With formal operations new games emerge that, like earlier games, allow necessary intellectual skills time to develop. Children now begin to debate, argue, and engage in what we used to call bull sessions. I believe that formal operations will not develop unless children have time to play with ideas in the same way they played with the objects involved in sensorimotor development and the social situation involved in "as if" or imaginative games.

I believe that when children are confronted with adaptive demands before they have had time to play, the manner in which they develop skills is very different than if they have had the luxury of exploring and experimenting with skills and the consequences that play provides. Skills learned under adaptive demands may well be rigid and limited in application and be experienced with very different emotions than under play conditions. I will return to play as a topic related to psycho"therapy" in the last three chapters of this volume.

PSYCHOLOGICAL CONTRIBUTIONS TO ADAPTIVE DIFFERENCES

I do not wish to leave the reader with the impression that human adaptive paradigms, that is human consciousness, are solely the product of biological and social functions. Although these variables dramatically shape conscious experience, they are in no way capable of predicting emerging differences in an individual's adaptive appraisals. With development and with reflective consciousness, the individual becomes increasingly capable of creating differences in his outlook and coming to new conclusions based on his or her reflections. Some human beings are constantly inventing new ideas, new theories, new skills, and new paradigms while all around them their fellow human beings do not.

I have stated a number of times in this book that not Skinner nor Freud nor Maslow nor any other theorist can account for how he made the discoveries that eventually found their way into the textbooks defining our field. Human consciousness seems to be infinitely self-regulating even though we have as yet no idea as to when or how these leaps of consciousness are made. Once new appraisals are created, all later adaptive behaviors to the same situations may well be remarkably different than if these new ideas had not come into existence.

I believe that there are psychological principles responsible, at least in part, for these changes in psychological functioning.

One source of these principles may be understood to emerge from the way in which we human beings seem to experience the flow of their lives. Each of us seems to take our experiences and tell a narrative (Spence 1982, 1987) about them. Murray Pollster (1987) suggests that human life can be conceived of as a novel and has his patients write such a novel as part of treatment. It is the telling of one's story in the presence of another that recontextualizes the story and allows insights and discoveries to be made. Schafer (1980), Strenger (1991), and a host of psychoanalysts now see psychoanalytic therapy as the telling of stories and narratives with the goal of changing the story and with it the future appraisals of the storyteller.

The narrative each of us tells emerges with reflective consciousness. The structure of the story changes with the emergence of operations. Each new set of experiences changes both the structure of the story and its content. The content of experience, as we interpret it, becomes incorporated into the ongoing narration and its evolution. In turn, the narrative determines much of the experiencing of the individual. Constant dynamics therefore exist in the interplay of reflective and nonreflective experiences.

The constructed sense of self changes as a function of being both the storyteller and the principal object and actor in the story. Differences exist as to whether the story places the individual as important or unimportant in the history and construction of events, as hero or villain, as victim or perpetrator, and so on. The story differs, too, if as it is told the narrator is consistent, is concerned with the listener, and experiences the self cohesively rather than if the narrator cannot tell the story consistently, experiences the self as fragmented, and tells the story without regard to its context.

The narrations we tell have many functions. They bind the past, present, and future together into a meaningful whole as well as construct the self as a part of the time line. Spence writes that our truths of the past are narrative truths, not historical truths. None of us can know directly or tell of our experiences in the first two years of life, when our story began. More and more of the past appears in our story as it relates to our later years, but it is constantly worked and reworked in our narrative. Missing events may be filled in, and events once in consciousness can disappear as needed by the demands of the narrative.

The present and future are interpreted at any given moment in term of past constructions. We also extend ourselves into a future that is in part constructed as we would wish it to be, as well as how it might be in terms of its congruence with present realities. The emotion hope exists when individuals feel that their future can be as they wish and want it to be. Behavior is vastly different when individuals experience hope as part of their adaptive paradigm, compared to when hope is missing as an element in constructions of the future.

Our story in part contains events experienced as true and those once experienced as fiction now made true. We constantly embellish, enhance, omit, and just plain make up events. This aspect of a narrative creates the myths that are a part of every human adaptive paradigm. Myths may intertwine seamlessly with scientific theories, making it impossible for a listener to tell where one starts and the other begins. Included in our narrative are ideologies, utopias, and other aspects of the myths that organize and direct so many aspects of our lives.

Every story has a moral tale to tell as well. Life is fair or lacking in justice, people are good or evil. Our stories have happy or sad endings. Some stories are told as if there is neither beginning nor ending. Without hope there may be no dreams of the future, only a story told of moment-to-moment happenings and therefore lacking direction, purpose, and ultimately meaning.

Stories will speak of democracy or authoritarian hierarchies. They may tell of the trials and success and failures of human beings or the action of superior and inferior beings. Gods and demons may people a story revealing a perception of others as worthy and unworthy. They may describe beings revered and hated or loved, shunned, or attacked. The story may speak of human beings motivated by experience or motivated by the type of person they are. There may be a search for truth in observations or the revelation of truth from authorities endowed with perfection, omnipotence, and omniscience.

The narrative of any individual contains a series of experienced facts that exist either as information or knowledge. Facts experienced as information are independent of a person's adaptive paradigm. Information does not lead to action. Information comes and goes. Knowledge involves facts that are experienced in terms of the operating skills of the individual. I may possess information about many things, but my facts concerning therapy are organized as part of an adaptive paradigm containing a variety of activities that seek specific goals.

Individuals become aware of facts and incorporate them into their knowledge to the degree that they enhance or threaten some aspect of adaptation. Individuals may utilize defenses to treat knowledge as information. Every therapist has had patients tell their life story as if the horrors and joys it contains had happened to someone else.

I close this chapter by stating the goals of the next two. In Chapters 8 and 9 I enter the world of the DSM. I first try to demonstrate the authoritarian and judgmental nature of what I call "the big book of bad names" and then selectively discuss some of its diagnoses as individual differences in adaptive paradigm. Chapter 9 interprets schizophrenia and other serious diagnoses as adaptive modes of being in the world.

IV

REDEFINING DIAGNOSES

8

"DIAGNOSIS" I: THE NEUROSES

The present system of psychotherapeutic services is increasingly driven by a medical model that utilizes the metaphor of mental disorder to describe and explain certain personal adaptive paradigms. These paradigms are so judged because of the individual's mode of experiencing his or her world and/or because of the skills he or she utilizes when acting upon it. When individuals encounter the mental health system, they are initially evaluated and then diagnosed. Ostensibly they are then treated according to the demands of the diagnosis. At present, the collection of mental disorders is contained in the *Diagnostical and Statistical Manual of Mental Disorder*, third edition, revised. DSM IV is reportedly nearing completion and, unless a major scientific revolution takes place, will be replaced by V, VI, and so on.

I have several goals for this chapter. First, I would like to establish the judgmental and totally unscientific nature of the material that comprises the symptoms and disorders in question. Second, I would like to present some of these disorders as the personal adaptive paradigm I believe them to be. *Paradigm*, I believe, is a more scientific metaphor, which represents a much better choice than disorder. Third, I would like to discuss which types of paradigm are included in the DSM and in this context suggest some of the political and intellectual biases inherent in the selection process. In general, I will try to place the DSM in the social context in which it belongs and thereby make sense of why it exists in the form that it does.

Let me begin with a single diagnostic category, Oppositional Defiant Disorder. If one diagnosis is seen as a series of judgments, then the entire operation and set of diagnoses must also fall under suspicion. I quote from the DSM III.

I emphasize each and every term I consider to be a judgment, that is, someone's personal opinion as to the goodness or badness of something along some dimension that establishes worth.

> The essential feature of this disorder is a pattern of *negativistic, hostile* and *defiant* behavior without the more serious violations of the basic rights of others that are seen in Conduct Disorder.
>
> Children with this disorder commonly are *argumentative* with adults, frequently *lose their temper*, swear and are often angry, resentful and *easily* annoyed by others. They *frequently* actively defy adult requests or rules and *deliberately* annoy other people. They tried to blame others for their own mistakes or difficulties.
>
> Manifestations of the disorder are almost invariably present in the home, but may not be present at school or with other adults or peers. In some case, features of the disorder, from the beginning of the disturbance, are displayed in areas outside the home, in other cases they start in the home, but later develop in areas outside the home: Typically symptoms of the disorder are more evident in interaction with adults or peers whom the child knows well. Thus, children with the disorder are likely to show little or no signs of the disorder when examined clinically. (emphasis mine)

Diagnostic Criteria of Oppositional Defiant Disorder

A. Disturbance of at least 6 minutes during which at least five of the following are present:

1. Often loses temper
2. Often argues with adults
3. Often actively defies or refuses adult requests or rules.
   ex. refuses to do chores at home
4. Often deliberately does things that annoy other people.
   ex. grabs other children's hats
5. Often blames others for his or her own mistakes
6. Is often touchy or easily annoyed by others
7. Is often angry and resentful
8. Is often spiteful or vindictive
9. Often swears or uses obscene language. (56, 58)

The following words are used as adjectives to describe the child. They seem to me to fit the criteria of judgments, as they represent personal opinions that establish worth or value: "touchy," "spiteful," "vindictive." The next words also seem to be judgments, but this time they describe behavior: "hostile," "defiant."

These judgments of the child and his behavior are then called descriptions of a mental disorder. The disorder itself is a judgment of a pattern of behavior, in the opinion of some authority doing the judging. In this case the overall term *disorder* does not even refer to a description of behavior but rather a series of judgments about the child's behavior and the child himself or herself.

If these are judgments and represent the opinion of authorities, who are the authorities voicing the opinion? The authority of the opinion is based on the voices of the psychiatrists who themselves are utilizing either descriptions of behavior or more likely the judgments of teachers and, mostly, parents who are the ones disturbed by the child's behavior. In any event I assume that these opinions represent adults who are teachers and parents. They do not seem to take into account the opinions of the children so judged.

Not only do the opinions, judgments, and descriptions of the child's own experiences not influence the disorder presented, but the psychiatrists involved go so far as to define the phenomenological outlook of the child with no evidence that the child was asked to corroborate these opinions. Consider, for example, "Deliberately does things that annoy other people." As there is no evidence that any given child is so motivated, where is the evidence? As is typical of hierarchical systems in which authority substitutes judgment for description, we see thoughts placed into the consciousness of those being judged.

The judgment of the authorities seems to find offensive children who defy authority and not those who slavishly (my judgment) conform to adult authority. If one asks the children in a classroom who has the problem and who therefore is disordered, they might well tell us it is the "bootlickers" who have the problem. (Bootlicker Disorder?) These same children might tell us that they admire the child who is brave enough to argue with the teacher.

As the diagnosed child is motivated by his disorder, he has now been totally decontextualized. He is not reacting to actions his parents or teachers might have initiated. His behavior cannot be the result of fear, anger, love, or hate of the events in his home or school as he experiences them. Flawed morality explains it all, and only the child is flawed. Teachers and parents have no flaws, that is, until they are decontextualized and judged according to the adult section of the DSM. Is the child reacting to a divorce or a parent who drinks (Alcohol Disorder) or to a parent who hears voices and has been recently hospitalized (Schizophrenic Disorder)? Are these issues important or relevant? Not according to the descriptions of the disorder that belongs to the child.

Judgments of behavior do not lend themselves to the precision that can be developed from descriptions of behavior. Judgments allow variables to be ordered nominally; interval and ratio measurements cannot be developed. Therefore, each and every symptom begins with "often," as in "Often loses temper." Often according to whom? How frequently is often? Is it often according to teachers, parents, or psychotherapists? We are told that at least five of the symptoms must be present for a "diagnosis" to be made. Why five? Why not any two or all nine? Clearly five is as arbitrary as is often. Finally, the "disturbances" must have lasted at least six months. Why six? Why not two, three, or four months or one year? I could go on at length but will limit myself to one more unscientific aspect of the DSM. What kind of illness appears only in some contexts and not others? Can I have an ulcer at work and in the doctor's office but not at home? Does a broken leg appear, disappear, and reappear as I move through my day and its events? What kind of illness or disorder disappears when it is "examined clinically"? I would suggest that disorders do not disappear but that behavior does change when individuals feel it is in their interest to behave differently! The readers can now judge for themselves whether or not a disorder exists for which a medical treatment is required.

THE SUBJECTS OF THE DSM

Who are the individuals judged by DSM? This is a critical question, as it is the unwanted, incomprehensible behavior of a group of individuals that provides the basis for the list of diagnostic disorders. By decontextualizing the processes of behavioral description, we do not ask about the processes that select those whose behaviors are judged. One is left with the impression that the DSM represents the entire range of human abnormalities. It is likely that the individuals who are the focus of psychiatry do not represent the full range of human adaptive efforts but only a segment of unknown groups and individuals.

I would suggest that the poor are represented more frequently than the wealthy, the socially weak more frequently than the socially powerful, women more frequently than men, and so on. I would suggest that the closer one gets to the individuals whom C. W. Mills (1956) called "the power elite" and Philip Reiff (1966) referred to as "the cultural elite" and President Eisenhower called "the military industrial complex," the less likely it is that their unwanted behavior becomes grist for DSM diagnosis. In part I believe that two groups, both rather limited and unrepresentative of human variability, comprise the sample pool from which the DSM derives its material. The first group represents the powerless and the marginal group who find themselves in an involuntary arrangement with the mental health system. My experience has been with two subsets of this involuntary group. The first are children whose behavior deviates from standards of academic success and obedience to authority. The second are people marginally related to society who hear voices, see things that only they see, and when they become enough of a nuisance to friends, family, and society are "hospitalized" and diagnosed "schizophrenic," "bipolar depressive," and the latest darling of diagnosis, "schizo-affective disorder."

The second group of individuals who are diagnosed are those mostly middle-class individuals who experience a crisis in their adaptation and who have learned that under such circumstances therapy can help. It is the second group who voluntarily come to treatment; as a self-selecting group it is no more representative of the broad stream of human adaptive styles than the first. It is this second group who comprise the patients with the least serious diagnoses who pay their bills, see therapists privately, and are most sought after by the bulk of therapists who dream of lucrative private practices.

I will limit this chapter to the diagnosis of the voluntary patient population. A psycho"therapist" does not see patients who come to the system involuntarily and, unless the therapist can convince a captive patient to come voluntarily, does not even administer a treatment. I will attempt to demonstrate in the rest of this chapter that, depending on when a therapist encounters a patient, that is, when the patient decides to seek therapy, the diagnosis assigned to the patient can be virtually any one in the DSM. This will be made clear in the following paragraphs.

I will discuss the more serious diagnosis in the next chapter with an eye toward again demonstrating how little such diagnoses are worth in helping people and how dangerous they can be as sources of stigmata and blocking the scientific understanding of the patients' adaptive mode of being in the world. In both cases it is my main goal to demonstrate that what we describe when we use these diagnostic categories are not illnesses or disorders but the end results of individuals' struggle to master their world until the moment in which we first encounter them.

Voluntary Patients and Their Diagnoses

Let us examine the voluntary group that finds itself judged in the DSM. We must ask why people come to treatment in the first place. I believe that people seek therapy when they discover that their emotional suffering (that which represents their experience of adaptive failures) is in some way a function of their own mode or style of struggling to adapt. These individuals realize, often without a clear capacity to reflect or verbalize their awareness, that their thinking, action, goals, or interpersonal relationship contains some information or knowledge that is not in keeping with the narrative story that they have constructed to make sense of their lives. Whether descriptively or morally they are doing something wrong and bringing grief of some sort into their own lives.

These individuals understand that their problem is not economic, political, or medical but psychological in nature. Such awareness always grows out of some new reflection on their own personal adaptive paradigm and how their paradigm influences the processes of adaptation. I believe that these insights are relatively rare and, from a historical and cultural perspective, brand new. Psychology is a new field, and the aspect of psychology that asks individuals to examine their own phenomenological experiences and skills is the newest element of a new field. Thus, the DSM reflects a tiny element of the human population.

In those societies (or subsocieties) where psychiatry and psychology have not evolved or gained favor from at least some of its members, the same unwanted patterns of behavior will never be either diagnosed or treated. Mental illness is relevant to our historical epoch and our social situation. Mental illness and treatment are socially constructed, and the people who seek out treatment share the basic constructions of those who provide it.

DYNAMICS OF ADAPTATION: DIAGNOSES

In this section I link the reasons people seek out therapy with the diagnostic names they will be called when they get there. In writing this section, I have to fight certain assumptions that have only recently become available to my reflective consciousness. These assumptions involve my belief that people come to therapy because they are mentally ill and that their illnesses are the result of various childhood experiences. But my theoretical assumptions have very little to do with individuals' own phenomenologically experienced reasons for seeking help.

Although my perception of the patient contained hidden value judgments and favored explanation based on their past lives, the patients enter therapy because they see problems as rooted in the present and having the potential to affect future plans. Adaptive paradigms may be understood to have begun in the past, but failures are experienced as immediate and related to the here and now. Our stance is directed from the here and now to the future. To understand why an individual experiences a crisis now, it is often necessary to understand how the individual experiences his future, not his past. Therefore, much of my training in clinical psychology and psychoanalysis tended to preclude my understanding of the crisis that brings people into treatment.

A second problem is related to the first. DSM III and all other diagnostic systems create a picture of individuals that not only is decontextualized and lacks the individuals' phenomenological experience of their own crisis but is also static in relation to the flow of time and space. Individuals experience themselves as moving through time and space in a way that is peculiar to themselves. Life never stops happening! A crisis is experienced as continuous, and the individual has to deal with the totality of an unexpected and uncontrolled flow of events.

Each individual is constantly engaging some situations and avoiding others. Each seeks to encounter some individuals while avoiding others. New skills are developed, while old skills may be lost. Some situations create problems that are solved, while others are solved only in the preoperational fantasies of defensive operations. As the individual moves through time and space, the narration that binds past to present and projects the future is written, rewritten, edited, maintained, or discarded.

At the point at which individuals decide on psychological help, they must be experiencing an event different from all other events. They must also be experiencing their solutions to events as different from all other solutions. Not only does the event appear overwhelming and terrifying, but all previously used skills, including the psychological defenses, cannot be successfully used either to "make the event go away" or prevent the individuals from becoming aware of their own modes of dealing with adaptive struggles. The individual experiences a problem that will not be solved and needs that cannot be satisfied.

The experience of such an event can be focused upon in a number of ways. Individuals may try to focus just on the event, but for the first time be forced to examine the emotions (which define needs and problems) that now cannot be denied, redefined, or resolved. Individuals may not find it possible to act in their typical ways to avoid these emotions or obliterate them as in past experience. At such a moment the past may take on a new light and the future be experienced in totally new ways. Individuals may now not be able to incorporate the experience of these feelings and their own responses into their ongoing narratives of life and the images of self that correspond to that narrative. All the politics, science, and especially a lifetime of carefully nurtured myths fail to allow individuals to describe, explain, predict, and control either the new events that created the personal adaptive crisis or the new experiences that are their own responses.

How do we express and preserve the passions, conflicts, terrors, joys, and problems that are individuals' experience of life and understand why they seek therapy within the terms of their experience? Not with the science as it is presently composed. DSM III might have some usefulness, but not as it is currently comprised and utilized. I believe that to understand our patients we will have to turn to a mode of scientific understanding that better matches that of the patient's own understanding of life. I believe that a modified form of art will be necessary in this endeavor. It is the novelist who tells the story of lives in which phenomenological experiences are maintained. It is the poet who creates metaphors and images that come closest to expressing those core inarticulate and fleeting experiences that determine moment-to-moment behavior. It is the composer who creates the sounds that best reflect human emotion.

But the artist expresses the universal in a single case. The composer and poet express in modes not really amicable to science with its needs for quantification and statistical analysis. What we must do is to save both science and art through the heterophenomenological methods already but inadequately described. I am most daunted by the demands I perceive are mine, if I am to explain human behavior. My scientific colleagues will mock my science, and I know that my artistic effort will at best embarrass me.

On the following pages I create the fictional characters of Mr. and Mrs. Everyman. I create a history for each as well as a contextualized present, trying to breathe life into them by capturing a small portion of their consciousness.

But I describe each as a personal adaptive paradigm shaped by biology and embedded in social contexts, all of which have had a history that extends back even before each was born. In that way I can describe their lives according to the scientific principle already outlined.

I realize that my "Everyman" and "Everywoman" are really no man and no woman. I realize, too, that they are bound by the experiences of my past, present, and expected future, which are limited to my culture and my historical epoch. By generalizing their similarities I am forced to ignore their uniqueness. Because of the limitation of space and my own lack of talent, I hope to create only enough of the picture to give a flavor of that which is required to begin to understand the processes of psycho"therapy."

I propose to create a scenario that describes the psychological development of two people within the context of a moderately authoritarian-totalitarian social system. I will trace the development of their adaptations both intraphysically, by discussing the individual's thoughts and feelings, and interpersonally, connecting where I can one system to the other. I will discuss the development of their skills: cognitive, motoric, and defensive, and describe some of these adaptations and some of the dynamic costs of living in the style in which they have come to live.

I will then create situations that at any moment in their lives represent the unsatisfiable needs and unsolvable problems that will promote a decision to seek psychiatric help. According to the problems they are struggling with, the defenses and skills that are in operation, what they tell their doctor at the time of their first visit, and what the doctor observes, they will receive a diagnosis. I hope to show that all or nearly all the available DSM diagnoses can be appropriately used on the same persons, depending on when the individuals appeared for their diagnosis.

From this, the reader will see that the diagnoses of DSM III are in actuality descriptions of an individual's adaptive paradigm as seen from a third-person perspective at a given moment in time and in a given context. What the reader will have to decide is whether or not under these circumstances these descriptions are helpful to understanding or helping patients. As for myself, I believe that the whole of the current DSM enterprise must eventually be jettisoned.

THE DYNAMICS OF ADAPTATION:
MR. AND MRS. EVERYMAN

Mr. Everyman is forty-five years old. He is a partner in a "big eight" accounting firm in New York City. He owns a home in a Westchester County suburb, a second home for summering in a seaside community, and several fine automobiles. Mr. E collects automobiles. No sooner does he take possession of a new car than a deep sense of dissatisfaction enters his awareness and he begins planning for his next dream car. Mr. E has been married for twenty-two years and has three children. His eldest son attends a fine Ivy League college, and his younger son, the middle child, is a good student at a private high school. His daughter, however, has just been brought for a psychiatric evaluation after she refused to study or attend classes, clean her room, or do her assigned chores and was caught smoking marijuana in the school bathroom.

The psychiatrist to whom Mr. and Mrs. E have brought her in order that she be "straightened out" cannot yet decide whether she is an Oppositional Defiant Disorder or a Conduct Disorder, Socialized, Non-aggressive. Mr. E wonders what has gotten into his daughter of late. She was always just like her mother, and it is impossible that his wife would ever "act crazy" as his daughter is now doing. Mr. E feels burdened by involvement with the psychiatrist. He is outraged at the cost and vaguely worried about his daughter. He does believe that she will "grow out of" this behavior and could be back to normal if she would "just stop hanging around with such a bad element."

Mr. E worries constantly about money and is ever more burdened by how much things cost and how much others want from him. No one thanks him for all he does for everybody, and there is no one with whom he can share his burdens. There is no one to talk to because everyone is "too stupid" to understand a man of his intelligence and capabilities. His male friends and coworkers would not understand because they are "jealous of his achievements." He would never give any of them the satisfaction of knowing that he has moments of weakness when he feels overwhelmed and at times terrified.

Mr. E does not know that every one of his friends feels just about the same about their lives as he does about his. They would love to "nail him" for the way he "lords" it over them with his cars, house, and money and the "arrogance" with which the "bastard" treats everyone, especially his "poor, sweet, depressed wife." Thus, while Mr. E would never express his feelings of weakness, none of the men with whom he is in a life-and-death competition would ever hear his confessions except with concealed pleasure.

Mr. E. has felt as he does now for as long as he can remember. His father was a self-made businessman who always told his son, "You have to look out for yourself in this dog-eat-dog world." "No one will show you mercy," said his father, and only "weak fools" would show concern or feelings. Mr. E never remembers his father asking for mercy or anyone ever extending any. Mr. E's father reminded his son of all the things he should do and must do if he were to emulate his father's success and not make the mistakes his father had made as a youngster.

No one ever asked Mr. E what he wanted to do, least of all his father. It was expected that he would attend college and enter the business world prepared for an entrepreneurial role. When Mr. E did take up the violin in junior high school, his father let him know in no uncertain terms that music was for "sissies" and was a "waste of a real man's time" in his search for economic success.

Mr. E learned that his father was no man with whom to argue. As with the violin, he gave up any expression of his own uniqueness to please his father. He could not bear his father's scorn or his father's rejection when he deviated from his father's commands. As a child he feared the belt with which his father threatened and occasionally hit him, but as an adult he found his father's stony silences even more difficult to stand up to. He did not know and, like his father, could not articulate that his father treated him as an extension of himself and that his failures and successes were perceived by his father as his own. He never knew how proud his father was of him when he did what he was supposed to do and was successful. (He never heard his father say so.) He did know, but could not say, that if he surpassed his father's abilities, he would disappoint, anger, and hurt his dad.

All his life Mr. E tried to please his father, but most often he saw that he failed. He saw his life as a struggle to be "good" and do as he ought and fight the impulses toward music and art, which he enjoyed only in secret. He would rather die than let anyone see him cry when he listened to Rachmaninoff. All of his life he felt afraid as he struggled harder and harder to avoid feeling like a failure; yet he never could relax, enjoy his achievements, and feel like a success.

Mr. E feared being exposed as a fraud and laughed at. He had a chronic sense of guilt that he wasn't good enough and a perpetual resentment of all those who took from him and never recognized either his mastery or his goodness. When an economic slowdown occurred, Mr. E could not sleep. He worried day and night about his business. Had he chosen at the juncture to seek professional help he might have been diagnosed as having a Sleep Disorder. Had he told his doctor that lately he had increased his drinking significantly and regularly consumed two martinis before dinner, half a bottle or more of wine with dinner (only the finest), and a cognac (or two) after dinner, his therapist might have diagnosed him Alcoholism Dependence: Psychoactive Substance Use Disorder.

For some time Mr. E had been feeling dirty and had been taking numerous showers and washing his hands. He thought this peculiar, but such patterns of behavior comforted him in their ritual control of emotions and thus he never really told anyone about this. If he had sought help for this problem he would have been diagnosed Obsessive-Compulsive Disorder. Or if he had told a therapist that, when he returned home and found that his wife had not cleaned up or even gotten out of bed that day, he became so angry that he punched holes in the walls, his doctor might have diagnosed him as Impulse Disorder, specifically called Intermittent Explosive Disorder.

Mr. E had also begun to blame the "niggers" and "spics" for the economic slowdown, but even if he had told this to a therapist he needn't have worried about being called a bad name. There is no Bigot Disorder. Had Mr. E told his therapist that he often thought that these lowlifes had it in for just him, he might have been diagnosed Paranoid Disorder. Lately, Mr. E has been feeling a heaviness in his chest for which his doctor (that quack) can find no medical causes. Had a therapist heard this, he would have diagnosed Mr. E with a Psychosomatic Stress Disorder. Mr. E did not tell anyone that he could not live this way anymore and that if the symptoms in his chest worsened and his business went under, he might well commit suicide. He thus avoided the diagnosis of Major Depressive Disorder.

Mr. E does not understand that his core feelings toward life and himself had not changed since he first lost touch with his fears. At that time he began to see them as weaknesses and started a lifelong struggle to prove to himself and his father that he was a success and a perfect son, husband, father, businessman, and citizen. He has little awareness that in his central relationships he perceives the world through preoperational eyes, extending his moral labels toward himself and others without seriation, in black-and-white fashion. What he least understands is that the more he tries to overcome the human feelings that are called weaknesses and the more effort he puts into being perfect, the more he is in a "search for glory" (Horney 1950). He is therefore trying to maintain a fiction of an idealized self-image that adds ever more burden and failure to his life. He is engaged in a "vicious circle" in which he brings about the very conditions that he is trying to escape.

Mrs. Everyman married Mr. E when she was eighteen years old and had just graduated from high school. As soon as she met Mr. E, who was considered a "good catch" by friends and family, she abandoned her tentative plans to attend a junior college and become a dental hygienist. In the words of her best friend, she now "had it made" as she will be taken care of for the rest of her life by her handsome, powerful husband. Mrs. E has always nurtured an unspoken sorrow about not developing her own economic skills. She had been a straight-A student in school and somehow knew that, even though she was called "smart for a girl," she was as intellectually able as any male she had ever met, including her husband.

Mrs. E was born to upper-middle-class parents who, unlike Mr. E's father, had not had to struggle to "make it." Both her parents could trace their bloodlines back to the early colonial days of the nation's history. Mrs. E grew up surrounded by proof that her family was superior and perfect in every way. Her home was immaculately clean; the family lived a punctual life that was the envy of all who were familiars. They did charity work which proved their moral worth even more than did their homes, cars, and the overall success made so effortlessly.

Like all young ladies of breeding, Mrs. E was raised never to shout, to argue, to complain, or to say that she was in any way unhappy. Rather, she was to demonstrate ebullience, friendliness, happiness, and charm and always remember to smile, smile, smile. She was a beautiful child, a golden possession of her mother and especially her father. She learned very quickly how terrifying the disapproval of her parents could be. Anger was her enemy, just as fear and helplessness were her husband's. Her parents were most rejecting if she was disobedient or if she argued and asserted herself in any way that conflicted with her familial role. She learned that she must never have a bad temper. As long as she was cheerful, spontaneous, popular, and good in school, she met the conditions of her worth and her parents were doting and pleased.

It was said of Mrs. E that she was "perfect like her mother" and more important "a credit to her father." As she grew older, she did well in school and became a cheerleader and one of the most popular and well-behaved children in the estimation of her grateful teachers. She was always careful with her eating for fear she would show too much weight. Being fat was almost as big a sin as showing temper. If she were fat, who would possibly want her, especially when it came time to be married?

Mrs. E always felt hungry—or at least the emptiness that grew and shrank inside her could be temporarily fixed by sweets or creamy foods. During her teenage years she felt the pressure of being perfect but never complained. She began to eat secretly, sometimes consuming huge amounts of food. To control her weight and avoid expressing the badness and observable fat, she began purging herself with diuretics, laxatives, and forced vomiting. If Mrs. E had thought this behavior abnormal (many of her friends did the same, as did some of the most successful models in society) and reported it to her doctor, she would have been diagnosed Eating Disorder and Bulimarexia.

When Mrs. E played with her brothers she found herself tolerated, and at times she enjoyed herself enormously. She would run around with them, yelling and calling out in her role of their imaginative "as if" games. Her father would demand of her mother that she control the noise made by the children, especially Mrs. E, who was "getting out of control" and behaving like a "savage." Over the years, Mrs. E, responded to the demands upon her and, while she could not articulate the principle, she did know that what she expressed was not mean-ingful communication but meaningless noise. Mrs. E stuck to the prescribed regimens and basked in the glory of her physical beauty and quiet, composed, and noncomplaining demeanor. (Had her parents sought professional advice for her tomboy behavior, she might have been diagnosed Gender Disorder.)

When Mr. and Mrs. E met and fell in love, each thought their happiness was complete and would last forever. (Everyone agreed that they were the perfect couple and had it all.) To this day, no one has ever heard them fight or seen Mrs. E angry or Mr. E upset with Mrs. E. They are envied by all except their children, who know that their father rarely talks to their mother and that they both sleep in separate bedrooms. They hear their mother cry much of the time as she sits and watches endless hours of television. (Television Withdrawal Disorder?) They know how unhappy she is as she continually complains to them how no one understands or appreciates how good she is, especially to her own children. "I have given up my life for you," she says, "and what gratitude do I get in return?"

When Mrs. E overheard Mr. E speak with his attorney about possible bankruptcy, Mrs. E felt intense panic. Mrs. E determined that she would get a job and help out, but she didn't know what she might do. She had her lifestyle to maintain, and the children needed her (although she did not know for what they needed her or when). However, it was the first time Mrs. E experienced a wave of the emotion known as anxiety. Anxiety, Mrs. E did not know, is an important emotion that occurs whenever the individual faces an adaptive crisis and cannot describe, explain, predict, or control that which needs to be described, explained, predicted, and controlled.

Mrs. E began to experience anxiety when she left the house. She became so disabled by the experience that she soon refused to leave the house alone. She would perspire, breathe heavily, and find her heart pounding and her chest constricting. As she did not know what was happening to her and did not know what to do about her emotions, which were experienced like an invasion of something alien, she developed anticipatory anxiety about her anxiety. She constricted her actions and limited her range of activities. If she had told a psychiatrist about her emotions, she would have been diagnosed Anxiety Disorder: Agoraphobia. She would still not have known that her anxiety was a powerful motivation to examine her life with its few honest truths and many lies, deceptions, myths, and secrets.

Early in their marriage both Mr. and Mrs. E felt reborn in the presence of the other, but as time passed he began to criticize her ebullience, demanding that she control herself and remember her age, status, and so on. He would insist that she was immature if she tried to protest or more likely plead for his understanding. Mr. E hated it when his wife pleaded as it represented weakness. He hated even more the disrespect that her attempts at humor or political arguments represented to him. (Mr. E was an avowed liberal and often argued vociferously for the rights of the poor and other downtrodden groups who through no fault of their own were born inferior. It was said of Mr. E, as it was said of Ivan Karamazov, "He loves humanity, he just hates everyone he knows.") He often wondered why his wife could not accept just being his wife.

Mrs. E remembers an incident that seemed typical of their relationship (although she could not say why). They were driving to meet friends for dinner in a restaurant in another town. Mr. E was clearly lost. He always drove the car, even though Mrs. E prided herself on her ability to drive. She asked him, quite respectfully, if he should not ask for directions. He had turned to her with rage and contempt on his face and screamed at her, "You shut up—what do you know—do you think you can tell me anything?" She had felt tiny, helpless, stupid, and angry. To the present day she describes the event as one in which "Something died in me toward him and toward myself. The thing that upset me the most is how I sat there half smiling and half crying and then played the role of the perfect wife that evening at dinner."

As the years passed, Mr. E had less and less to do with his wife. In his eyes, she was useless. He had long since begun to have affairs with younger women who "made him feel more alive." All his wife now "made him feel" was angry. (His wife complained that he "made her feel empty, useless, and sad.") Neither partner was aware that each experienced the other as in control of his or her own emotions.

Mrs. E felt ever more empty as the years unfolded, and as she looked in the mirror she saw signs of aging that led to a horrible feeling of doom. Often she had the experience that she didn't exist in some way, except in those moments when someone gave her a compliment. Early in her marriage sex was an important activity, as it allowed her a feeling of control over her husband's behavior as well as a feeling of being needed by him. Sex has never been satisfying for her, and now she feels too ugly and worthless to ask. Mr. E had stopped desiring his wife. During bouts of drinking he failed to achieve an erection. If both partners had told about these feelings, each would have received a diagnosis of Sexual Dysfunction. For her, Female Sexual Arousal Disorder. For him, Male Erection Disorder.

In recent years Mr. E has been having nightmares of killing people and being killed. This, if reported, would be diagnosed Dream Anxiety Disorder. Mrs. E kept complaining about her health, and because her doctors gave her recognition for her complaints she kept on complaining. Her doctors found nothing wrong even after the most exhaustive tests. As long as they believed that she believed she was truly ill they diagnosed her as having a Somatoform Disorder. Mrs. E finally admitted to her internist that she knew in her head that she really wasn't ill. Her diagnosis was changed to Factitious Disorder with Physical Symptoms. During Mr. E's economic trouble he developed an ulcer. His medical doctor did note in his records the diagnosis Psychological Factor Affecting Physical Condition.

Like her husband, Mrs. E is trapped in a kind of experiential time warp in which she brings about the very fears she so desperately tries to avoid. Mrs. E perceives being alone in her helplessness with the same terror as her husband fears being helpless in his aloneness. Whereas he denies these feelings and avoids them by dominating others, particularly his wife, she denies and tries to avoid her terror by being compliant and agreeable and defining such modes of behavior as proof of her goodness. The more compliant she becomes, the more she complains and martyrs herself in the name of goodness. The more she martyrs herself the less useful she is, and therefore the more easily she is rejected and discarded. How can she be pleasing to others if she experiences herself as not existing?

Mr. and Mrs. E are each other's worst nightmare. She cannot assert herself or experience herself as an agency. She can be of use neither to herself nor to her husband. She cannot ask or demand recognition from her husband for her thoughts, needs, or accomplishments. Her husband can not get the comfort or recognition he needs from his wife. He cannot accept such comfort, as it represents weakness, but also he cannot see his wife as capable of comforting him. The more he belittles her in order to prove his worth, the more worthless she becomes in terms of his need to be helped or admired by someone of real value. How can one be admired by someone whom one does not admire?

Why do Mr. and Mrs. E bear with lives that are increasingly unbearable? They know about therapy and yet do not choose to seek it or something else to change their lives? Why do they live lives that we see as based on self-deception, lies, abuse of self and others, and a constant set of human interactions that are based on what might be called emotional blackmail? Let me briefly outline some of the complex intrapsychic and interpersonal reasons they continue to live as they do and then describe the events that finally brought both into the orbit of the mental health system.

An individual is a biological, psychological, and social being. Each person is each of these simultaneously. Each system can be understood by the rules created to explain it as a system. Thus an individual can be simultaneously described in biological, psychological, and social terms. Each system both parallels and interacts with the other system. A change in one system affects all other systems. Each biological individual sees the world through his unique vision and experiences that vision as true. Simultaneously each individual is a member of a family, community, nation, and the world. Each individual has a multiplicity of social roles in the variety of social systems of which they are a member. Therefore, each and every adaptation can be described in terms of an individual's appraisals, emotions, and all of the social roles and situations in which the psychological experience takes place.

Each action and adaptation performed by an individual has moral significance in the eyes of the individual and in the sociological relationships in which they take place. The punishments and reinforcements of society are called discipline by psychologists and sanctions by sociologists. We are rewarded and punished for following and breaking the rules of our social system. Each role we play is simultaneously seen from a critical perspective by members of a given social group in terms of its privilege, the value of the skills demanded by social roles, and the social power these skills represent in terms of status and prestige.

Mr. and Mrs. E must experience one or both of two conditions if they are to risk their current psychological and social adaptation. Either their current condition is intolerable or a more profitable condition seems attainable. To make significant life changes both individuals would have to deal with profound psychological and social considerations. They would have to make these changes both descriptively and morally, struggling all the while with moral terms and metaphors that have long since replaced the descriptive ones.

Change would involve at least the following:

1. A reflective awareness that their mode of experiencing the world is not the only perspective that exists would have to precede any attempts at change. To the degree that sensorimotor and more important preoperational modes of appraisal predominate, no such determination would be possible. Mr. and Mrs. E do possess formal operations, although most of their lives are lived with preoperational modes of experience. Those patients who disturb society or experience the world from the lens of preoperational thinking are those who enter the mental health system involuntarily. While Mr. and Mrs. E have no other perspective with which to evaluate themselves and each other than the one they utilize, each does realize that that perspective is not the only one that might exist. Thus, when Mr. E seeks therapy he states, "Something is the matter with me!"

2. Change would also involve confronting and describing the emotions that have long since been defined either as weakness, disrespect, or moral badness. They would simultaneously have to accept that all their lives they have pursued certain skills to the exclusion of others. Mr. E never learned how to play the musical instrument he once desired to play. Mr. E has never developed any skills that might be called leisure skills. He cannot really play. He can run a business and intimidate people but not delegate responsibility and negotiate. Mrs. E, too, never completed school. If she now desired a life without Mr. E, what would she offer a prospective employer? In general, if they separated, Mr. E would discover that he has never learned to make coffee or cook an egg, while Mrs. E would not know the dipstick on her car engine from the release on the gas cap. She knows how to dress, put on makeup, flatter others, laugh at bad jokes, plead, and cry. To what adaptive situation, other than her present life, can these skills apply?

3. Both individuals would also have to run the risk of losing important social relationships if they sought to change their lives. Mr. E makes real money that solves real economic problems for himself, Mrs. E, and his children. To change his life is not only to risk social sanctions but also to learn new social roles that might risk his economic and political standing in the community. With the potential loss of income comes the potential loss of social status and prestige that such changes might well entail. Mr. E had been voted "Businessman of the Year" by the local chamber of commerce, while his wife was "Fundraiser of the Year" for a local charity. They are both valued members of a church, which represents a powerful source of identity, stability, and social sanctions.

Mr. and Mrs. E both can tell the story or narrative of their lives. That story contains the intellectual and moral myths that explain and justify their past, present, and future. To change their lives is to confront those stories and to discover the lies therein. To scrutinize one's narrative is to create a need to tell a new story, confront new moral truths, rewrite history, and plan a new future. This added to the demands of experiencing oneself anew, learning new skills and new social roles, means risk, risk, risk.

Chapters 11 and 12 discuss what the Es might gain from changing their lives, but it is clear that there is much in each individual's life that mitigates against these changes. The total weight of their lives demands very good reasons for changing, even if much pain already exists as a reason for doing so. What then provided the stimulus for both to enter the mental health system if the events already described were not sufficient for them to do so? What unique experience convinced each that he or she could not any longer tolerate their current mode of adaptation?

Just as the Es were assimilated into the social structure that nurtured, rewarded, and punished them, so too did each try to assimilate each other into the myths of the other. Each demanded faith, belief, and obedience to the rules and expectations each set for the other. These rules and expectations were never consciously reflected upon as rules but operated as powerful determinants of the adaptive paradigms of the other. And just as the Es shaped each other, both then shaped their three children as they had been shaped by their own parents.

Time and space forbid me to describe the operation of the family process as it affected each child and drew him or her into being an Everyman. I will focus just briefly on one of the three, namely, the youngest and the only girl. As a parent, Mr. E now saw as reasonable many of the role attributes of his father. He saw the inferior child from the eyes of the superior adult and could apply his father's role as he had observed it throughout his childhood. Even if he wished to raise his daughter differently than he was raised, he would have to invent a new role for himself as a father and confront many of the same issues that inhibited other change.

The same could be said of Mrs. E's mode of being a mother. Neither Mr. nor Mrs. E knew that their own parents had felt as helpless and overwhelmed by the demands of parenthood as they felt now in assuming their own parental roles. They had no way of reflecting on the fact that each felt like a child playing at being both an adult and a parent. Each was frightened and unreflective and thus could not even begin to evaluate the dogmatic and critical demands for obedience they made on their children. Mr. E demanded and criticized, Mrs. E begged and cajoled, unaware of their need to enlist and assimilate their children into the Everyman way of life and thinking.

Things went reasonably well with the Everyman's children, except for their daughter. From the beginning, she experienced difficulties in finding her assigned place in the family hierarchy. Perhaps she was born with neurological differences in sensitivity. Perhaps her differences were in her basic psychological mode of appraising situations. In any event she seemed to require a different adaptive niche from the one into which she had been thrust. Since early childhood she had alternately been described as either a "free spirit" or a "disobedient brat," depending on who judged her.

Mr. E found himself responding warmly to his daughter's rebellion and simultaneously abhorred her disobedience. Mrs. E found her daughter a good listener. She never realized how much and how often she confided in her child, seeking both sympathy and recognition. A family therapist observing their relationship might say that a role reversal was taking place in which the child was being burdened by a premature parental role.

The daughter found herself burdened and flattered by her mother's confessions; she felt guilty at her sense of failure in helping her mother and angry at her mother's attempts to manipulate her. She saw her father as a tyrant, and when she rebelled she did not realize how much support she received from her father for her rebellion. Her brothers thought their father's inconsistency was unfair and wondered why he was so much more strict with them. But as time passed, the daughter found herself more with her friends than at home and dreading the time she had to spend with her parents.

It was in high school that she found a home in that group known to the school administration as the dropouts, delinquents, and losers. In that group she found emotional release in drugs and powerful social approval for getting high. As her grades plummeted, her frantic parents tried to control her. They did not know that sociologically their daughter was already deeply embedded in a new, powerful, and very different social structure than the one represented by their family. They could not articulate that this group had more power in their child's life than they did and that society was allowing the counterculture to operate independent of all the major cultural institutions of which society was composed.

Several years after their daughter dropped out of the tenth grade to "hang out," the Es received a call from the police that she had died in an automobile accident. The police added that they were not sure what had happened but, as there were no skid marks and the boy who was at the wheel was driving at a high speed, the couple had either fallen asleep or committed suicide. Drugs had been found in the car, but neither youngsters had significant blood levels of the drugs found.

As an aftermath of the grieving process, both Mr. and Mrs. E found their way into the mental health system. He saw a private therapist, to whom he had been referred by his cardiologist after suffering angina pains. The therapist diagnosed Mr. E Adjustment Disorder with Mixed Emotions. Soon after her daughter's death Mrs. E began to hear the voice of her daughter calling to her. She was hospitalized involuntarily and was diagnosed as a Schizo-Affective Disorder. With those diagnoses this chapter closes.

9

"DIAGNOSIS" II: THE PSYCHOSES

This chapter discusses the diagnoses considered to be the more serious of those found in the DSM. In the last chapter, I generated the diagnoses that in earlier DSMs were generally termed the *neuroses*. This section discusses the diagnoses referred to as the *psychoses*. I will argue that these patterns of behavior, especially the pattern of activity known as schizophrenia, are adaptive modes of experiencing and being in the world and as such represent a variety of personal adaptive paradigms.

Of all the mythical medical entities contained in the psychiatric catalogue, none is more precious to the clinical field than schizophrenia. The "bizarre" patterns of behavior, the often frightening hallucinations and delusions are all self-evident proof to the clinician that mental illness and disorders exist. Moreover, with schizophrenia there is implicit hope, if not more evidence than for other diagnostic categories, that neurological and biochemical disease can directly account for the syndrome. With a belief in the medical basis of the disorder intact, there are few reasons not to use chemotherapy to treat the illness. This makes schizophrenia not only the justificatory backbone of psychiatry, but also an enormously profitable enterprise for both medicine and the drug companies who find strong economic incentives to be involved with the field of psychiatry.

In the last chapter, I tried to demonstrate that any individuals, depending on which problems they were trying to solve and which methods were being employed to solve these problems, could be diagnosed with any of many diagnoses. If my observations are correct, it is also true that any one of a very large number of individuals struggling to adapt to very different situations, needs, and problems might be diagnosed with any diagnosis. Schizophrenia might not be a single disorder, or based on any single pattern of behavior. Rather, it may well be that a wide variety of adaptive modes and paradigms can be labeled and judged schizophrenia.

Even believers in the disorder are forced to struggle with the possibility that the above analysis is correct. In an editorial that began an issue of a psychiatric journal, devoted just to the diagnosis of schizophrenia, the editor, Jan Fawcett (1993: 102), writes,

> For those clinicians in practice over the past 30 years of the post-chlor-prozamine era, not much positive has seemed to happen. We have essentially spent this time learning about the limitation and hazards (extrapyramidal reactions, tardive dyskenesia and neuroleptic malignant syndrome) of the very medication that initially brought hope to schizo-phrenic patients and their families. We watched state hospitals change from overcrowded snake pits from which people never seemed to return to underfunded revolving door operations. Despite the promise of Community Psychiatry we have watched the homeless mentally ill increase to a conspicuous population.

What Dr. Fawcett seems not to understand is that the very presence of psychiatry as it creates "schizophrenia" may be at the forefront of many of the problems he describes. Igbal et al. (1933: 217) begin to give lie to the myth (although they do not experience themselves doing so) when they write, "The composition of the Schizophrenia Syndrome varies across individuals, and even within individuals over time." They continue, "In addition to progress in the nosology of schizophrenia, the past decade has seen an increasing appreciation of the phenomenological diversity of the disorder. Schizophrenia still lacks a simple defining feature and instead is marked by a diversity of symptoms including disturbances in perception, attention, thought affect and motor be-havior." In short, any and all aspects of any individual's personal adaptive paradigm can be judged and a diagnosis of schizophrenia can be made.

DIAGNOSIS OF SCHIZOPHRENIA

If there is no schizophrenia, what are the symptoms described as comprising the illness? If we read *symptoms* to be "unwanted behavior of unknown motivation," then we begin to unravel the mystery of the disorder that is not a disorder. An excursion through DSM III reveals a list of specific behavior and attitudes clustered together to comprise a disorder. But if we examine each aspect or symptom of the cluster, we see that we are dealing with the same illogical unscientific problem that existed when we examined Oppositional Defiant Disorder.

Just as with Oppositional Defiant Disorder (see Chapter 8), a decontextual-ized, ahistorical list of human activities is juxtaposed and declared to be symptoms or representative aspects of a disease. If we examine the DSM we see sets of symptoms forming the lynch pin of schizophrenia. First in the set, we find any seriously odd behavior that cannot be explained as belonging to socialization in another culture. If one talks to oneself, dyes one's hair blue, toilets oneself in public, or otherwise demonstrates bad manners and poor personal habits one is suspected of schizophrenia.

The motivation for behaving in these odd ways is not asked about, as the motivation is assumed to be the illness itself. Some years ago a homeless person named "Billy Boggs" was taken off the streets for defecating on Third Avenue in front of Bloomingdale's department store. The justification for her incarcera-tion was that she was schizophrenic. When asked why she defecated on the street, Ms. Boggs replied that she was homeless and did not have a bathroom. It was also clear that if Ms. Boggs had defecated on Eleventh Avenue at night, rather than on Third Avenue, she would not have called such attention to herself and would have remained "homeless" rather than "schizophrenic."

The central core of schizophrenia, however, is established by the presence of delusions and hallucinations. *Delusions* are false beliefs. Most human beliefs are false, either in that they cannot be empirically verified or in that individuals lack the faith to accept them as true. To the believer of any given religion, the believers of all other religions have false beliefs. To me, the concept of schizophrenia is a false belief. Prior to the invention of the delusion, most false beliefs were sin, blasphemy, apostasy, and heresy. In secular society they are delusions and thus an indication of schizophrenia. That people make up beliefs that cannot be substan-tiated cannot be disputed. That they require medical attention for false beliefs certainly can be disputed. The question is, why do people invent ideas that cannot be substantiated? My answer is that they need these beliefs in order to describe, explain, predict, and control their world and satisfy needs and solve problems that cannot otherwise be satisfied or solved.

A *hallucination* involves perceptions that can only be experienced by the perceiver. It is one thing for an individual to deviate significantly from the beliefs of his fellows in a culture; it is quite another not to share the sensory perceptions that comprise shared reality. When an individual hears or sees things that only he or she can hear or see, it seems to create intense anxiety for everyone involved with that individual. Yet despite calling the individual who hallucinates psychotic or schizophrenic, what do we know of this experience or the motivations for its occurrence?

Ghazi Asaad (1990) has written on hallucination, not as secondary to schizophrenia but as a phenomenon. Although he refers to the hallucination as a symptom, the symptom may refer back to a variety of causes. Thus, individu-als can hallucinate because of the excessive use of alcohol or other drugs, including hallucinogens, because of organic brain disorder or eye and ear disorders, or because of intense human emotions. It is not uncommon in extreme grief for a loved one to be seen during the period of mourning. Asaad differentiates between hallucinations and pseudohallucinations, in which the individual knows that he/she is hallucinating.

If we examine the historical record and anthropological evidence we know that in other times and other societies hallucinations are sought after rather than feared. Much of religious ecstasy and the use of hallucinogens are part of a search for hallucination, which represents the achievement of making contact with the spirit world.

Asaad suggests that there may be a threshold for hallucinations, one that differs from person to person and within individuals based on health, fatigue, and other factors. Laing (1982) has long maintained, as does Asaad, that a large segment of the human population can and does hallucinate. This may be true even in our society, where discretion and fear of labeling insure that individuals do not talk about various hallucinatory phenomena. We know very little about the range of individual differences in states of consciousness, both between and within people, because there is so much pressure to maintain a public state of consciousness that is socially approved of.

Hallucinations have a developmental history as well. Analysts have long believed that the hungry infant will hallucinate his bottle when hungry. Developmental psychology suggests that the different experience of imaging and perceiving takes time to develop and as a result young children experience images, dreams, and fantasies as real. Hallucinations or experiences similar to hallucinations are a part of childhood, and their diminution and separation from "normal" conscious experience are topics still shrouded in the deepest mystery. Throughout this book I have argued that mental illness does not exist, in particular, that schizophrenia does not exist but that hallucination, false beliefs, and unusual behavior do. I would like to turn now to some theoretical explanations as to why people construct "fantastic" stories for their lives, hallucinate, and otherwise behave in ways others wish they would not. I will discuss these psychological phenomena for what I believe they are, namely, defenses that are part of individual adaptive paradigms.

However, the first question to be addressed in regard to hallucinations and delusions as defenses involves the issue of neurological involvement in these phenomena. Can schizophrenia (the collective term I will use for the phenomena) involve brain pathology and still be seen as an adaptive mode of experiencing the world? I believe the answer to the question is, very possibly, in some cases, yes. The issue of brain pathology must be dealt with because there is compelling evidence that it is involved in some cases of schizophrenia.

BRAIN PATHOLOGY AND HALLUCINATIONS

Over the years hundreds of biological markers have been put forward to differentiate those who hallucinate and those who don't. None of these markers has been consistent in differentiating schizophrenic from nonschizophrenic populations. The search for such consistency is still short of reaching its goal, although evidence continues to grow that brain pathology is involved with some cases of hallucinatory and delusional activity.

Sharif et al. (1993) summarize the results of brain-imaging studies in schizophrenia. Small but significant differences between schizophrenics and normals exist in the enlargement of the lateral ventricle of the brain. Other studies reveal enlargement of the third ventricle. Some studies utilizing computer axial tomography (CAT) and magnetic resonance imagery (MRI) also reveal cortical atrophy of about 3 to 5 percent in some studies. Psychiatry is excited about somewhat more consistent findings that reveal changes in temporal lobe size, especially the left temporal lobe, in schizophrenic populations. The use of positron emission tomography (PET) has shown inconsistent results in differences in the metabolic rates of schizophrenic and normal brains. We find that newer studies rarely replicate the findings of older studies. Neurological differences may well exist in some unknown proportion of those who hallucinate, and this proportion may in fact be greater than in a population of people who do not hallucinate. Let us for a moment assume that a greater number of hallucinators have brain differences, disturbances, or damage than those who do not hallucinate. What does such a fact signify? It signifies that a correlation exists between hallucinating and brain differences and/or brain pathology and that this correlation is very far from perfect.

If a correlation does exist between schizophrenia and brain pathology, that still does not establish a cause-and-effect relationship. Let us examine some relationships between brain differences and unwanted brain behavior that might exist. First, it may be true, as Dr. Asaad and others suggest, that hallucinations are the direct symptoms of brain pathology. If this is so, those hallucinations have no meaning psychologically. They play no role in the adaptive struggles of the individual. As I have argued earlier, these hallucinations are neurological symptoms and thus part of a true medical illness or disorder.

A second interpretation of the correlation between brain damage and hallucinations can be developed as follows. Individuals are born with or develop brain pathology due to viral infestation, allergies, or physical damage and now find the struggle to adapt much more difficult than they would had not the damage or brain differences existed. Perhaps these brain differences (such as forebrain injury) make the emotions harder to modulate and control. The increased intensity of emotions such as fear might then lead to an increased need to employ defenses such as "delusions" or hallucinations. If this conclusion is true, we can see the hallucinations as part of the adaptive struggle of the individual. Because of the presence of brain pathology, the role of the therapist is changed dramatically and made much more difficult.

A third interpretation can also be made. Children subjected to terror, isolation, or other extreme forms of stress and duress may develop brain differences as a result of their attempts to cope with the stress. One of the standing assumptions of the medical model is that brain structure influences behavior. The only way to test this hypothesis would be to do a longitudinal study that begins with differentiated groups of brain injured and non–brain-injured, follows their development, and notes who does or does not hallucinate in each group.

To my knowledge such a longitudinal study has never been made. As I noted earlier, DSM III is based on highly biased sampling methods. It includes a specialized group that is self-selected and another that is involuntary in its participation in medical science. The sampling procedures of all medical sciences are similarly biased. All of our studies employing electroencephalograms (EEG), PET, and CAT scans and the like are based on self-selecting and otherwise biased populations. We have no idea just what a large random sampling of the citizenry would reveal as to the size of ventricles, cortical structure, or neurochemical functioning.

We can add still another explanation of the correlation in question. Long-time hospitalization, homelessness, or being homebound or otherwise living a lifestyle bereft of hope, dignity, and stimulation may be the cause of the brain differences found in those who hallucinate and are thus labeled schizophrenic. Are studies of brain differences made before or after these individuals have been taking the powerful neuroleptics known to cause brain damage by their toxicity? Is it possible that the brain damage found in schizophrenics is the result of being schizophrenic? (I would like to compare the result of brain injury studies on schizophrenics to those of individuals experiencing prison sentences or being held hostage or who have otherwise been deprived of their freedom for extended periods of time.)

We cannot conclude that schizophrenia is a brain disorder. I shall therefore continue developing the hypothesis that delusions and hallucinations are dynamic, meaningful behaviors engaged in by those whose lives have taught them different truths and demanded different solutions to life's problems and different modes of satisfaction of their basic human needs. I will pursue this hypothesis by asking after the nature of noesis and noema required by these desperate acts of survival, understanding, dignity and sanity.

DYNAMICS OF ADAPTATION: SCHIZOPHRENIA

The behavioral patterns described in the DSM are those of an individual's adaptive mode in being in the world. Schizophrenia is a way of being in the world. If we describe schizophrenia this way we can certainly say it is different in a statistical sense than the ways of being of us who live in the world and are pledged to be, more or less, "normal." We have to ask then what accounts for the differences between those who are adapted in one way and those adapted in the other. We must do this descriptively if we are to gain understanding into the differences. We must put aside our judgments, which requires of us that we stop calling these individuals schizophrenic.

Why might people engage in behaviors including the kind of thought patterns described/judged as schizophrenic. We do not know. Our ignorance is perhaps more profound about this group of individuals than about all the others with whom we deal in the mental health system. First, our contact with these individuals is often not of the patients' choice. Often these individuals frighten or disgust family and friends until they are judged sufficiently crazy. They are then brought into the system involuntarily. Sometimes they arrive in handcuffs and in police protection. I agree with Laing (1967b) that a patient's initiation into the expected role of schizophrenic is one that represents a "degradation ceremony" or, as I call it, a ritual dehumanization. Being hospitalized and diagnosed schizophrenic is one more significant step in the life of an individual already made into a nonperson.

Moreover, in my experience with such individuals, their desire is to comply with the external demands made upon them by society and the mental health system, but not to engage in a treatment process. I theorize also that these individuals are filled with self-hatred and doubt and perceive themselves as defective in permanent and irredeemable ways. We do not get to know them as we might Mr. Everyman, not only because our labeling of them precludes understanding and taking them seriously as people but also because they give us little opportunity to understand the thoughts and emotions that motivate them. As our research paradigm is basically flawed and our treatment process compromised from the outset, our knowledge of this disorder is conjectural at best. Therefore, let me conjecture.

With every "seriously disturbed patient" I have worked with and also have gotten to know (a relatively small percentage of those worked with), I was told of a childhood filled with interlocking features. First was a sense of massive threat producing unremitting fear, terror, anxiety, and a feeling that one is and will always be different and defective. The second feature was the individual's perception that there was no way out of the terror-inducing situation. The third element, not reflected upon by the storyteller, was that the only way out required the pervasive use of sensorimotor and preoperationally based defense mechanisms.

Why such terror in childhood? Often no events are described that can account for such intensity of emotion. It may be that in some cases there are brain differences that somehow lower the threshold of emotional arousal and allow operation of the world to be perceived in such a way that fear is induced. I have long felt that such sensitivities exist in certain individuals, involving not only pain but how intense affect appears phenomenologically to the individual. A number of patients report feeling overwhelmed by colors, sounds, or even people.

In an autobiography Donna Williams (1992) writes of earlier memories of trying to lose herself in "bright spots of fluffy color" that were a "barrier against the intrusive gabble" of human beings around her. Although Ms. Williams longed for emotional contact, interactions "terrified" her. Such terror may be induced, but it may also stem from the peculiarities of brain organization, perceptual and emotional thresholds, and the intensity with which human contact is experienced. Such an individual would have no external stance from which to reflect on her mode of experience and little choice but to seek to adapt to minimize her terror and optimize some form of communication.

Ms. Williams reports that what the clinical mental health field calls autism was for her an adaptive private language. Rocking, handshaking, and even hurting herself were expressions of her need to prove she existed and to gain some form of social recognition. Ms. Williams reports that her mother did physically and psychologically abuse her, but secondarily to her autism. The emotional experience of terror in one so sensitive to pain must have deepened and increased the need to withdraw as a means of adaptation.

From patient after patient diagnosed as seriously disturbed, I have heard stories not only of experiencing the world differently but also of being the victim of extreme violence in childhood. I believe that we are now coming to recognize the degree to which violence is used in authoritarian-totalitarian family adaptations. Those of us who make up the fields of the helping profession often complain of loneliness, isolation, and being misunderstood in childhood. But for me and most of my colleagues there was little experience of extreme violence in childhood and little basis for its conceptualization in our theories. The only major writer I know of who has dealt seriously with the issue of terror in childhood is Alice Miller (1984.). Recently, as child abuse has become a popular subject, more attention has been given to the issue.

Several patients I worked with repeat similar experiences of being attacked by parents repeatedly and ferociously. They report experiences of total helplessness when parents become angry, followed by intense rushes of terror. As the years progressed, these patients reported that at the first hint of terror, they became psychologically "empty" and "numb." One reported that as her mother beat her she would achieve a total depersonalization. She could remember actually "climbing out" of her body and feeling nothing as her mother beat her with fists, belts, sticks, and shoes.

Some individuals grow to enjoy the experience of detaching and induce this under any and all stressful conditions. One person reported learning to be totally helpless and "without will," submitting fully to the authority of any who demanded anything of her. Another feared that during her detached state she might "go off" and so lose conscious control with herself that she might never come back.

All of the individuals being discussed had found ways to alter the basic perceptual experiences of pain. We have no idea how this is achieved neurologically or at what possible organic cost. Psychologically the patient who was told continuously by her mother, "I wish you were dead," adopted a stance toward life that she believed would please the mother by denying her own desires to continue living. She would engage in a litany of self-abnegation and denial. She would punish herself by going hungry for long periods of time but would not feel the hunger. Ultimately, this individual constructed a view that life was hopeless and empty and that she was worthless and undeserving of even basic desires. As she could not stop desiring she was in constant guilt. When she was hospitalized for suicidal intent she was diagnosed Major Depressive Disorder.

But there are situations more desperate than those already described involving fear and terror. In some situations the individual is not only physically terrified but also enjoined to think certain thoughts, feel certain emotions or drives, or accept definitions of self that leave little in the way of positive moral worth. Even worse, they are enjoined from thinking, feeling, or even experiencing themselves as subject agencies. It is the adaptive solution to what Bateson (1978), Haley (1976), Berger (1978), Whitaker (1976), and others have called the *double bind* form of communication, and double-bind interactions. It is also theorized that double binding leads to those patterns of behaviors and mode of subjective experience that are called schizophrenic disorders.

A double-bind communication is one that contains an internal contradiction. If the communication is a command, the command is contradictory. No matter what the individual does to obey the command, no matter which of the contradictions he obeys, he must fail to please the authority doing the commanding. Thus, a father says to his son, "Listen to your father; do as you want to do." If the son does as he wants to do then he cannot listen to his father; if he listens to his father he cannot do as he wishes to do. The individual cannot do the right thing and, as father gets ever angrier at his son, the son is confronted with a problem that cannot be solved in relation to the father.

Double binds can occur in any situation. As a teenager I remember a number of instances of calling a girl up for a date and being told, "I'd love to go out with you, but I'm busy this week." Which aspect of the message does one listen to? However, after several repeats of "I'd love to but. . . ," I had several choices. First, I could unravel the double bind. I knew "I'd love to" was said to be polite and that the "but" contained the real message. Second, I could at any time leave the field of play and not call this young lady again.

Children, however, cannot leave the home or school where parents and teachers are responsible for them. Moreover, they are also often enjoined by the parents from unraveling the double bind. If a child accuses the parent of being unclear or upsetting them (they certainly do not have the linguistic capacity to recognize a double bind for what it is), the parent has power to punish the child for such moral allegations. Often, double-bind messages put the child in conflict with his own psychological processes. "Go to bed; you are tired," "Eat your food; you are hungry," place the words of the parent, who is experienced early in life as omniscient and omnipotent, in contradiction with the child's own feelings of hunger or of fatigue. It is possible that a child will believe the parent for fear of punishment or rejection and now must find a way to contradict his or her own most basic experiences. Whatever solution the child uses to solve this problem is doomed to create even more contradictions or internally experienced double binds. How does a child who has said, "I hate my brother," come to grips with the contradiction created when he believes his mother, who demands that he believe, "You really love your brother."

Not only can children be placed in a double bind but their very thought processes can be attacked at the same time. "I know what is good for you," "You don't know your own mind," "What's the matter with you for thinking such a thing," "This hurts me more than it hurts you," and "I'm doing this for your own good" are statements that can create powerful internal contradictions if they are backed up with threats of violent punishment or rejection. Perhaps the most common double bind and one of the most difficult to resolve is "There is nothing to be afraid of." Like all defensive solutions the consequences of any defense bring about the short-term experience of satisfaction and solved problems but long-term experience of ever more difficult problems. The parents who utilize the double bind are themselves trying to solve the problem of raising their own children. How overwhelmed must such an individual feel when confronted by the demands and needs of his or her child, that he or she would in turn demand that the child have no needs or demands unless given permission to do so by teachers or parents. Essentially parents who demand loyalty in this way are exercising a totalitarian demand that the child's very experience of the world be under their control.

In Orwells' *1984*, those who oppose the will of the state are brought to the Ministry of Truth for reeducation. As O'Brien tortures Winston Smith, he explains to him that it is not enough for him to behave loyally to the state and say all the right things. He must, if the state demands it, agree that $2 + 2 = 5$, and believe that in fact $2 + 2 = 5$. Before being released from his torture he must convince his captors that he hates his former girlfriend and loves Big Brother (the state's figurehead leader). By book's end, Winston has betrayed his former love and loves Big Brother. He experiences himself as nonexistent except in the eyes of the state.

The parents who utilize the double bind are in effect demanding such a loyalty of their children. Often they are embedded in political systems that demand the same of them. In our country such a civil political process is not in operation, but many belong to religions that demand loyalty in much the same way. All religions define sin in some way, but some equate sins of thought and feeling with sins of doing. Children are taught to imagine a God that looks human and lives in a real place called heaven and reads their minds. If they have "bad thoughts" God will hate and punish them. True to the preoperational notion of such ideas, punishments are more terrible than can be imagined and are inflicted by God forever. Psychology has long recognized that the so-called delusions and hallucinations of schizophrenics were of a religious nature but have ignored the possible link between the schizophrenic adaptation and the demands made upon the individual by his or her religion. I believe that many children who are subjected to demands for total loyalty are embedded in a home life that operates with such rules and that the home is contextualized by religions that operate with the same preoperational literalness. These religions set up the same kind of loyalty test as the parent and state, defining loyalty as a will-lessness in personal experience.

The third factor involved in the creation of severe diagnoses begins with an individual seeking to leave or control a situation in which there is an experience of having no way out, except by utilizing defenses. Although defenses may always be employed at such moments, in these cases only defensive solutions are available to the individual. The Everymans' could always conform to the demands made upon them and then develop skills that would be amply rewarded by family, friends, and society. Although defenses abounded in their experience of reality, they shared realities with others that were mutually pleasing to themselves and the others. Until the death of their daughter, the Everymans could always find a way to utilize the nondefensive aspects of their paradigms in satisfying needs and solving problems. Defense and nondefense, lie and truth, existed side by side until the death of their daughter exploded the lies with which they maintained their lives. For Mr. Everyman, therapy with another human being became another nondefensive way out of his predicament.

The people discussed previously were bound since childhood in situations that did not provide a way out through social acceptance of someone else's moral rules of behavior. For example, a child who experiences her mother sitting on her body, banging her head on the floor while she screams, "Why don't you die?" has at that moment little with which to form compromises. Or a young boy who cannot discover just what rule he must follow to please his father, who refers to him continuously as "that useless bag of shit" and then chases him around the house with a leather strap, has to utilize unusual and creative means to cope with the situation.

In addition, the defenses involved in the behavior of those diagnosed "psychotic" involve the extensive utilization of sensorimotor and preoperational modes of appraisal and emotional expression. Sensorimotor distortions occur continually, whereas preoperational thinking becomes rooted in a wide number of appraisals that comprise those most basic to self-image and the narrative that comprise those personal stories. Why does the individual use such primitive defense mechanisms? I believe part of the answer comes from the very motivation to use these defenses in the first place. The individual is desperate and unable to do otherwise. Part of the answer may also lie in the young age of the individual when terror, confusion, and anxiety are first experienced. As with all other defenses, the desire to avoid pain and please those powerful in one's life has the unforeseen consequences of producing the very pain and helplessness that one seeks to avoid. By experiencing oneself as beyond pain, one creates an endless sea of pain. Biologically, psychologically, and socially, life becomes attack and defense, accusation and judgment of self and others. Denial of physical needs of pleasure and pain becomes constant activities. Laing (1967a) has best described these appraisals, defenses, and their consequences as "knots"—knots that envelop the patient, the therapist, and all those with whom they interact in an endless self-confirming set of hypotheses experienced as completely true.

How do individuals solve the problems inherent in such terrible demands? "I think," said Decartes, "therefore I am." We might have added "I feel, I need, I solve problems, I observe, I explain, I predict, and I engage in a myriad number of acts of control, all of which prove I exist." How does one contradict such basic levels of experience? How does one reduce terror when the sources of terror are those supposed to be the sources of comfort? How does one satisfy one's needs for recognition and protection by one's family and community and achieve an experienced state of nonexistence? Although the next paragraphs will describe what I believe are such attempts, I must add that such solutions can never be permanent or stable. To experience oneself as nonexisting must instantly clash with the experience of trying to not exist. Thus, the double bind sets in motion a moment-to-moment set of conflicts that keep the individual busy, focused, and unable to engage in any other set of activities.

At the same time such individuals may create fictions, believed by them to be true, that everyone in the world is persecuting them. Such a statement not only is a preoperationally overextended idea but creates conditions that counteract the terrible experience of having to be nothing and no one. The utter helplessness of being watched by all of humanity, God, the universe itself as it sends spaceships to Earth is negated by the same idea, which makes one the most important figure on heaven and earth.

The belief that one is God or Jesus Christ, Moses, George Washington, or some other revered and mythological character achieves much the same ends. Who can be more powerful yet be guiltless in his use of power than God or Jesus Christ? Who can be more above reproach than the source of morality itself? The children of Everyman constantly complain to their parents, "That's unfair." Their parents tell them that their claims to justice are unfounded. Although the children know that the rules their parents create favor the parents, their parents set about to convince them that the rules really favor them, the children. Often siblings developing in such conditions will learn to blame and attack each other. As the children we have just been speaking of cannot even think, "It's unfair," their need to absolve guilt requires a more urgent and ideosyncratic solution. "I am Jesus Christ" announces an individual who is now guilt free.

Hallucinations often accompany the delusions that I will at this juncture refer to as "Religions of One." Delusions are fabrications of beliefs; hallucinations are fabrications and reconstructions of experience itself. Every hallucination that I have ever been told of seems to make adaptive sense if one places it in the context in which it has an adaptive role to play. For example, a woman hears God commanding her to write poetry and then telling her that she is an immortal poetess. As a child, this individual was beaten mercilessly for evidence of pride, a mortal sin in both her mother's and her church's judgment. Who, however, can disagree with God if he does the commanding and then provides a judgment of the poem's excellence? Another woman is abandoned by her husband with two small children. This same woman was raised in an impoverished agrarian community in Puerto Rico and regularly attended church where she was told to listen to God and beware of the Devil. As a child her grandmother beat her regularly "to keep the Devil away from her" and one time inflicted serious punishment because the patient refused to acknowledge the grandmother's vision of the "holy mother of God." The priest conceded that it was childish "willfulness" that prevented the child from seeing the holy vision.

The woman was sexually abused at age four and raped at age six. She fled Puerto Rico as a young teen to escape the beatings of her grandmother, only to come to New York where she was raped twice the first year she was here. She married a man she believed would protect her only to be beaten seriously by him on numerous occasions. The beatings stopped when he abandoned her and soon after was arrested during the commission of a violent crime and sent to prison. One afternoon during a snowy cold winter the patient, left alone with two small children, feeling totally overwhelmed by her responsibilities, and feeling she must be the worst person in the world, heard a voice command her, "Kill the children." These voices, coming from the outside, provided a solution for her immediate problem. Without the children she could be free to get a job, meet a new man to take care of her, and reduce the terror of her economic and human responsibilities. The woman at first believed God was commanding her to kill the children but later decided it was the devil. Her neighbors heard her screams. The police were called. The children were placed in foster care, and she began to find her permanent place in the mental health system.

A woman was raised by a frightened mother who was abandoned by her husband, the child's father, after years of abuse and drinking. Her mother told her that she was a "special child" sent by God to take care of her (the mother) and her brothers. The child grew up constantly fearful of displeasing her mother and God as she felt driven to see to it that neither her mother or rebellious brothers were ever unhappy. After years of such goodness, in which she never "hated or wished her mother and brother dead even once," she began seeing Jesus Christ. She began to have long deep discussions with "her savior" concerning her moral role in the world. These discussions were often interrupted by a "devil" that attacked her and Jesus and at times created terror for both of them. During the two years or so the patient engaged in these discussions she was repeatedly hospitalized. The hallucinations ended (and have not returned now for several years) when she and Jesus defeated the devil and Jesus said to her, "Relax and just be human; you do not need to be perfect." Commanded by Jesus to relax, the woman could now tell her mother that she would not be available to help take care of her as she used to. She stated that for the first time in her life she did not feel the need to be perfect or driven in the pursuit of her success as well as keeping her mother happy and her brother out of trouble. The burdens were lifted but now the woman states: My life is over. I can never do any of the things I used to do, like work or entertain or be in stress in any way because my psychiatrists tell me if I do I will get sick again.

In each of these individuals the delusion and hallucinations had a clear adaptive function. Even if brain injury of some kind was involved in creating the terror and confusion that led to such desperate adaptations, the thoughts, actions, and perceptions are all organized, purposeful, and intensely meaning-ful. Moreover, they are all adaptations to moral problems and needs, just as they are attempts to describe, explain, predict, and control certain events of a social and nonsocial nature. They are attempts at meeting needs and solving problems and often they are successful but, as with all defensive solutions, create the very difficulties that they seek to avoid.

The consequences of utilizing defenses that protect one's basic experience from the control of others or protect one's basic thoughts and emotions from an experienced annihilation bring about the very catastrophe being avoided. One consequence of fabricating a personal autistic world is that the individual increasingly loses contact with the world the rest of us, at least to some major degree, experience as real. When the patient negotiated with Jesus Christ, she did not have to negotiate with the living people who comprised her social world. The skills one develops are in fabrication, not discussion, debate, or even argument. Assertions in the arena of the shared world of experienced reality give way to private assertions of one's individually created world.

The overwhelming helplessness and terror of having to defend the very basis of one's consciousness are expressed in the grandiose experience of the individual's fabricated experiences. But any attempts to reach these individuals or directly to influence their defenses can produce retaliation in which one experiences one's own annihilation. Thus I once said to a patient who was listening to voices tell her she was evil and sinful that there were no voices but mine and hers. She paused a second and said to me, "No! The voices tell me that you don't exist, your voice is unreal." I believe this was an attempt to assume godlike powers to deny deep-down weakness. But the basis of any human contact between us was lost. Whenever an individual either reconstructs or fabricates major portions of experience, he or she ultimately creates the obliteration of self and experience that he or she seeks to avoid. Not only do such "schizophrenic" adaptations achieve their ends and produce such unintended unsequences but so too do attempts to control emotions and thoughts with alcohol and other chemical means. The longer these defenses are utilized and the longer they form the control basis of an individual's existence, the more difficult are the problems of engaging other individuals or reengaging life in some other ways.

As the years unravel and the control with the social world remains weak or nonexistent, the more the individual feels compelled to avoid that world. The fears that are avoided become harder to face. The skills of avoidance become more effective and reinforced while the skills of assertion into the social world grow even more atrophied. The days and hours of life as lived become emptier, more banal, and more trivialized and are filled with increasing spans of economic difficulties and political submissions.

A middle-aged woman who had been hospitalized on and off for many years since her first breakdown at age eighteen appeared for a session one day with a glossy 8 x 11 professional photo of herself taken at age seventeen. She stated "When I was 18 I was ready to become a movie star. Now all I can do is sit by my kitchen table, smoke cigarettes and stare into space. What is my life and where has it gone?" Several moments later she said, "I'm lonely, I think I'll bring back the voices."

How does one "treat" a person whose personal adaptive paradigm works in such a manner? How does one convince an individual to reengage life and develop skills that are required of a life in an economic and social setting.? How does one negate the roles created during the years of being a patient in which the status of the individual was that of an invisible nonperson? How does one help an individual who believes that her "poisonous thoughts" are created by a "poisonous brain" and that only a life without struggle or challenge and filled with endless hours waiting for the next pill to control her poisonous brain can keep her from further hospitalization?.

I will turn next to the topic of treatment and suggest that prevention may well be the best cure. I believe that the medical model must be rejected and patients must be helped to develop an attitude similar to that evinced by Odile Tomacek in a letter published in the comment section of the *American Psychologist*. She writes (1990: 550) of her fear and disgust upon learning that psychotherapists are looking to cure her schizophrenia.

> My initial reaction in reading the article was immediate revolt and panic
> at the idea that some people are striving under false cover of scientific
> goals and laudable intentions to "eliminate" people like me who are happy
> and proud to be the way they are. My Schizophrenia makes me be in such
> a way as I can accept myself and it is not my fault if the rest of the world
> will have little to do with it. To speak of "eliminate" is rather strong and
> reminiscent of Nazi philosophy. . . . I do not wish to be a so-called "nor-
> mal" individual at all.

Were I to devise a treatment for schizophrenia, it would be to help every individual experience the "disease" as an acceptable but often burdensome mode of being in the world, just as Tomacek does.

V

THE PRACTICE OF PSYCHO"THERAPY"

10 _____

PSYCHO"THERAPY": CONTEXTUALIZED

THE MYTHS OF PSYCHOTHERAPY

The philosopher Martin Tamney (1991) points out that scientific revolutions are both forward looking and backward looking. Breaks with the past cannot be understood without reference to the context that past ideas represent for the newer theories that break with them. Once a new paradigm emerges, however, it exists in conflict with the representatives of the very paradigms that gave rise to the new. In the ensuing struggle, the new paradigm is used to establish an agenda for the future with which existing paradigms cannot compete. If that agenda is fulfilled, then the new paradigm is dominant until it too is supplanted by ideas it gives rise to that are incompatible with what is dominant and traditional.

I have developed the theme that each individual is a scientist and that each of us goes through crises that may give rise to personal paradigmatic revolutions. What is true of scientific revolutions is also true of personal upheavals. Some of my struggles in relation to the past, present, and future have emerged as a result of my developing a paradigm of therapy based on nonmedical concepts.

To undergo a personal scientific revolution is to experience the world anew. It means a rejection, to some degree, of one's own past phenomenological experience and behavior and a simultaneous rejection of the morality that, of necessity, relates to those experiences and modes of behaving. The way we see the world and the way we live can be understood scientifically but can and will always be judged morally. To experience the world anew is to find oneself seeing the world as fresh and yet strange. The guidelines and rituals that defined life before the paradigmatic revolution become useless in guiding one's behaviors. Although some personal revolutions were guided by my parents and teachers and my own thoughts, the present revolution, in my middle age, places me in the company of some writers (Szasz, Laing, Mahoney, and Sarbin, to name a few) I have never met—and of a few others.

My rejection of the medical model is based on an awareness of a large set of issues that relate to not only the psychological theories that guide therapy but the techniques of therapy as well. Our field, its theories and/or applied endeavor, deals with the central moral issues important to humanity. Simultaneously, our field confuses its contentions and its values more than any other field. I have become increasingly aware of how my training helped foster this confusion in myself and how I played my role in the furtherance and maintenance of that confusion. My awareness has led me to insights on how these problems affect my life. My discovery of solutions for the field began, however, with personal solutions that dramatically affect how I live my life, especially in my role as therapist.

Psychologists have the same scientific and moral needs as anyone else. They are enfolded and contextualized by other human beings with scientific and moral needs. As for most other human beings, the social context in which psychologists operate and are trained is more authoritarian than democratic (even though lip service is given to democracy). Psychology and psychotherapy are filled with examples of the authoritarian, which are denied and then claimed to be objective science. Unless we in the field separate our science and our morality, base our theories or practice on science while justifying science, or practice on a democratic humanistic morality, our travails will continue.

The root of our scientific confusions begins with the peculiar nature of our subject matter. It is ourselves. We must understand ourselves and others, and we must be morally correct. Everything we seem to learn about ourselves and others appears to be cast in moral terms, our own needs to be right, truthful, worthy, and good. No one has a greater personal need to be correct than a scientist, whose social worth is dependent on how correct he is. No one has a greater need to be correct than people who claim to want to help in the lives of others. Not only do we as scientists have self-esteem riding on our knowledge, we have the lives of others riding on our skills. The temptation to be correct in such circumstances appears overwhelming.

Even as I call what I am writing a theory, I experience it as the truth. What I know and what I feel are at odds. As many others, I find that when I'm least sure of my knowledge, I argue in favor of it with most intensity. That and a tendency to present myself as morally superior because of my knowledge represent part of my most serious moral failings. My own struggle in recent years is to argue strenuously for the ideas I believe in, but never at the cost of the self-esteem or worth of those whom I debate.

One insight that has guided my behavior involves the realization that if one develops a new idea then one must battle for its continued existence with the same energy that led to its creation. The battle need not be done in defensive arrogance, but unless the fight is fought there can never be new knowledge. Those who assert new ideas, whether as patients or as scientists, must always do so in the conviction that they are right, or they will not sustain themselves when the onslaught of criticism begins. To study art or science is to discover that all of the creative people we now revere were attacked for their ideas in their time.

Galileo, Darwin, Freud, Einstein, Beethoven, Stravinsky, Picasso, Matisse, and a host of other pioneers were loathed in their own time. Each discovered the Buddhist truth: For every new idea a thousand soldiers guard the past. Yet, not only did all have to fight staunchly to define their ideas but all had simultaneously to struggle, as I do, to finalize their order and establish themselves as "authority." Each sought to feel the joy of certainty as well as to reduce the pain of doubt that is the constant companion of new discoveries. Each must have, as I do now, enjoyed the sense of independence and power that new discovery brings, as well as learned to hate the sense of isolation and loneliness that thinking differently than one's peers and colleagues creates. I find that the need to be certain, to be correct and morally acceptable to one's peers, appears in many more guises than in arrogant self-virtue. Throughout my career I have noted that, for every figure such as Freud, ten thousand followers claim correctness in his name. I have earlier noted that those higher in the social hierarchy dominate those lower in the social hierarchy who see submission and faith in the leader as their proper mode of being in the world.

No field has had more leaders raised to cult status on the basis of their personal merit than our own. Throughout the 1960s, as I went through college and graduate school, I noted these battles and their sequelae. Freudians, Adlerians, ego psychologists, Sullivanians, Horneyians, Kleinians, and later Kohutians all claimed a kind of godhood for their leaders. Each school demanded that the rest acknowledge its brand of psychoanalysis to be the one true analysis. I once recommended a book to a well-known Freudian analyst, who asked me, "Who analyzed the author?" When I stated, rather astonished, that I had no idea, the individual said, "I'll pass. I never read anything unless I know who the analyst of the author was."

Training in one or another of these "church sciences" revealed their tyrannies. I twice applied to analytic training programs but rejected each when I was told my own analysis (three times a week for three years) could not count because of the affiliation and/or lack of stature of my analyst. I would have had to submit to three more years of analysis with an approved analyst. I do agree that therapists benefit from the experience of personal therapy (if only to know how it feels to be the recipient of the process), but I abhor the idea that therapy should be forced on anyone. I argue that therapy under coercion is no therapy at all.

I soon learned the folly of arguing that I did not need therapy. To say that one has a problem is to admit a preconceived truth. To say that one does not have a problem is to be guilty of having a bigger problem. I now freely admit to having a mental illness that has been suspected by many since I started advancing the arguments in this book. I have Psychiatric Diagnosis Denial Disorder.

The battles in the field extend beyond the borders of psychoanalysis. Academics who do research (often sterile, meaningless, and rarely capable of being replicated) look down upon clinicians of all types, who in turn often have contempt for academics. Behaviorists soon entered the fray. Analysts and other "dynamic" psychotherapists had nothing but contempt for the behaviorists, who in turn called psychoanalysts a variety of bad names. Humanists enshrined Carl Rogers and Abe Maslow and often looked down their collective noses at both the behaviorists and the analysts. In each area the dominant theorists were declared geniuses, the equivalent to intellectuals of being called God. The adherents of each school achieved certainty and moral rectitude by slavish adherence to their leaders' precepts. If one examines the content of those theories, the often excellent and overlapping ideas are cast in implicit moral terms. As my own early allegiance was to psychoanalysis (of no clear school or type), I shall begin my moral analysis with this theory. Freud's ideas are filled with moral hierarchy. Not only are patients people with "weak egos," "dominant ids," and "inadequate or over-controlled superegos," but as Hannah Lerman (1986), Jessica Benjamin (1988), Nancy Chodorow (1978), and others point out, women are seen as inferior to men. Men are innately "active," women destined by their anatomy to be "passive." Freud (1930) also worried about the lifting of repressions that control the "instinctual masses," which would place civilization itself at risk.

Maslow discusses human needs but places them in a hierarchy of higher and lower needs. Courageous people surmount life's difficulties and rise through the hierarchy. Reading Maslow, one is reminded frequently of the inherent moral superiority (and self-congratulations) of the self-actualized individual. Only B. F. Skinner's ideas are truly democratic. We are all machines programmed by the processes of operant and respondent conditioning. We are all equal, but all equally not human.

Throughout my education and training I found much that made sense in each theory and am proud of the voracious reading I did in each area, although I never became a true believer in any school or theoretical persuasion. I discovered that each of these schools was monolithic only from a distance. I kept meeting teachers and therapists whose own personal ideas transcended the schools to which they were nominally adherents. I discovered that when one got past the public pronouncements and political wrangling and sat quietly with a friend that the personal, privately held differences each individual had with the collective were profound. If one counted up the differences, one found that privately there were no schools at all.

I discovered many individuals who resisted both their own desire for certainty and deification and my need either to deify them or attack their authority. They remained scientists, able to help me establish warm, friendly, caring relationships with them. In these circumstances individual differences in beliefs transcended group belief in uniformity and group think, while personal bonds rose above theory, moral rectitude, ideology, and utopian vision. It is this set of discoveries that I struggle to keep at the forefront of my thinking and work with colleagues and patients.

As the years unfolded, the authority of psychoanalysis, behaviorism, and humanism collapsed, although too slowly for any of us to notice that it was happening. Cognitive psychology arose, and my own studies in Piaget and developmental theory led me to try to interpret cognitive theory with psychoanalytic notions of ego, adaptation, defenses, and "unconscious thinking." I discovered the work of Rotter (1966), Beck (1967), Meichenbaum (1974), Bandura (1989), and others who combine behaviorism and cognitive psychology. (However, these individuals persisted in calling their patients bad names and referring to their beliefs and modes of thinking as "irrational.") I was introduced to the work of the family therapists, which helped me to begin to contextualize the active developing individual.

But as the old tyrannies collapsed, new tyrannies arose more distasteful than before. The battle between psychiatry and psychology began to grow. Instead of the prize to be won being the right to be trained as psychoanalysts, the new prize involved the right to diagnose patients with pseudomedical terminology. As this is written another phase of the never-ending struggle has begun, as two Air Force psychologists have been declared fit to prescribe neuroleptic drugs. The new tyranny, the medical model, seems to intrude itself into more and more areas of all our lives.

The battle was joined by the social-work professional, whose presence has provided democratization of the field at levels of intellectual mediocrity undreamed of in the 1950s and 1960s. Psychiatrists claimed moral superiority over the psychologists, who in turn claimed superiority over the social workers. To this day, comparison of the salaries of the three members of the "team" reveals the nature of the moral hierarchy of the mental health system.

I have become aware in recent years that more and more job advertisements for psychotherapists ask for either the Ph.D. or MSW degree. I react to this with fury and despair. Is not the scientific training of a Ph.D., which takes a minimum of five years and requires a research degree, different from that of an MSW, which is based on a year of courses and a year of field work? Not in the field of psychotherapy! There seems less and less room for theory, science, and philosophy in a field that is dominated by calling people bad names and developing techniques for curing imaginary afflictions.

I must make clear that the problem is not with the field of social workers. The social-work profession is filled with decent, caring people, many of whom make fine therapists. The problem is that our field is rooted in a lie that constantly threatens to overwhelm the best intentions of those who work in it. Therapists seek to understand people that they might understand themselves and become empowered to live their lives in different ways. The lie of mental illness results in workers more often than not seeking to control unwanted behaviors and creating the conditions that make people puppets, obedient to the will of others. In such a moral hierarchy, standards of education and skill can never be set. The resultant anarchy allows anyone with any credentials at all to find a foothold in the endeavor.

Psychiatry is a moral-philosophical enterprise that pretends to be a field of medicine. Psychiatrists trained in medicine find themselves defensively pretending to practice medicine while they make moral demands on the socially marginal people with whom they work. The pressure and social costs of this travesty are incalculable. Psychologists are trained in research, philosophy, and theory. They now pretend to be miniature medical personnel, giving up the best and finest of their beliefs for the lies and defenses of psychiatry. Social workers are trained in social theory and the practice of helping individuals adjust to the complexities of the social system. When they become clinicians they give up their legitimate training and join the mutual lies of psychiatry and psychology. The personal and social costs mount!

The resulting confusion, anxiety, fear, and guilt are played out in relation to the lives of the people with whom we work. Because decency and concern are so often present, the members of the confused, unhappy profession are constantly casting about for direction and guidance. Although science is always available as a way of dealing with our problems, defenses abound. Solutions are found in confounding our moral notions of what "should be" with our empirical experiences of "what is." We become certain or arrogant or turn to the "genius-gods" of our profession. We claim moral superiority over the nonpersons we create when declaring them to be mentally ill.

As the Freuds, Skinners, and Maslows disappear, new defensive arrangements have appeared in our field. What more and more therapists have seized upon are the growing number of writers claiming to have invented techniques to cure specific mental disorders. The generalized ideologies of the past have given rise to a new cult that I refer to as the "clinical engineers of techniques." More and more practitioners are guided by a nontheoretical approach called *eclecticism*. Eclecticism is often a babble of loosely organized, poorly articulated ideas and techniques that are justified by the simplistic pragmatism, "They work." How they work and toward what ends are asked ever more rarely. As new "diseases" are invented, as the economic bases of the field erode, ever more therapists seek skills and techniques in a desperate attempt to do something that works. For example, a group of colleagues recently spoke excitedly of a workshop based on the hypnotic technique of Milton Erikson. They were ecstatic because Erikson had worked out an elaborate system of fooling patients into adopting his goals and values. The patients' resistance is overcome without their ever knowing how and why. Do we professionals wish to see ourselves as fooling people into behaving as we wish, under the justification, "I know what is good for the patient," and, "Morality has nothing to do with the issue—we are only curing mental illness"?

I will not attempt to review the growing literature of techniques. More and more ingenuity is being utilized to change people's moral orientation without either an understanding of how changes come about or an attempt to justify the morality of the means and methods of reaching that change. As the number of unquestioning, aphilosophical workers grows, as the expertise of the techniques of behavior change improves, the closer we get to what Szasz calls the "therapeutic state."

My concerns, however, are with the intelligent, kind individuals who work in a profession that runs counter to their real interests as they desperately try to become good psycho"therapists" or psychoeducators. Their scientific and moral needs cannot and will not be satisfied by reading how-to books on the cure of mental disorders. I am therefore ready to begin a formal description of the process of psycho"therapy" and help the readers ascertain the degree to which they are already therapists who might wish to walk through the door (metaphorically speaking) into a nonmedicalized scientific and humanistic profession. First, I must briefly discuss another obstacle to this transition, the manner in which therapists are trained.

THE TRAINING OF PSYCHOTHERAPISTS

How would one learn a craft such as psychotherapy if its methods and goals were to be articulated both scientifically and morally? Can one learn to do a complex job by reading a book on how to do it? How do medicine, law, and education, for example, train their professionals in the craft that defines their professional lives? Let us note that physicians and attorneys are licensed in the practice of medicine and the practice of law. In our own garden of delights, separately trained personnel are licensed to use the titles of psychiatrist, psychologist, and social worker. What is to be practiced is never defined. Almost anyone can call himself or herself a psychotherapist or counselor. No professional licenses confer that title.

I raise this issue because I believe that many of the problems discussed in this book grow out of how we train psychotherapists, even though these problems derive from lies that underlie the field. Michael Polanyi (1958) suggests that no one can tell another how to do a complex skill because no one knows how he or she does it. Each of us knows what we are doing as we do it, but as so much of any activity is tacit to the activity we cannot say how it is done. A piano player who tries to concentrate on how he or she plays the piano will not be able to play the piano. The skills of a craft are tools directed toward an end result. The tools point to the end result and do not call attention to themselves. If we concentrate on the tools (provided they are accessible to our attention), we cannot concentrate on achieving the end result.

Polanyi points out that scientists learn science—and I include medicine and law in this example—by doing science. Novices do their learning as apprentices to a master scientist. It is through the process of imitation, identification, and role modeling that scientists learn to do research. I learned the role of scientist by being apprenticed to some of the finest research psychologists available, including George Klein, Robert Holt, I. H. Paul, and perhaps most important my thesis mentor, Donald Spence.

I learned to do therapy, however, by trial and error, as does virtually every other therapist. In the name of the morality of confidentiality, therapists almost always work alone even from the time they begin as neophytes either in a graduate program or some kind of internship or externship. This fact underlies our field's inability to develop and transmit a consistent working paradigm for psychotherapy. It works hand in hand with the discoveries of the competing schools and professors and helps explain why therapists are so desperate for direction in their life-or-death activities. Between the lies that undercut our field and the isolation in which it is learned, our field is chaotic and inconsistent. It is also why I have to agree with Jeffrey Masson (1988) that most therapists are deeply suspicious about what other therapists do and just as deeply defensive about their own activities.

Masson points out that most physicians have a number of other physicians to whom to refer family members or themselves. Lawyers also have access, in their own thinking, to a number of other attorneys that they trust. As an educator I know many other educators (as does my wife who is also a teacher) whom we would trust to educate our own children. But that is not so with therapists. Even with people I like, the number of those I would trust as a therapist is very small. I believe those feelings are reciprocated by most other therapists. Therefore my experience echoes Masson's. What are the reasons for this anomaly? As we invent ourselves as therapists, ultimately share what we do with very few others, and work in a moral quagmire of our own myths, we have little faith in our field, its ideas, or its participants. Ultimately I believe, we do not even trust ourselves.

The books written on techniques are written about what people do after they have stopped doing it. When we write about therapy, we are not doing therapy but are writing. Writing after the fact allows us to report selectively and defensively. It permits us to present ourselves in the most positive and effective light. As most of us do feel uneasy about calling people names (most therapists will not easily share the diagnoses they make of their patients and refuse to share progress notes with them as well), there are everpresent reasons for us to justify our activity defensively.

Most important, perhaps, in addition to our suspiciousness and mistrust of our own field, is the inability to teach others how we do therapy, a process that would open up our techniques to debate, scrutiny, and the processes of natural selection in which the best techniques can gain access to the majority of the field's adherents. We remain a fragmented, frightened group, isolating ourselves into little tribes of proponents of this technique or that and timidly but stubbornly suggesting that we and we alone possess the best therapy. Ultimately each therapist is an island unto himself or herself, isolated from a larger whole that does not even exist.

Other activities, such as writing, must be learned alone. A writer cannot take an apprentice, as writing must be done away from the presence of others. Yet with writing, we have the products of the writer to evaluate. As if therapy's problems weren't great enough as outlined, with our field not only is the process invisible but so is its product. We have no way of demonstrating the effectiveness of any given therapist. Although much research exists to demonstrate that therapy does have real and even positive effects, there is no way to evaluate the work of any given therapist. This deepens our suspicions of each other and therefore of ourselves and demands of us defensive solutions to our professional problems. (Thus each therapist claims that there are no bad therapists, only resistant patients whose original pathology was underestimated.)

I am now ready to begin to describe the process of psycho"therapy" and how it has helped me resolve many of the problems described that plagued the earlier part of my career. Again, I believe many therapists are already practicing in the way I do but often lack a conscious justification and language. I believe that despite our claims to hundreds of different therapies, our constant "diagnoses," and the continuing public battles between professionals and schools of therapy, private interactions of therapists and patients are more similar than any of us can imagine or that an interested reader will learn about by pursuing our literature.

The following represents a personal view of the process of psycho"therapy" that involves a psychological theory and a humanistic moral justification. Much of what passes for psychotherapy does not do so and has never been therapy. The reader will recognize that the main roots of therapeutic techniques lie in psychoanalysis and psychoanalytically oriented treatment, although many of the techniques also derive from family therapy, cognitive and behavioral treatments, and the growing field of what is being called health psychology. I do not consider myself eclectic in that all of the techniques I utilize grow from a theoretical position that is capable of describing their interrelationships and how they influence human change processes.

PSYCHO"THERAPY"

Psycho"therapy" is an educational process between two or more people, one of whom is called therapist and the other patient. These individuals work together toward changing the personal operating paradigm of the individual referred to as patient. Psycho"therapy" is an enterprise directed by the science of psychology and justified by the tenants of humanistic morality. It is a process that has a historical and social context with political, economic, spiritual, and creative ramifications. As a process, psycho"therapy" is embedded in the everchanging social, political, educational, and religious institutions that comprise a society. It is both affected by and affects the totality of the social enterprise of which it is a part.

Psycho"therapy" has grown out of the period of history known as the Enlightenment and the scientific revolution, and has found its place and most fertile grounds in the democratic, capitalistic, technologically advanced societies of the West. Neither the Enlightenment nor the scientific revolution occurred universally, and the social and political institutions they have created are always in danger from within and without. To live in a democratic-scientific society is to live with the knowledge that each human being has to be free to make the major decisions of how to live and then to take responsibility for the consequences of those decisions. There is, however, a constant desire on the part of most individuals to increase their freedoms and avoid their responsibilities.

In trying to solve the problems of increasing personal freedoms and decreasing personal responsibility some individuals seek to dominate others while reciprocally some seek to be dominated. As discussed in Chapter 2, some seek to increase their freedom at the expense of the freedom of others, while those whom they would dominate may seek to decrease their responsibilities by relying on the freedom and power of others. Some seek to be more than human, some to be less. Some seek gods while others wish to be gods. Psycho"therapy" is a process inimical to all those desires. It begins with the assumption, "We are all more human than otherwise" (attributed to Harry Stack Sullivan) and holds that the legitimate and moral use of power is to help empower others that they too may have both the freedom to live as they choose and an acceptance of the responsibilities to match.

Psycho"therapists" are historians enough to understand that the century in which they live has given rise to more freedom and liberty and more tyranny and horror than any other. We live in a century that has seen the rise of Hitler and the advent of the holocaust. We have watched as Stalin bestrode the empire of communism and the whole world armed itself with weapons of such mass destruction that the power of the gods to destroy all life was fully realized by human beings. Few in our field have attempted to understand how the very fabric of our culture has been shaped by these realities. Robert Jay Lifton (1979) has provided us with some theory as to how we have been affected by the mass terror we have allowed ourselves to live under. We have also seen in our century that the democracies have had greater staying power and have out-produced and out-educated and created more wealth of every kind than the totalitarian societies that have evolved among us. With the collapse of communism and the Soviet empire there have been those who have declared a victory for democracy and free-market enterprise (Frances Fukuyama, 1992). Yet new tyrannies grow, even as these declarations are made and even as the fruits of democracy, science, and humanism would appear to have the day.

When I was in high school, I read George Orwell's *1984*. I not only was terrified by the prospect of life under a dictatorship but was even more frightened by Orwell's ability to draw so inevitable a picture of how strong and enduring such a dictatorship could be. It was clear that any individual has a point at which no more pain or terror can be tolerated and will believe anything if it means the removal of fear and pain. Apparently, I was not alone, as almost all the intelligentsia of Western society were surprised by the collapse of the Soviet Union and how completely that defensive mode of life and myth had consumed itself.

But I read another book in high school called *Brave New World* by Aldous Huxley. Subsequently, Anthony Burgess (1978) published *1985*, in which he warns us that the real tyranny of our age may yet turn out to be Huxley's vision. It is as a psycho"therapist" that I fight to see to it that our society does not enter a Brave New World with the mental health profession leading the way.

I have watched in my lifetime as we human beings have gone from worshipping God in hopes that He would reveal knowledge to us, to worshipping the state in the hope that politicians would save us, to the modern worshipping of technology in the hope that computers, robots, genetic engineering, and biochemistry will save us from ourselves and provide us with the good life. It is this latest vision that the psycho"therapist" must face and be willing to fight with his patients.

Fukuyama (1992) worries that with the end of political history human beings will lose their creativity and seek creative comforts as they define the good life both materialistically and in terms of the absence of pain. Philip Reiff (1966) was concerned about exactly the same thing as he lamented the passing of Christian morality with the great visions it gave to life, compared to the small safe comforts offered by psychotherapy. I watch with similar concern as the triumphs and tragedies of life, the genius of creativity and madness, the villainy and the victimization, are reduced to mental disorders, while ever more effective drugs are used to roboticize people according to some bureaucratic definition of being well adjusted.

If we throw off the notion of mental illness or disorder, we throw off as well any myth concerning the "well adjusted" or "normalcy." We begin with the assumption that all human beings are as different as they are similar and that, if they live according to a humanistic morality in self-chosen democratic social structures, there emerges a new set of goals for "therapy." Those goals are the experience of those human differences according to the highest standards of excellence, which define the creative life and the life of the artist.

The therapeutic relationship itself grows in response to vast changes in how people choose to live or find themselves living in our modern urban, technological, and scientific society. The ties to the farm are broken, and we move where our skills are needed. Ties to church and community become easier to disrupt, and in general the comforting dogma and ritual of religion have less hold on the lives of a growing number of individual citizens.

With the rise of science, those who speak for science have become the new prophets of how to live. As human needs for structuring, community, and guidance remain constant and the social contexts that traditionally satisfy those needs erode and change, therapy has become increasingly popular and necessary to the population at large. Therapists are more visible and more important to society. It is important that our profession recognize that they are becoming part of what C. W. Mills (1956) calls "the power elite."

Therapists are increasingly a part of people's families; indeed, we are often their only family. We enter into intact families and become an integral part of the political, economic, and religious functions of that family. We are seen on television giving advice and setting moral standards for people with all manner of adaptations and unhappiness. The book stores are filled with hundreds of volumes on how to live, marry, discipline children, and die. We are indeed deciding whether or not our culture becomes a society of artists or drones living in a brave new world.

Psycho"therapy" is a recontextualization of human experiences that follows humanistic rules. It permits individuals to have time and place to explore the thoughts and emotions that define who they are as human beings and solutions to life problems and need satisfaction. The patients find themselves involved in a human relationship in which the moral goals of the therapist are to understand the life experiences of and paradigmatic solutions employed by the patients thus far in their life. To that end, patients find that they are asked to talk about their lives, tell their stories, and reflect upon thoughts, feelings, skills, and social roles in order that they may begin to develop a new theoretical understanding of their lives and their lives' contexts.

The patient has an opportunity to learn because of the basic scientific attitude of the therapist to his life struggles. This attitude is well expressed by Donald Campbell (1975: 1105):

When an evolutionary biologist encounters some ludicrous and puzzling form of animal life he approaches it with a kind of awe, certain that behind the bizarre form lies a functional wisdom that he has yet to understand. I believe the case for sociocultural evolution is strong enough so that psychologists and other social scientists, when considering an apparently bizarre, incomprehensible feature of their own social tradition, or that of another culture should approach it with a similar awe, expecting that when eventually understood, when our theories have caught up with it, that seemingly bizarre superstition will turn out to make adaptive sense.

Two notions in the Campbell quotation need explication. The first is that the apparent mental disorders of the patient are the result of developmental struggles to adapt in contexts that are initially unknown to the therapist. I have already tried to provide a theory that begins to conceptualize the nature of developmental solutions that are in our judgment bizarre and maladaptive. The use of defenses and magic to achieve adaptation usually means that what the therapist is seeing is the creative use of preoperational thinking, with the unintended effect of locking the individual into a time warp that began the moment the defenses were utilized and were found by the individual to be immediately successful.

The second explication involves a recognition on the part of the therapist as to the depth of his or her ignorance and helplessness in dealing with the problems created for him or her when he or she seeks to undertake therapy. The theory guides the work of the therapist, but the theory is subject to constant revision in the face of the information provided by the patient. The therapist must be aware that he or she knows very little about the actual circumstances of the patient's life, the mode of experiencing of the patient, the neurological and biological basis that underlies the patient's mode of experience, and most of all any real notion of the causality of human change process.

In Chapter 7, I explored the emergence of individual differences in human consciousness. How human beings make decisions and what decisions they are capable of making at any given moment are clearly under the influences of their biological and sociological contexts. As human beings make so many unpredictable decisions and the number of factors impinging on those decisions are so vast, we must recognize that we may never know enough completely to predict human behavior. Ultimately our theories will become probabilities and take on the characteristics provided us by chaos theory (Prirogene and Stengers 1984).

Let me provide an example of the ignorance in question with an individual with whom I worked. The patient was a young man of twenty-nine, who had lived in a family whose organization ranged between anarchy and totalitarian control. His father drank heavily and provided no direction or discipline, while his mother criticized and physically beat him for any little provocation. He described an incident that he claimed summed up his childhood. He had fallen off his bicycle and broken his arm. His father was unconscious from drink, and his mother slapped him for being so clumsy. "You made the problem," she told him, "now take care of it."

The patient went by himself to his family physician, who immediately drove him to an emergency room where his arm was set. The doctor then called the mother to find out why her son had sought medical attention without parental assistance. When the patient returned home he received a severe beating by his mother for "getting her in trouble with the doctor." The patient describes how by adolescence he was either in trouble with the law for violent offenses against others or petty criminality or was stoned on alcohol, marijuana, heroin, or any other drug he could get his hands on.

The patient dropped out of school and gave up all of the activities he enjoyed, one of which was painting. "I had a real talent," he reported. The patient lived a life reflective of self-hatred and rage toward the world as he sank even deeper in degradation, crime, and the mental health and criminal justice systems. His labels, which mounted up with each new imprisonment or hospitalization, included depression, alcoholism, schizophrenia, borderline personality, and manic-depressive psychosis as well as juvenile delinquent and psychopath.

At the age of twenty-nine the patient awoke on the Bowery on a Sunday morning, lying in the gutter covered with blood and vomit and having no memory of the days that had passed. He decided that his life had to end; this suicide attempt would now end in success. As he walked toward the Manhattan Bridge with every intention of jumping off into the East River, he passed an Alcoholics Anonymous (AA) storefront. "I don't know why I went in," he states, "but I did." He reported that he had been sober for two years, and although his health had already been compromised he would make the best of his remaining years. He had returned to school and earned his GED and was now in a City University of New York college receiving a degree in fine arts in painting.

The patient was seeking therapy because he had grown somewhat unhappy with AA. In effect, he described a process in which AA had built a floor beneath his feet so that he would not fall back into degradation and despair. But he had now discovered that the floor was also a ceiling. The belief that he was an alcoholic and could not leave the life AA recommended or he would fall off the wagon ran counter to his growing conviction that his potential as a human being was unlimited and that he could grow independently of AA even if risks were part of the task.

I took pleasure in working with this young man and seeing the growth in his scientific understanding that took place over the two years of our relationship. I wish to stress my profound ignorance as to why and how he changed his life with the decision he made that Sunday morning. Why then and not earlier? Why did he make a decision that so many others in his circumstances do not make? I have no answers. My theory describes and can provide a framework within which questions can be asked but cannot answer critical causative questions as to changes in human phenomenological experience.

Why do individuals undergo massive phenomenological shifts in such a sudden and apparently disjunctive manner? That such questions cannot be answered must humble us as scientists and force us to rest on a faith that the processes inherent in our human relationships are capable of fostering or creating such changes. What we cannot do is foreclose our ignorance by pretending that moral judgments are explanatory medical concepts, no matter how painful and anxiety-provoking our ignorance is. To do so would be to unleash the unintended consequences discussed in this book and to compromise our work as scientists and moral philosophers.

When we work with patients, not only are we ignorant but we are also aware that both they and we are enfolded in physical, chemical, biological, psychological, social, political, and economic developmental processes. Not only is life a mystery, but we are in awe as to the massive forces involved, which continue to unfold, affecting both our development and that of the person with whom we are to work. We are both ignorant and helpless to change the essentially random, often tragic, sometimes lucky, and always seemingly chaotic forces that have produced and continue to shape what we are. We are left with faith in the fact that people in relationships make a difference in the lives of others because of those relationships. We have faith that growth and phenomenological change can occur in people, leading to the exercise of a few more degrees of freedom in their lives because of our therapeutic interaction with them.

11

PSYCHO"THERAPY":
ALTERING ADAPTIVE PARADIGMS

In this and the next chapter, I discuss a variety of topics related to psycho"therapy" and its performance. These topics become important to the degree that the definitional demands of therapy make them so. They involve ideas and procedures that have changed in my own work, over time, as I have moved toward my present professional conceptualization. They involve activities that have left me feeling more successful as a therapist as well as more relaxed, joyful, and excited in doing clinical work. I make no attempt on these pages to provide an overall framework for others to follow or to specify techniques.

Psycho"therapy" defines a professional human relationship. To the degree that it is a human relationship, it is similar to all other relationships. To the degree that it is determined by the demands of a profession, it differs from all other relationships. Psycho"therapy" involves a human relationship that is guided by scientific concepts but follows humanistic rules of moral conduct. To the degree that "therapy" operates according to its scientific method and moral precepts is the degree to which it is often a unique human relationship and, in my opinion, represents a goal for all human relationships.

The effectiveness of therapy is determined by the degree to which this relationship is different from others that the patient has experienced and by the degree to which the therapist and patient can establish a relationship in which the patient experiences the difference. The core of the therapeutic process is found in the relationship that forms between patient and therapist and not merely in the technique employed by the therapist. The techniques employed in psycho"therapy" by the therapist are those that grow organically out of the therapeutic relationship. Techniques are, therefore, the behaviors of the therapist that emerge from his or her personal paradigm as he or she attempts to define a scientific-humanistic relationship new to the experiences of the patient.

The techniques of the therapist are the skills of his or her personal paradigm, of his or her being in the world in a time and place as defined by the encounter between himself or herself and the patient. I stress this point because so often therapists, casting about for "something that works," adopt behaviors that are imitative of some expert. As these behaviors do not grow organically out of the conscious experience of the therapist, and are not part of the primary appraisals of the therapist when he assesses his therapeutic tasks and goals with the patient, they feel artificial and unnatural. We have all experienced utilizing someone else's skills and being dealt with by someone whose behaviors are not natural to themselves. Neither party benefits from such an encounter.

To the degree that the therapeutic relationship is humanistic, both patient and therapist are seen as human beings of equal worth, who nonetheless have differences in experience, skills, and knowledge. No words utilized in establishing the therapeutic relationship suggest that the therapist is well or healthy while the patient is sick, diseased, disordered, or in any other way morally inferior to the therapist. A therapist is aware that if he is addressed as "Dr. Simon," his patient, if an adult, is "Mr. Jones" or "Mrs. Smith." He is not "Doctor" and she "Barbara," which from the beginning sets up a moral hierarchy of an authoritarian sort.

I as a therapist work with my patients (whom I increasingly refer to with the ungainly but more accurate phrase, "the people with whom I work") and do not do things to them. I do not work on them or speak about them behind their backs with other members of their family unless I get permission from them to do so. While my patients often perceive themselves as less than human—"I am crazy, weird, the worst, most stupid, lazy person in the world"—I struggle to resist their often vigorous attempts to entreat me to see them as they are used to conceiving themselves. Similarly, if they tell me they are "God," "Jesus Christ," "an immortal poetess," or "Moses," I will attempt to treat them and refer to them as simply human.

Equally as important is the fact that while I struggle to see myself as no better than my patients and try not to play the role of a god in their lives, I will not be treated as less than human either. I will not accept verbal or physical abuse, have my office destroyed or defaced, or be referred to in any way different than how I attempt to treat my patients. There are no moral justifications for me to be hurt or diminished in any way in the name of the patient's mental illness.

THE BEGINNING PHASE OF PSYCHO"THERAPY"

The initial phases of establishing a therapeutic relationship are critical and must be established as humanistic from the moment of first contact. As many patients at the mental health clinic where I work are assigned to me only after a diagnosis has been made and/or after a period of hospitalization, the manner of the initial contact is critical indeed if reversals are to be made in the destructive authoritarian labeling that has already taken place. Even private patients, who have had less of a chance of having been diagnosed, are so inculcated with the belief that mentally ill or sick people go to therapy that establishing a humanistic-scientific relationship does not begin with a neutral preconception.

In order that therapy be established as humanistic, certain conditions must be met. If not, therapy cannot be humanistic—and if therapy is not humanistic, it is not therapy. The conditions to be established are as follows: (a) The individuals who are seeking help are doing so freely, without coercion or blackmail and of their own choosing. (b) These individuals believe that therapy can help them make changes in their lives and thus they are or can be responsible for their own actions. (c) Therapy is a means to an end and not an end in itself. The therapy begins with the establishment of goals toward which therapeutic work is directed.

After appropriate social interactions take place, a series of questions establishes whether therapy is possible or whether some other psychological or social intervention might be appropriate. If therapy is not indicated or if I cannot in the early meetings with the individual create the conditions necessary to therapy, I will indicate this to the prospective patient. When I do so, these individuals understand rather quickly why therapy is not indicated and choose to disengage rather than continuing to relate to me.

When I was trained under the medical model, the rules of medicine applied to the notion of treatment. A physician may not refuse to treat a patient. Any illness must be treated in spite of the personal characteristics of the patient. The only reasons that medical treatment can be withheld are, first, conditions that make triage necessary and, second, when the nature of the illness or diagnosis prevents the physician from following the Hippocratic Oath, which in effect requires, "Don't hurt the patient!" Therapy is not a medical procedure. It is based on a relationship that must be subject to certain guidelines, and where these guidelines cannot be met there can be no "therapy."

Several questions must be answered affirmatively before therapy can begin. The first question is guided by the demand that therapy should not ever be coercive. Unless the patient agrees that he or she is seeking help of his or her own free will, I will not work with that patient. Thus individuals who are sent by parole officers or the courts, children and teenagers sent by frustrated parents (see Chapter 12 for a more extended discussion on working with children), or school officials, or husbands or wives coming under the threat of divorce do not provide reasons for therapy to begin.

I try to stimulate individuals' desire for therapy if they are not the ones who wished to see me. Often a session or two reveals that acceding to the wishes of others was merely an excuse or defense used by individuals to seek help for themselves. At other times the patient and I will hit it off and to the surprise of both of us begin a fruitful interaction. But if by the end of these initial sessions the individuals cannot say with some certainty that they are coming on their own, then therapy has no basis to begin.

Therapy, therefore, begins with an affirmative answer to the question, "How may I help you?" Patients who answer that they do not need help, as it is someone else who is unhappy with them, are not ready to be patients. At other times individuals will seek my services willingly, but not because they experience themselves to be in a crisis. These individuals are unhappy with the behavior of someone or something else. These people seek to confirm that the world, their spouses, children, teachers, society, and even God have the problem. They too are not ready to be patients.

The second question that requires an affirmative response if psycho"therapy" is to take place relates to the first. The first question establishes that the individuals seeking help recognize that they are in crisis and willingly agree to come. The second establishes whether or not these individuals see themselves as participants in the crisis. I might query, "In what way have you contributed to the mess your life is in?" Often an individual seems to me to be a genuine victim of some injustice who has played no role in bringing about the crisis. The question then becomes, "Do you feel you are handling the situations that have happened to you to your best advantage?"

Unless individuals can take responsibility for their problems and for their solutions, there can be no real therapy. Real therapy does not begin until an individual can articulate answers to the question, "If therapy is successful, in what way do you think you might be living differently (choosing differently, seeing things differently, feeling, acting, or behaving differently) than you are today?" Personal responsibility for one's own life and changing the paradigm that directs that life in whatever manner is necessary is mandatory for treatment to take place.

Often several issues are involved in helping patients take responsibility for both their life problems and their solutions. The first is that taking responsibility is rarely understood in psychological terms but is usually understood in moral terms. The question, "How were the decisions made that help create the morass that you are in?" is different from, "How were you bad or evil?" Similarly, "What happened?" "Who did what?" and "What were your motivations?" are all different questions than "Who is to blame?" and "Who is at fault?"

Responsibility can be understood in psychological terms even when the individual has actually done things to others that I consider to be immoral. As long as the individual can say, "I feel guilty," we are dealing with psychological issues and can move toward goals in which the individual atones, makes restitution, and, by understanding the background, context, and motivations of his or her actions, behaves differently in the future.

If I perceive a patient as morally deficient in some manner and if I cannot get past my own judgments, then I cannot, and perhaps will not, work with this individual. If patients cannot be helped to see themselves in psychological terms (see below) and can only judge themselves, they will be unable to benefit from procedures whose primary goals are to increase understanding. Often individuals who speak of their sins and other moral shortcomings want to confess and be forgiven for such sins. Perry London (1986) has well understood how a therapist may function as a "secular priest or cleric." I totally reject such a role for a therapist. If the patient has committed a real offense (as I experience it), if the patient is a real victim (as I experience it), or if the patient merely believes in his or her own badness because of how he or she was treated by others, real changes can come about only when "sin" is replaced with psychological concepts.

"I have a problem" cannot mean, "I am defective." "I have a problem" must mean, "I have something in my life that needs solving. I may have helped create the problem or life created it for me, but I do not know how to solve it. If I can learn how to solve it, I will." Therapists cannot but judge the guilt and innocence of their patients; but if they cannot frame the issues, for both themselves and the patients in psychological terms, then the patients may need a lawyer, a priest, a banker, or a politician—but not a therapist.

A therapist must resist either blaming or absolving anyone of any moral issues if therapy is to proceed as it should (my judgment). Masson (1985) points out, as have many feminist writers, that Freud made his female patients culpable for their adult life problems by (a) holding them responsible for the memories of childhood sexual abuse and then (b) declaring them not responsible in the name of neurotic libidinal wishes. Thus no one was responsible for what appears to have been genuinely heinous acts, especially on the part of the adult men who committed them.

More currently, I see therapists agreeing with patients that the patients are victims of others. They insist with the same vigor used by analysts to deny sexual abuse that abuse has taken place. Often patients do not remember being abused, and the evidence of abuse is negligible. However, the therapist insists that the abuse took place and that the patient as a victim has certain "rights." As society is culpable for victimizing the patient, the patient deserves compensation and support in the form of therapy, welfare, SSI, and Dr. Feelgood's patented feel-good medicine. The attitude is sometimes expressed that the victim has rights that can last a lifetime.

Although these actions do keep patients in a relationship with the therapist, what results is often as hateful and painful to the therapist as it is destructive to the patient. It is not therapy as I conceive it to be. In these and other cases the therapist acts as judge and simultaneously absolves some responsibilities while delegating responsibilities to others. The patient is sent on a wild goose chase to understand his role as perpetrator when there is none to be understood, or the patient is placed in perpetual dependency on those who feel they must make up to the patient for injustices.

Another element necessary for therapy to begin is the establishing of goals for treatment. The establishment of goals grows out of the patients' articulation of how they are seeking to change their lives. Goals established early in treatment may or may not be the goals articulated later on. But there must be a mutual recognition that both therapist and patient are working together of their own free choosing toward recognizable goals. Therapy, as I have defined it, must be a means to some end and not an end in itself.

Human relationships such as marriage and friendships exist both as means to an end (raising children, helping each other as it becomes necessary) and as ends. These relationships may exist for a lifetime. I have discovered that three of the critical roles of my own life must first be means to an end. These relationships must either self-destruct or change dramatically if they are to be successful. As a parent I must help my children develop to some point that they no longer need me. My goal as parent has always been to see my children not only able to take care of themselves but, if they choose, able to be parents themselves. As an educator my goal is to help my students not only to be able to be their own teachers but to go on, if they choose, to educate others. Finally, as a therapist, my goal is to help my patients be therapists to themselves and, in creating the rest of their relationships, be a therapist to others. In all three relationships the ultimate goal is to change the basic paradigm of the others so that these individuals live their lives according to different perceptions and different goals.

Only by establishing and reestablishing goals from the first session of therapy to the last can we avoid some of the problems already discussed. The goals that we set are never my goals but those articulated by the patients. They may have broadly stated life goals such as "I want a better job" or "I want more and better friends" or "I want to fulfill my ambition and be a successful therapist." Or the goal may be simpler, such as "I will clean my house," "take a bath before coming to therapy," "learn how to argue without screaming at another person," "begin to do my homework," or "finally go the dentist."

Often goals begin as simple reality-oriented goals and, as therapy is engaged and the paradigm of the individual changes, become replaced by broader and more ambitious goals. Goals are stated in behavioral terms as well as cognitive and emotional ones. "I want to feel better" always stimulates me to say, "Feeling better depends on doing something to feel better. What is it that you might do that might help you feel better?" The moment a patient states a behavioral goal I ask, "When will you begin?"

I do not ever force goals or determine them without clear consent of the patient. I do not determine how long therapy will last. Patients can work with me for as long as they wish, as long as the three conditions that allow therapy to begin continue as conditions. We work for as long as the patients feel a personal need to continue work, as long as the patients feel a responsibility and a faith that they can continue to progress toward goals, and as long as these goals can be articulated in specific behavioral terms as they relate to specific contexts.

Although I do not place a time limit on therapy, I do try to set specific lengths of time for patients to achieve certain goals. For example, a patient recently expressed a desire to have greater self-confidence. I helped the patient establish behavioral goals by asking what she would be able to do if she had more self-confidence. She replied that would be able to drive her car by herself. I then asked her if we might spend eight sessions to achieve just that goal. Therapy is, therefore, always focused and in a sense time-limited.

Melvin Fein (1992) describes the process of psychotherapy in sociological terms. He believes that therapy works to correct "defective social roles." Therapy helps the individual by providing (a) social support, (b) socialization, or (c) resocialization. It is clear as Fein describes the process of therapy that he is also describing how individuals think and feel both while participating in their defective social roles and as they learn to change the roles in question. The changes in thought and feeling occur as a result of support, socialization, and resocialization.

Fein's analysis has direct relevance for the theory being presented here if we shift the focus from the sociological to the psychological. The skills with which individuals act to adapt to their world are the very social roles that are formalized by sociological theory. People seek professional help because of crises in adaptation. The cognitive and motoric skills that they possess cannot, without help, make the necessary accommodations to permit the assimilation or need satisfaction or emotional resolutions that define successful adaptation. However, the therapy required can also be defined in terms analogous to Fein's support, socialization, and resocialization.

From the perspective I employ, people come to therapy for support, recognition, and comfort when emotions such as grief, despair, and fear result from illnesses, deaths, loss of job, or any personal or social catastrophe beyond the individual's ability to cope. People also come to therapy when they realize that they lack specific skills to deal with various day-to-day situations in lives that otherwise satisfy them. Parents who cannot deal with a child's rebellion, students who find they are failing in school, and people of all ages who discover that they are failing to find friends or mates or earn better livings seek help. Finally, people enter therapy when they realize that the lives they are living are going awry and lose faith in the cognitive and motoric operations of the very adaptive paradigm that defines the self in the world.

The degree of therapeutic intervention and the time it will take depends on whether individuals see themselves as the victims of capricious fates and cannot deal with the emotions aroused or whether they see themselves as participating in the failure of their own lives. Often individuals enter treatment feeling like failures and discover that their reactions to a crisis are similar to those of most other mortals. They will leave therapy as soon as the crisis is resolved. At other times individuals will seek help believing that they have hit a temporary road block in their lives and, after some reflection, reconsider the nature of how they have lived their entire lives. These discoveries are only made by the individual. I ask questions, they answer them; awareness does or does not grow.

THERAPEUTIC CONTENT

Some of the specific issues I raise in therapy have grown out of the ideas presented in earlier material. First and perhaps most important, I actively teach all my patients, to the degree that they can assimilate and accept the ideas, that mental illness is a myth, that there is nothing wrong with them of a psychological nature, and that they can either judge themselves or understand themselves, but not both at the same time.

I believe it is essential to "give psychology away" to patients and teach them what I know for their own use. I cannot easily describe the many ways I introduce this topic. The method depends upon the operating paradigms of the individuals when I meet them. A high school dropout with ten years prior hospitalization cannot be taught in the same way as a college-educated adult seeking to motivate a child to do better academically in school. Both can be taught the material and both need it. (The dropout may well take longer to learn the concept but needs it even more that the college graduate.)

With a patient, I might begin by introducing the theory underlying this book, by asking an individual who has referred to himself as lazy and stupid if *lazy* and *stupid* are descriptions of himself or judgments. What almost always amazes me is how many individuals intuitively know one from the other even though they lack any verbalizable definition of a description or judgment. I have helped individuals, in several sessions, monitor their language for the use of judgments that are acting as descriptions. Once the distinctions are made we can begin to trace the psychological and social consequences of judging versus describing and explaining.

I describe to my patients the differences among anarchic, authoritarian, and democratic social relationships and ask them to evaluate their own relationships according to these criteria. They evaluate their relationships with their own children, parents, friends, and professionals (such as physicians, teachers, and therapists). Once again, a majority of individuals grasp the distinctions and can easily analyze past and present relationships and the consequences of such interactions.

The difficulty patients have in giving up their usual mode of self-understanding is revealed when they ask, "If I'm not crazy, then what would you call me?" I suggest that they are now looking for another label and introduce them to the idea of a personal paradigm adapting to a social world of one type or another. I rarely use the words "personal paradigm," but I will say, "You behave in each situation based on what you see, think, and feel about what is going on about you and what you think you are able to do in a given situation."

As time progresses I provide information about perceptions, thought, and especially the emotions. I discuss the emotions as innate reactions to situations, in the same way that pain innately results if one bangs into an object. No matter how much you wish not to feel a painful emotion, the emotion is necessary for living in the world and can never be wrong, sick, or in any way judged as bad. What we do when we feel a certain way can be judged morally, but not what we think or, more important, feel.

The intent of my sessions increasingly relates to the information I begin introducing to the patient, while the process increasingly is directed by the personal knowledge this information comes to be for the patient. I cannot describe to the reader (nor prove) how profound and effective it makes therapy for an individual who both understands and begins to utilize these concepts. I have not kept statistics on improvement, but this information short-circuits much of the time that is usually necessary to help individuals organize and reorganize personal paradigms.

Some individuals cannot understand these ideas, and some cannot accept them. Some people are so used to living in the mental health network, have so justified their moral existence with the ideas that they are sick, so firmly believe they cannot change their lives or be held accountable for their actions, that they will not even begin to comprehend otherwise. For example, an educated woman (a published author), in her sixties, who had been in therapy and on neuroleptic drugs for over thirty years, reacted strongly to my suggestion that she was not mentally ill. She stated, "You sound like Thomas Szasz." When I delightedly replied that he was one of my intellectual heroes and asked after her knowledge of him, she stormed from the room, saying, "You must be as crazy as he is." So ended another in dozens of attempted therapies, each of which she ended the moment a therapist suggested change of any kind in her mode of living.

As I begin to teach patients about thoughts and feelings and as they begin to see themselves in terms of contextualized psychological processes, I actively confront any notion of dualism that they utilize in explaining their own behavior. I challenge the notion, "I can lose my mind." "Wallets and keys can be lost, psychological processes cannot." This dialogue introduces the patient to the idea of alternate states of consciousness and reflective consciousness. This reframes the rather fixed view people have of "going crazy" as a judgment to a contextualized psychological process.

For example a woman who was constantly afraid of losing her mind and becoming "nuts" began to understand the process of being so judged when she described her reactions to the severe beatings administered by her mother. "I wanted to go to another place," she stated, "where I could feel no pain. I was always afraid I would go to that place and be so lost in it, that I would never return." We discussed this natural and normal defensive maneuver. I affirmed her terror both of the beatings and the consequence of the defense and led her in a discussion in which she recognized that the process of detachment was under her control and only took place in contexts that inspired such terror. It is hard to describe her relief to know that she was the agent who controlled her construction of experienced reality and that with newly developing skills she need not any longer derealize or depersonalize. She understood that she could never develop mental illness in the same way as she could a cold or cancer.

The teaching of a theory and the learning of a new language and metaphors for describing oneself are only one aspect of ongoing therapy. As with many of the new concepts of analysis (Spence, Strenger, Schafer), I see the main process of therapy in terms of hermeneutics. All reinterpretations take place as the patients tell their stories. I have never met an individual who has led an uninteresting life. The patients' treatment of their life stories as a novel or work of art carries with it profound implications for human change and what I judge to be growth.

A variety of techniques can be employed to develop the skills to tell one's story and to increase motivations to do so. Conversation is the most common and effective means of getting someone to tell his or her life story. I have never been comfortable utilizing free associations, but with some individuals nothing better seems to exist. I have had patients write letters, keep diaries, and even make tape recordings as techniques to foster storytelling. (See Mahoney [1991] for a discussion of therapeutic writing.)

Generally, I am an active listener and utilize these techniques to help patients become more aware of the judgments and condemnations (of self and others) that prevent their stories from becoming an increased source of contextualized understanding. What makes storytelling ultimately effective—allowing reassessment of the past, the emergence of emotions, increases in reflections, and the growth of operational thinking—is the nature of the therapeutic relationships that develop as one person genuinely listens to another.

THERAPEUTIC RELATIONSHIPS

I have suggested that psycho"therapy" involves restructuring of an individual's personal paradigm or consciousness through a recontextualization of experience. The paradigm of the individual is in large measure a product of previous relationships. Therapy, especially where an individual seeks help in changing many areas of his or her life, may take a good deal of time. (I must reiterate that long therapies are all focused in time-limited, goal-oriented sequences.) As the therapist listens, making clear by word and deed that there are not to be judgments for what is said and felt, and as the patient experiences a genuine interest on the part of the therapist and also experiences being heard, an intense emotional bonding takes place.

How these individuals form a relationship and how they separate will either confirm or deny for the patients their previous conclusions about human beings and the skills needed to maintain relationships. As the relationship between therapist and patient develops, a struggle ensues in which both individuals attempt to assimilate the other into their existing operating paradigms. The degree to which the therapist offers a different way of seeing the world and relating to it and the degree to which the therapist wins the assimilative struggle are the degrees to which "therapy" will be successful.

Psychoanalysis has long been concerned with the nature of the therapeutic relationship and the struggle that ensues between the individuals so involved. The attempts of patients to utilize preexisting skills and to create with the therapist either the same type of relationship they have known or to create some idealized relationship are known as transference. The nonreflective response of the therapist to live up to the idealization of the patients, to be drawn into some mutually destructive interaction, or to act on other extratherapeutic needs with patients is known as countertransference.

One of the strengths of every school of analysis has come from the awareness of transference and countertransference. The psychological awareness of how two individuals may affect each other when defenses blind one or both as to the nature of their interaction and the unintended consequences that flow from such interactions fosters not only effective therapy but ethical and moral therapy as well. In analyzing transferences, in effect, one discovers either that one person is using another for his or her own needs without fairness or reciprocity or that one person is dehumanizing the other.

We have seen that often patients dehumanize others as they have been dehumanized because of being raised in anarchic or authoritarian-totalitarian homes, communities, and nations. Such a childhood leads one to experience others as either one's betters or one's inferiors. One's betters must be appeased, flattered, and pleaded with. One's inferiors must be ordered about, forced to act obediently, and so on. Moral labels replace psychological feelings to explain behaviors of oneself and others.

I assume that patients are patients in part because they have never experienced a humanizing, empowering relationship, or at least not one that dominated in the shaping of the personal paradigm. They not only do not understand such relationships but do not possess the skills to negotiate a democratic humanistic relationship. Transference flows from everything in the patient's past that has prevented a humanistic-democratic-scientific paradigm from developing. Countertransference is anything in the therapist's paradigm that leads him or her to plead with, flatter or appease, order about, or force and in general dehumanize himself or herself and/or the patient.

To discuss the sources of transference and countertransference is to repeat everything that has been discussed in this book. The number of definitions of transference and countertransference and the quantity of books and articles on the subject are beyond the capacitiy of the space I can make available. The topic is critical for the rest of my discussion, and I wish to delineate here the aspects of countertransference not usually found in the literature.

If one peruses the literature on transference and countertransference, one finds that various authors see these problems as developing because of unresolved issues related to early childhood and familial experiences. The Freudian stresses how unresolved oedipal problems create transference problems, while the Horneyan theorizes that unresolved basic anxiety and neurotic trends create transference. Other therapists see transference as resulting in issues related to attachment, separation, and individualization. Any and all of these areas may be legitimate sources of transference and countertransference.

Analytic discussions concerning transference and countertransference focus on early childhood and family as main sources and therefore fail to take into account many other factors that lead one human being to use and/or dehumanize another. These include social, political, economic, and religious factors. Feminist writers will insist that studying family relationships does not contextualize the roles played by men and women in society at large. The same concerns have been raised by those who feel that racist attitudes might permeate a society so completely that virtually no one recognizes the dehumanizing transferences and more critical the countertransferences that can develop.

My own concerns involve the myths and ideologies that permeate our field that have to do with the moral judgments we call diagnoses. I believe that the self-reflective therapist must understand the explicit and implicit dehumanizations that exist when we call someone "borderline" or "schizophrenic." When our own racist, sexist, and socioeconomic prejudices are factored into our diagnoses, then a massive countertransference may be in operation, one that is invisible to all concerned because it is so openly used and so central to the beliefs in which the field takes active pride.

I now return to a description of the continuing process of therapy. I began a discussion of transference and countertransference when I described the growing emotional bond between therapist and patient. The growth of such a bond and the separation that follows must take place according to the dictates of humanistic principles already described. It is this relationship that seems to empower the individual to become more scientific and responsive to democratic relationships. It is similar to the ideal relationships of childhood described earlier and endorsed by analysts and therapists everywhere.

The relationship between patient and therapist allows for the continuation (or perhaps the birth) of development along lines valued by the present author and others who agree with the tenets of therapy. I should like to turn to several developmental aspects of therapy as they emerge in the context of the developing patient-therapist relationship as the patient continues to tell his story and interact with the therapist.

WORK AND PLAY IN PSYCHO"THERAPY"

I have defined work as involving activities engaged in as a direct result of the adaptive struggle. When individuals employ their paradigm to satisfy needs and solve problems related to survival, social relationships, or creativity, these individuals are working. When individuals engage in paradigmatic activity for its own sake, they are playing. The importance of play and the consequences of its inhibition for development are an increasingly important topic for developmental researchers. See, for example, Göncü (1993), Kane and Furth (1993), and Gordon (1993). Play permits the development of experimentation and exploration based on interest and curiosity (rather than fear) and calls forth the development of reflection. Often, when we examine the products of artists and scientists judged to be creative, we find that their most admired achievements are the result of play. These individuals were lucky and insightful enough to be able to make choices that allowed for a life of reflective experimentation and the ability and willingness to pursue themes and variations of their own choosing.

As patients bond with therapists, as they tell their stories and find they are not judged, when they discover that their secrets are kept and that they are recognized and valued as human beings, then psycho"therapy" meets the conditions that permit play. The therapist cannot do for patients what parents might (and should) have done, but they can set up conditions that permit the patients to play. Freud's suggestion about free association meets my criterion for play: The individual is able to reflect on whatever emerges into consciousness and to follow these ideas without regard to the demands of formal logic, time sequence, or good manners.

In the next chapter, I discuss working with children and why I believe playing games with children is most often a costly waste of time. When adults play with ideas and the themes of their lives, the effect is most worthwhile. Human beings learn motor skills and basic physics by playing with blocks and other basic objects in our environments. We develop formal operations that permit science and reflective consciousness to exist by playing with words and ideas. I believe that the most significant achievements of therapy result from patients' ability to learn to reflect on their own emotions and behaviors and observe when they are satisfying needs and solving problems while utilizing preoperational thinking. It is to the developmental processes affected by therapy that we now turn.

DEVELOPMENT AND PSYCHO"THERAPY"

As patients tell their stories, and tell them more in terms of thoughts, feelings, and actions than in terms of judgments and morals, explanations of behavior emerge in terms of psychological causalities rather than of moral flaws in the characters and personalities of the protagonists involved. As bonding with the therapist continues, the therapeutic relationship develops as a context for the story being told to the therapist. The new context makes the story a new story. Simultaneously, these individuals begin to experience their current lives with a newly emerging paradigm.

The focus of "therapy" continually shifts from the events of the past, which helped shape the present, to the events of the present, which are often distressingly like the events of the past. The newly emerging ability (willingness) to reflect permits the focus of therapy to be the thoughts, emotions, and skills of the paradigms themselves, without discussing their operation in the contexts of past and present. The focus of therapy is often on the therapy itself and how and why it is producing the changes that it is. The relationship of patient and therapist is discussed as a prototype for other of the patient's relationships yet to be and from its differences from previous and contemporary relationships.

The more self-aware the patient and therapist are about what is going on between them, the more both can adjust and readjust their behaviors to one another as it serves the goals of treatment. Simultaneously with such changes the patient can begin to utilize the skills developed with the therapist in changing other existing relationships. Often patients will ask how to behave toward other people in their lives. As therapy develops and the patient asks, "What should I do or say?" my response will be, "What would I say to you?"

With the emergence of a new mode of experiencing life there inevitably appears a growing willingness to focus on the future as well as an increased tendency to let go of the past. Therapy is going well when the patient stops repeating the same complaints about his past as a victim and begins to deal with the present as a platform from which to make future plans. The willingness to discuss the future is not only a function of the development of formal operations but the emergence of the emotion of hope as well as faith that the future need not necessarily be a replica of the past.

As with the securely attached child, the patient uses the attachment process to develop the skills that allow ultimate separation. In the case of adolescents and adults, many of the explorations that begin to take place are not only of the physical world but of the past and of internal psychological processes as well. As with the developing child, not only does the scope of the patient's explorations begin to widen but they become more vigorous, adventurous, thorough, and inevitably creative.

Therapists have long recognized that many patients cannot or will not remember their pasts. Often the most horrendous events are described with total emotional detachment. The willingness to reflect on one's memories often produces a flood of forgotten events with emotions as fresh and intense as when the events actually occurred. (I disagree with the Freudian concept of the return of the repressed. The patient was always conscious of what had happened but was unable and/or unwilling to reflect on the event for whole periods of life.) The terrors, rage, guilt, and shame that led the individual to withdraw reflective consciousness in the first place are experienced in ways that turn memories back into knowledge rather than the kind of sterile information they had become.

As emotions begin to appear in relation to the patient's story they also begin to emerge in daily life and in the therapy room as well. It is as if the patient comes alive. Work must be done during this phase to increase the patient's reflective ability and thus the ability to remain conscious of these emotions. Simultaneously, I will help the patient not only to remain conscious of emotions but to develop skills of expression that are in keeping with humanistic moral principles. Often I will stop patients who have begun to accept and deal with a newly emerging emotion and ask them to reflect on how old they feel at that moment. It is remarkable for patients to become aware that they are feeling helpless, terrified, or humiliated in the same way they felt these emotions at the moment they were aroused years ago in childhood.

The discovery by patients that they have been experiencing various people and situations in the same way since childhood is a profound one. It is equally disconcerting to learn that their experienced responses are essentially the same as when they were children as well. One patient expressed the feeling that it is as if she has been frozen in time! These insights lead to the planning of new ways of engaging existing relationships. There is often an increased willingness to bring various family members into treatment to help the patient learn a new set of interpersonal skills, such as debating and negotiating without screaming, begging, hitting, forcing, or blackmail. Parents learn to ask after the feeling of family members rather than assuming the other's conscious experience or, worse, telling the other what he or she is thinking or feeling.

Often friends, spouses, and children of "patients" are delighted in the newly emerging person with whom they are dealing. Often the patient's relations are disappointed and unwilling to accommodate to the new perceptions and skills of the patient. It has been my experience that as many relationships are terminated as are newly renegotiated as a patient undergoes a personal paradigmatic revolution. The next chapter discusses how family and friends who become hostile to the new skills and values of the patient become enemies of therapy itself and seek to undermine or terminate the process.

ISSUES RELATED TO "THERAPY" OF THE EMOTIONS

Individuals who begin experiencing certain emotions are often terrified not only of specific feelings but of the experience of emotions. Anger is often such a feared emotion. During the preoperational phase, particularly in authoritarian homes in which corporal punishment is used, many children learn that anger is a very destructive emotion. They learn that when people are angry, they hit, verbally attack, and do other things to create terrible pain and humiliation. The emotion is experienced as inseparable from the physical attacks associated with it, and thereafter the feeling of anger is avoided at all costs.

To get angry is to destroy the other; to experience another angry at oneself is to risk destruction. An individual may either shrink in the face of angry emotions or explode toward others while denying that anger is motivating the explosion. The attack may be justified by saying, "You make me do it," "I was only disciplining," or "You needed a beating or a good yelling." But anger as an emotion is not felt or recognized as an emotion and never reflected upon as an experience. Women are often thought not to feel anger, as part of a societal constellation of values that suggest that women are the gentle nurturing sex and should not assert themselves.

The emotional mate to anger is fear. Anger and fear are both responses to perceived threat. Anger stimulates a "fight response" while fear generates "flight." For many men fear cannot be tolerated, as it is equated with being a coward or being annihilated by other males who are themselves exhibiting anger. The very feeling of and reflection of fear cannot be tolerated and are often covered by explosive anger. Many other emotions cannot be tolerated by various individuals. Because of a variety of defenses employed by people, the emotions have neither been clearly experienced nor reflected upon as basic experience.

As emotions emerge, as they must if psycho"therapy" progresses, I teach a theory of the emotions to patients, using Socratic techniques and other devices. I instruct them that their emotions are aroused by their perception of what has been and is going on in their lives. Emotions once aroused may be painful, but they are part of what makes people human; if accepted and acted upon, they offer some of the best guidance available as to how to respond to a situation. I suggest that once an emotion is aroused it can no more be ignored or turned off than if the individuals had struck their shinbones against a desk or chair and are in pain.

I make clear my belief that emotions may be pleasant or unpleasant but are never good or bad, they just are. It therefore makes no sense to call oneself (or allow anyone else to call one) crazy, sick, evil, or any other judgment for what one feels. I make clear that I am here for them when they start to feel and that they can trust me not to judge or hurt them because they feel emotion. Patients are encouraged to verbalize their phenomenological experience of their emerging emotions. Patients coming alive with affect have said, "If I start crying I'll never stop"; "If I get angry I will kill the whole world"; "If I tell my wife I need her she will absorb me and take away my life"; "If I give up control of my emotions I will fall into an abyss"; and "If I feel, I will be swept away, be crazy, be put away."

My response usually affirms that what they are calling crazy I believe is genuine sanity. If they fall into an abyss they will find solid ground beneath them. If they allow themselves to "die" they will be reborn. It is critical for the therapist at this juncture to feel completely comfortable with patients' newly expressed emotions. Therapists who believe in mental illness, loss of control, and other metaphors that reinforce the patient's fears will not be able to carry through in this phase of therapeutic work.

Simultaneously with what can be called cognitive restructuring of emotional experience, I teach meditation techniques and deep breathing exercises that allow both a sense of control as emotions are felt and a mode of reflective consciousness normally missing from the patient's life (and from Western society in general). Buddhism is a most interesting religion in that it teaches mindful observation, a mode of experience that not only provides what Benson and Klipper (1976) call a relaxation response but also allows individuals a consciousness of emotions without the worry of acting out or the loss of control so feared in our society.

One of the emotions that all patients must learn to accept and manage is anxiety. Anxiety is emotion that occurs whenever a person's paradigm ceases effective adaptation. Anxiety, I instruct my patients, stimulates a search for new answers and new skills. Like all emotions it is the result of human evolution and is necessary for continued adaptation. There can be no paradigmatic growth without anxiety. Anxiety is very painful, I suggest to my patients, but also very good for them. In fact, the reasons they have anxiety are the same reasons they have sought treatment. Without the beginnings of change in their mode of experience there would have been no anxiety, and without anxiety there would be much less motivation to search for new answers and skills in satisfying needs and solving problems.

I teach my patients not to fight anxiety, but rather to give themselves up to it and let it take them to new truths. I involve a metaphor of a riptide at the beach. The more one fights a riptide, the less chance one has of reaching the shore. By moving with the tide one discovers a point at which it ends and from which one can easily swim to shore. I have patients practice meditative breathing and mindfulness and allow the anxiety to flow through them. I have taught individuals to say aloud, "Anxiety is my friend—it hurts but will not hurt me." I further ask them to free associate or write down all that comes to mind when anxiety is felt and as it passes. The results almost always are illuminating, increase bonding and move the therapy rapidly along its course.

What I am teaching many patients is the opposite of what they have learned from psychiatric nomenclature about sadness, anxiety, fear, guilt, and the like. Emotions, particularly strong anxiety, are called symptoms and disorders and are increasingly controlled by drugs. I have had a number of patients leave therapy with me for more traditional clinical interventions. Some individuals will work with me and take antianxiety compounds as well but most of my patients eventually give up all medications voluntarily and with great relief. Let me again make clear that these psychotropic drugs are no more medicines than are alcohol and marijuana. A medicine is a drug that treats an illness. As anxiety is not an illness, these drugs are just drugs.

The emotions are in general the stepchild of psychology and even more specifically the field of psychotherapy. I am gratified to see an increasing number of books and articles dealing specifically with the emotions in psychotherapy and suggest that Greenberg and Safran's (1987) excellent discussion on the topic is a good place to find a much more thorough explication of the issues than can be developed here. If, as one reads their work, one substitutes *adaptational struggles* whenever one sees the word *disorder*, the material becomes complementary to the present discussion.

ISSUES RELATED TO PREOPERATIONAL THINKING

Patients with serious diagnoses are usually individuals who appraise much or all of their life events with preoperational or even sensorimotor perceptions. One of the unstated goals of therapy is to help those individuals develop formal operations. I have already suggested that activities such as conversation, debate, and storytelling foster the playful use of language and help develop formal operations. Posing problems to the patient that require inductive and deductive reasoning also stimulates operational development.

Often I will utilize techniques to challenge preoperational statements and to stimulate the use of operational thought. For example, self-appraisals that are based on preoperations lack seriation. Patients will say, "I am the laziest, stupidest, or worst person in the world." At such moments I will employ a Piagetian task to challenge the notion. I will ask patients to choose the best and worst persons who have ever lived. Jesus Christ and Adolf Hitler are commonly chosen. I then ask patients to place themselves on the continuum and then justify their placement with the actual achievements, good or bad, that justify their choice.

JESUS CHRIST————————————————————**ADOLF HITLER**

Patients ready to argue how bad they are often are taken aback, although one young woman recently stated, "I didn't do well in school and I always upset my parents." I will take up the nonseriated "always" at another time and simply wait. Few patients continue to insist they are the worst and show enormous emotional relief as they begin to evaluate themselves operationally.

Information and education that stimulate operational appraisals can come from any source and when they take place have a profound effect on therapy. I begin suggesting to people quite early in treatment that they return to school and complete high school diplomas or attend college full or part time. I often suggest books to read and stimulate patients to read and write poetry. I am generally amazed at the number of uneducated patients and students I have met who do write powerful and emotionally meaningful poetry but will show it to no one. I try to include such efforts as an integral part of treatment.

THERAPEUTIC OUTCOMES

I would like to describe some of the changes that begin to occur as patients tell their story and reappraise past and present events, both in the presence of the "therapist" and as operational thinking begins to be utilized.

A reduction in egocentrism is one such change. The story of past abuses is reappraised when individuals see these from a distance and through operations that reorient causality. Although they retain the belief that what happened to them was unfair, they discover that they are not to blame for most occurrences. They move from the worst villain to have lived to victim. After assimilating rage and hurt, emotions appropriate to being victimized, they further discover that their parents or other abusers were often victims of the same process.

Although nothing undoes what was done, the individual begins scientifically to reevaluate the processes involved. A number of patients discover that what their parents did to them was no more personal or a function of themselves than if they had been hurt in an earthquake.

The reduction in egocentrism is matched by an increased experience of differentiation from the environment. Individuals feel themselves to be both objects of events and subjects of action. Just feeling the freedom to think and the related experiences of emotions brings an enormous sense of being reborn and an increase in feelings of personal power. As skills develop, the sense of power increases. There is an increased experience of the unexpected and of novelty. The individual feels simultaneously differentiated from surroundings and yet more related to these surrounds through choice and emotional reaction. Many clients have expressed intensely passionate feelings about just being alive.

A reduction in egocentrism also reveals a reduction in overgeneralized appraisals of self and others. When I described the Everymans, I suggested that to be everyone is to be no one. We are often embedded, by the demands of others, in common identities. Thus, before we are ourselves, we are men or women; black or white; Christian, Jew, or Muslim; American or foreign; or normal or schizophrenic. Being so bonded and attached is comforting and defining, but all comfort and definition also limit and set boundaries. We (who are not first "I") see those who are not "we" as the "others." If we then declare ourselves either morally superior or inferior we find ourselves in an authoritarian-totalitarian hierarchy.

As patients increase their sense of subjective power and differentiate judgment from description, they conceive of themselves as individuals. Human beings who belong voluntarily to this group or who become human beings born with certain physical characteristics that differentiate them from others. The families the patients belong to are comprised of individual members who are free to stay or leave as development continues. The behavior of mother and/or father is not the destiny of the patient (which is the belief of so many patients and nonpatients alike).

The development of a sense of agency and the reduction in preoperational thinking lead to a reappraisal of causality. Individuals stop saying things like, "You made me angry," and begin to articulate statements such as, "You did thus and so and I am angry at you for doing it." Oftentimes, such reappraisals, made from the developing vantage point of what I would judge to be adulthood, no longer even conceptualize the offending actions as threatening and thus fear and anger are resolved.

Another important development that occurs with the emergence of operations involves the conservation of self and others. One no longer hears people say, "You've changed," when another gets angry or upset in some way. One now hears the question, "What has upset you?" There is no longer the immediate assumption, "You are mad at me—I didn't do anything wrong." One hears less frequently, "You don't love me—you never did." Finally, there are fewer of the unreflected conclusions that grow from such dialogue: "I will not exist without you," followed by panic, despair, tantrums, drinking, and so on.

Patients' evaluations of life and its goals change from concern with abstract notions of perfection that are dominated by "should" to concerns for wants related to a more empirically determined "what is." With an increase in subjective agency and the skills to realize goals, the individual is able to create subgoals or short-term goals necessary to achieving longer-term goals. As they now have more humanly achievable standards of success, individuals pace themselves realistically and are less driven and more able to relax. Often they begin to experience better health with improved eating and sleep patterns.

Individuals no longer find themselves frightened of starting tasks, as tasks are understood in terms of their components and need not be undertaken all at once. One discovers that these individuals no longer have to make up elaborate excuses as to why they procrastinate doing homework, cleaning house, or looking for employment. Success and failure are no longer experienced as total, and the self is no longer evaluated in terms of the hyperbole demanded by grandiose overinclusive evaluations.

Patients display less fear either in asking for help or in risking themselves in solving problems on their own. The defensive maneuvers described by Horney (1950) begin to disappear. No longer do individuals feel compelled to dominate others in order to demonstrate personal power or to be dominated by others in order to feel safe. I have had male patients admit to fear and seek the comfort of wives and girlfriends or make doctor's appointments for long-overdue physicals, while female patients have begun to assert themselves, enroll in college courses, or insist on driving even when husbands and boyfriends were with them. One of the most interesting sets of changes occurs in relationships to money, which represents power and success in our society.

As interests develop, as hope begins to be felt, and as individuals begin to conserve time, long-range plans are developed congruent with the future principle. Existential needs appear, allowing for wholesale reorganization of life's activities. Life goals are experienced not as achievable but as end points that dominate and direct life, give purpose and meaning to day-to-day activities, and create justifications for suffering the travails and sorrows that life inevitably brings.

What is perhaps most joyful to experience as a therapist is patients' discoveries of their own passions and the fruits of their own struggles as they find their own unique expressive voices. It is the emergence of genuine creativity that is for me one of the ultimate goals of psycho"therapy." Individuals become aware of what only they can envision and then realize their visions according to the highest standards of excellence. It is the knowledge that one can produce both uniqueness and quality that gives life its most joyful moments.

TERMINATING THERAPY

In *Analysis Terminable and Interminable*, Freud (1937) argues that analysis may never be over because defenses will always be utilized by the individual and neurosis is everpresent in the human condition. Although psycho"therapy" does not cure neuroses, it does help individuals become their own persons, capable of loving, growing, and actualizing. As such goals are never fully realizable, from that conceptional point of view it can be argued that therapy is interminable. However, my hope is that the patient will become his or her own therapist as soon as possible. Therefore, though therapy with the professional is terminated, the patients' therapy with themselves will never end.

I accept patients' desires to terminate, however, at any point that they wish it. Although I ask patients to make clear, if they would, the reasoning behind their choices, I never suggest that they are making the wrong decision, even if I believe this to be the case. I will try to get patients to understand the consequences of termination, as I understand them, which form the basis of my disagreement with them. However, I will make no judgment as to their making a mistake. I will not suggest they are demonstrating resistance, poor judgment, or psychopathology! I certainly will not repeat what a respected therapist claimed to say to patients he believed were terminating prematurely: "I cannot be responsible for what might happen to you if you stop."

As neither I nor that therapist will be responsible for the lives of our patients, whether they are in or out of treatment, I do not believe that forcing or frightening them to remain is ever the right thing to do. I usually say that I shall respect their decision and if they ever wish to return to therapy with me or wish a referral to another worker, they are free to contact me. Some of the most gratifying treatments in my professional life have been with individuals who have worked with me a number of different times for varying lengths of time.

PSYCHO"THERAPY": REMAINING ISSUES

I end this book by discussing another group of topics central to therapy. I formulate some answers to the critical issue of therapeutic effectiveness. I ask whether child therapy can exist given some of the tenets and beliefs of the psycho"therapists," and how the therapist can be of service to children. Finally, I argue that psycho"therapy" cannot exist without a principled confidentiality and suggest that confidentiality barely exists in the field as it now is practiced. I close the chapter by returning to the myth of mental illness and the role it plays in the life of professionals working with their patients.

DOES THERAPY WORK?

One of the questions asked by therapists and students of therapy concerns therapy's effectiveness. Therapists who do day-to-day work are convinced of its powerful effects, while critics of the process (Eysenck 1952, 1965; Gross 1978; Masson 1988) point to data that suggest that therapy is of very limited effectiveness. Even when data exist to demonstrate a real measurable effect of therapy, that same data suggest that all the varieties of therapy produce similar effects and that the effects of therapy seem to be similar to changes attributed to nontherapeutic relationships such as friendships and interactions with teachers, ministers, and nonprofessional support groups.

The discovery that nonprofessional interaction can help in a person's life as much as professional therapy is used by critics to deride the process further and is viewed by proponents with a kind of confused depression. Therapists will say, "But I know therapy works, why can't research prove it?" The answer to this last question, I believe, grows organically out of the preceding chapter. The question of whether therapy works or not is a meaningless question. If one is dealing with an illness, it certainly makes sense to ask if a drug or treatment can cure or otherwise ameliorate the symptoms of the illness. Therapists do not deal with illnesses but rather try to influence the adaptational struggles of human beings in the context of human relationships. To ask, therefore, if therapy is effective is to ask whether or not human relationships matter and under what contextual conditions they matter the most. Psycho"therapy" is first and foremost a human relationship, and if it works it is because the therapeutic relationship was of such a nature that it mattered, both in terms of the patient's overall human relationships and in the context of the history of those relationships. The techniques of psycho"therapy" are those behaviors that define the nature of the relationship between patient and therapist; each behavior alone, out of context, can be expected to produce little measurable effect. In fact, my argument is bolstered by the consistent evidence of research on therapy that reveals that what matters most in therapeutic effectiveness is whether or not the patient and therapist like and respect one another.

Therefore, the question to be asked concerning therapeutic effectiveness relates to the factors that produce a relationship capable of leading to real changes in the paradigms of those it purports to affect. Before I discuss what I believe to be the factors that enhance psycho"therapy" and its effects, I wish to continue discussing the difficulties that researchers would have in demonstrating or refuting that therapy is effective. Any aspect of an individual's paradigm may be changed by therapy: how one thinks, the developmental rules that govern one's appraisals, how one feels, what one feels, how one expresses emotion, and the skills with which one acts to satisfy needs and solve problems. Current research techniques are far too unsophisticated to take into account the range of phenomena that might be measured to define success or failures in treatment.

As therapists set specific behavioral goals during therapy, might not researchers pay attention to these as an index of success or failure? They might, but it is important to note that goals are constantly shifting within each individual's therapy and certainly differ from person to person in separate therapies. I believe success would have to be measured from individual to individual. Cross-individual studies would be extremely difficult to accomplish and generalization very hard to come by. Until psychological researchers take seriously single case studies, I believe research in this area will remain marginally fruitful.

Ignoring all these caveats, I believe that current research implies that therapy has an effect on people's lives and that the effect overall is significant but not terribly great. I now turn to those factors that increase or decrease the potential of the therapeutic relationship to bring changes to various individuals' adaptive paradigms. I also hope to support the idea that the best and most we can hope for from therapy across people are modest changes in human behavior, given the nature of the human condition and the societal context in which the human being operates. Occasionally, however, therapy can make a profound difference in the behavior of individuals. I will return to the issue of therapeutic expectations later.

We discussed some of the factors that can determine the nature of the patient-therapist relationship when we discussed transference and countertransference. A therapeutic relationship will be effective to the degree to which both individuals are able and willing to allow a humanizing, change-inducing relationship to occur. When therapists see patients as hopeless victims, life's failures, schizophrenics unable to grow, then the likelihood that the therapists can seek life-affirming, growth-inducing relationships is not great.

Similarly, if patients live in an autistic world of their own imagination, see the therapist as less real than the fantastic characters of their own creations, and will not risk the necessary pain to respond to the genuine efforts of the therapist to develop a meaningful relationship, then therapy has little chance of inducing change. Only when therapist and patient can see each other as important and experience the thoughts and emotions of the other as real can a relationship form that can lead to the growth of scientific and humanistic personal experiences.

Beyond the internal issues that exist between therapist and patient that induce or limit relationship development, many other issues determine therapeutic success and failure. These factors, which might be considered extratherapeutic, relate to the contexts in which patient and therapist live and work when they are not with each other in the therapeutic environment (Simon 1981). An individual who remains deeply embedded in the existing relationship that helped create the crisis in the first place will develop intense conflicts with the therapist as the therapeutic relationship begins to have effect. I will discuss resistance below, but for now merely suggest that patients fight therapy not only to protect their existing paradigms, but also because as they begin to experience life differently, develop more skills, and try to live differently conflicts erupt in their social relationships.

Therapy rarely induces change in one individual alone. Like any life change in one person, the change reverberates through all the relationships in an individual's life. A teen living at home may enter therapy and be deeply affected by the therapeutic relationship. However, if the parents and siblings who provided the context of the patient's development are not involved in the patient's therapy, they may see the change in the patient as anything but positive. The family's ongoing functioning represents adaptive success to at least some of its members. A teen who behaves differently may well not comply with various family rules. Family members might then put enormous pressure on the teen to withdraw from or change treatments.

Change is especially problematic when children are involved in therapy. (I argue that the therapist greatly increases the chances of therapeutic success by turning the child's therapy into a family treatment.) But similar problems occur whenever the social matrix of the patient objects to the changes occurring in the patient's paradigm. I have had patients involved with religions, gangs, and other closely knit groups who sought to change their lives but either withdrew from therapy or otherwise tempered our relationship when conflicts arose with existing relationships. Gangs, cults, and families do not remain neutral when a member begins to shift loyalties from the authoritarian structure that binds their members together. Patients will report that suddenly they are being called sinners or crazy or traitors as well as threatened with ostracism or even corporal punishment.

Another crucial determinant of the therapeutic relationship is the degree to which an individual is involved with drugs, alcohol, or other potent self-medications. Therapy threatens a lifestyle based on drugs and alcohol. When drug or alcohol usage is socialized and reinforced by group participation and affirmation, a potent force exists against the development of a humanizing psychologically oriented relationship. In general, therapy is not possible until patients have taken steps to detoxify and to modify their use of drugs and alcohol.

If one views the changes promoted by therapy in terms of an individual's social roles, one sees that therapeutic change threatens any set social relationships that form the context of relationships of the individual involved in therapy. Fromm (1980) pointed out that psychoanalysis was a revolutionary idea and a revolutionary process to the degree that it fostered changes in the social roles of the individual being analyzed. However, any individual who, as a result of either doing or receiving analysis, challenges the roles that society values unleashes a counterpressure to nullify the effects of analysis. Freud not only experienced such counterpressures but apparently may have succumbed to them. The invention of the Oedipus and Elektra complexes shifts the focus of analysis from the roles played by parents (and society) in the etiology of their children's problems to the fantasies of the children while under the influence of their own innate sexual desires.

One can ask about the very meaning of change in this light. When do social groups (in society) accept and foster therapeutic relationships? Clearly, they do so when our field functions as society would have it function. When the values of the therapist are in agreement with the values of society, conflict between the two will be minimal. When the values of the therapist are in conflict with the patients' contextualizing relationships, conflicts will be maximized. When the families who send members for therapy have those members returned to them more accepting of family values, they will be supportive and nurturant of therapy. I have earlier argued that adjustment and normalcy are conservative concepts and that often therapy works toward having the patient conform to the demands of his or her social milieu.

Psycho"therapy," with its emphasis on scientific and humanistic relationships, is almost always in conflict with the values of most societies, which are almost always organized along authoritarian lines. Therapy rarely works, since most of the individuals sent for therapy are sent by families and institutions hostile to therapy. Most therapies are not psycho"therapy" in that they seek to help individuals adjust to the demands of their families, schools, and society at large. Most of the therapists I know are psycho"therapists" who are almost always in conflict about their work and disappointed about its outcome although most do not reflect on their feelings in the terms outlined here.

George Albee and his associates (1988) have suggested that therapy does not work and that therapists should consider redirecting their efforts at the prevention of mental illness. From the lens of the present theory it is clear that Albee recognizes how fragile the efforts of the therapist are when confronted by the powers of the collective society. However, there is nothing to prevent. There is no mental illness, only individuals who fail to live as society would wish them to. Albee is therefore exhorting our field to change society itself, a noble but daunting task. Albee is clearly a humanist who wishes that society would operate according to his values.

Even if psychology, psychiatry, and social work were to unite and begin the political processes of changing society, I'm not sure they could agree on the goals of change. The values of our field often mirror the society in which we all function, particularly when we label people mentally ill and seek to have them adjust. When members of our field do criticize the values of society, I find some of the advocated alternatives driven by ideologies and utopian visions worse than what we now live by. Most often the social countergoals of our field are expressed in the same decontextualized, overly abstract terms, as are the majority of concepts I have already criticized. I often wonder if the fads that come and go with such bewildering speed, advocated without historical, intellectual, sociological, economic, religious, or moral justification, plague other fields of endeavor to the same degree they do ours.

I do not think our field is quite ready to advocate a brave new world and thus prevent mental illness. Many in our field, for example, will advocate "greater independence" as a goal for our endeavors, without asking after the meanings of independence. Does the development of independence take place with an awareness of those affected as an individual becomes independent? Does independent ultimately mean that an individual is to be isolated from others and ignore the obligations he or she has already undertaken? Cushman (1980) has pointed out that, with another set of judgments, independence can mean alienation. The very independence advocated by psychotherapists has contributed to what he calls "the empty self."

Similarly, the goal of many in our field might be to help individuals achieve "increased self-esteem." Many in our field advocate, in my opinion, a kind of empty narcissistic quality of self-adoration rather than that self-esteem should be based on genuine achievement or self-sacrifice in the service of family, community, or country. Whenever I see children being told how wonderful they are for achieving the simplest of skills or simply "being," I wonder what standard of excellence these children will develop or whether or not they can ever be concerned with other than themselves.

I agree with Albee and others who realize that people are adversely affected by their childhoods and society and that therapy will never have the impact that society has had on these individuals. But I am also quite convinced that our field will have little to offer to the dilemma until we have a science to be reckoned with and have justified our science with clearly stated moral and ethical goals. At the present time, I see our field as often being just as destructive to the individuals it purports to help as the society it often criticizes. I also see the field as destructive to some of the best virtues of society that have nurtured us as individuals and allow us to share much of the wealth and power of society. Philip Reiff (1966) has demonstrated that the triumph of the therapeutic attitude has produced as much to lament as it has produced causes to cheer.

Is psycho"therapy" successful? My experience says it is. When I work with individuals who develop the values and skills that I believe in and can effect changes in their own lives because they have the power to do so, I find therapy powerfully effective. I do not have any scientific means, however, of proving my contentions. How often do I experience such success? Not very often, and with very few individuals. Working with people once or twice a week after they have spent a lifetime developing skills and values other than those I advocate and being rewarded for these values and skills by family friends and society makes that work a fragile force for change indeed. But I can see no alternatives to my present mode of work but to keep inducing change in one patient, one student, and one colleague at a time.

CHILD THERAPY

There might be no area in the field of psychology in which the promises made are more undermined and corrupted than in our work with children. It seems to me that much of what is wrong with our field and much of what is being (or could be) made right exist in relation to the still-growing tendency to diagnose and treat children. I have long felt that the moment therapists take children into a room and leave parents and other family members in the waiting room we are demonstrating our field's worst ignorance, arrogance, and countertransferences. It is reasoned that the therapist will do something to the child that only a therapist can do and that this activity will restore the mental health of the child. There is often little capacity or interest in asking about the consequences of such actions vis-à-vis the parents, schools, and society when those children leave the therapy room.

I need not repeat my contentions concerning the lack of logic in decontextualizing children and then implicitly blaming them for their personal adaptations to the family, school, or community situation that has judged their adaptations to be inferior or bad. The children we see are not sick but in search of love, kindness, self-expression, and justice. (The children we see have already begun the litany of virtually all human beings: "It's not fair" and "Why me?") The children we see are often well adjusted to their families, which makes adjustment to any other social institution impossible. Or, the children we see are in rebellion against social situations whose operative principles are such that these children should be labeled heroic and courageous instead of sick. I need not repeat that to all too many therapists all these possibilities are not in evidence and play no role in the therapists' activities as they close the door behind them and exclude the principal players in these children's lives.

I would like to concentrate on the possible aftermath and unintended consequences of not working with the parents or schools that originate the complaints against the children. In addition, I would also like to elucidate the consequences of not examining our refusal to withdraw our efforts to get the child to adjust to reference groups whose values, if examined, are abhorrent to us.

What takes place when the therapist and child engage each other in the therapy room? I shall speak from personal experience, the only experience open to me. Discussions with a number of individuals who work with children seem to corroborate my own description of events. Children under eleven basically cannot reflect on their own motives and thus insight cannot be a goal or be part of the process of therapy. Children can well describe what happened, but no further analysis can take place.

Moreover, therapists discover still other impediments to work with children. Children are rarely, if ever, in therapy of their own choices. Therefore, therapists discover that they are agents of somebody else. The people for whom therapists front, often parents, unhappy frustrated teachers, and school officials, have been unable to get the children either to comply with the rules of home or school or to live up to social and academic standards. Therapists often find that their goal is to induce children's compliance with people or institutions they neither know personally nor necessarily agree with.

Children will often tell therapists that the reason they are being sent for therapy is that they are bad. The children are of course right on target with their explanation. However, therapists redefine bad as mental disorder and good as mental health. Not only does therapy now have a single acceptable outcome but the outcome is completely moral in nature. Given these facts, the interaction between therapists and patients often becomes nonverbal, as verbal interactions are not only not productive but are based on the distortions of meaning introduced by the therapists. Therapists must now introduce a nonverbal level of interaction with the children to fill up sessions and prevent their interactions with the children from becoming completely hostile and noninteractive.

Children usually learn that therapists have even less power than their teachers to make them comply with demands and standards. The therapist who usually sees a child for forty-five minutes a week has little to offer in the way of inducement or aid to improve skills, other than a pleasant forty-five minutes. The therapist, now usually at wits end, begins to engage the child in "play therapy." My clinic has a whole room full of wonderful toys and games referred to as therapeutic toys and games.

I have spent years at a time playing games with children. They have liked me and I them. Playing games with a child is fun and rarely demands of the child the kind of behaviors others find disobedient, rebellious, obnoxious, or failing. (Sometimes children do show a real integrity about not complying with their parents' or teachers' "agents" and will neither speak nor play games.) A year or two of playing games often leads to a lovely relationship between child and therapist but little change in the areas of concern to those who sent the child for treatment. Such children read no better, sit in their seats no longer, do not eat their vegetables, still hit little brother, and have not once cleaned their rooms.

Occasionally, however, the therapist demonstrates to the child that he or she is on the child's side. The child begins to complain about parents and teachers, often in convincing terms. What is the goal of this process to be? The child has absolutely no power to exact changes at home or at school. There is, as I have already described, only one possible outcome of therapy acceptable to parents and school, and that is the child's compliance. What is supposed to occur when an adult outside of the family and unrelated to the school supports the perceptions and values of a "disobedient" child?

The sociological implications are staggering. Parents hear from their children how they play games with the therapist. Parents are often confused by the information but, like most people in society, defer to the authority of the therapists that these games will eventually bring about desired changes. Parents watch as their children bond to adults outside the family, confide in these outsiders, and are happy with these outsiders. Neither the therapist nor parents ask about the consequences of such events for the family. The family is, from my perceptions, being undermined. The therapist becomes the good guy, the parents the bad guys. "My therapist talks to me and daddy does not." "My therapist has fun with me, my parents do not." "My therapist is funny and competent, my parents are not."

I ask my colleagues why they do not teach parents the skills that they have developed with children. I ask my colleagues to analyze the reasons that parents so often have so little fun with their own children and see them as moral burdens. I ask colleagues to gauge the effects of their activities on teachers and parents as well as children. If they try and force the "resistive" child to comply, they are one more incompetent judgmental adult in the child's life. If they play games with the child they show up the rest of the adult world for the incompetent and judgmental individuals that they are. My colleagues have yet to answer any of these questions.

I can add a bit more evidence to the contentions just outlined. One excellent and popular therapeutic game is the "Thinking, Feeling and Doing" game developed by Richard Gardner, M.D. The following "important notice" is found in the game: "The teaching, feeling and doing game was designed to be used only by mental health professionals in their therapeutic work with children. Use of the game by parents with their own children is therapeutically contraindicated."

As a human being and especially a parent, I have always objected to the professional demeanor that bespoke godhood and the attitude that I am part of some instinctual mass incapable of learning what the professional knows. To discover that I am an inadequate parent who cannot learn effective parenting skills because only professional therapists have access to such skills is particularly vexing indeed. Let me again state my original premise: Therapists who take a child into a therapy room and exclude the parents undertake not only an impossible task but a morally reprehensible one at the same time.

If a child does not have parents, such interactions with the therapist might teach the child that kind, sympathetic adults do exist who can both listen and have fun with children. But this is not therapy, has nothing to do with medicine, and fixes little in the child's life. The child still needs parents, teachers, and others who will sympathetically and humanistically interact with the child for more than forty-five minutes a week and be there for the child through all the crises, large and small, that comprise the child's growing up. I keep this all in mind when I see children in the role I refer to as "rent a dad."

I have stopped seeing children for therapy. (I do play the role of "rent a dad," but I have little faith in its positive effects on the lives of children growing up amid anarchy, violence, betrayal, drugs, and the features of modern urban life that enfold so many youngsters.) I now work with families or, more usually, with the parents of the children sent to me. Some of my techniques and goals have turned my work with children from the most frustrating and guilt provoking to the most joyful and, I believe, effective work I do.

One more note before I describe my current work with children: There are therapists who use behavioral techniques to gain a child's compliance to home or school and rely on what is euphemistically called *aversive conditioning*. Electric shocks, locking up the child in "time-out rooms," and a variety of other pain- and fear-inducing conditions also work in gaining the child's attention and compliance to institutional rules. I believe that as a humanist I have a duty and a right to call such activities torture and the therapists utilizing these modes of behavioral technology torturers. Torture does work. But torture and coercion have no place in the field of psycho"therapy" no matter how frustrated we are with "defiant" children or how artful the torturer is in achieving his or her ends.

When a child is brought to me, I see the problem as not "in" or "with" the child but between the child and other members of his or her social world. Often I discover that the "bad" child is but a diversion for parents who fear examining their own marital problems or judgments of self that stem from their own family origins. Often parents bring children because schools demand it. The parents will feel sorry for the children who have to deal with teachers who scream at them, overcrowded classes, or other children who are bullies. Often those parents experience themselves as children in relation to the school, and even though they sympathize with their children they are too afraid to do anything but comply with the school's demand for therapy.

Often parents tell me that something is the matter with their children. They have tried "everything" to get them to "be obedient," "do his homework," "listen to the teacher," "clean her room." Having tried everything (nagging, screaming, hitting, threatening, grounding, and endless hours of lecturing that begin with, "When I was a child") and found nothing that worked, it stands to reason that the child must be defective. When a person is defective, it is also a priori true that medical attention of some kind is needed to fix the damaged child.

I recognize that most of these problems result from schools and families operating along authoritarian lines and blaming moral flaws in people as the sources of all interpersonal difficulties. Teachers, parents, administrators, and children are all caught up in systems and modes of thinking that will not allow humanistic resolutions of conflicts. Unable to appeal to one another and ultimately lacking the power to force each other to comply, people become anxious and desperate with one another.

I recognize as well that children do not ask to come to therapy, that they lack the wherewithal to take responsibility for changing their lives, and that I can set few reasonable goals with them to do so. I also realize that I will do nothing, except in desperation and in the last resort, to hurt the family of which the child is a part. Five billion years of human biological and social evolution have led to the family as the main means of raising children, and nothing social scientists or government bureaucrats have created seems adequate to replace the family.

After listening to parents' complaints, I begin reframing the issues from ones in which problems define moral defects in children, to a definition of problems as things that require solution. At this point the parents involved make a decision. As one woman screamed at me recently, "If you are suggesting that I have a problem and my kid doesn't then you are not for us and you are a [expletive]." She left. Other parents recognize that the child is doing what the child wants and that they have the problem of figuring out how to get the child to comply.

Unless parents are committed to defining their children as morally defective, they feel relieved to discover that there is nothing wrong with either their children or any other family member. They begin to discover that it is not their children who are "out of control" but they who lack control of their parental roles and goals. It often becomes a source of genuine relief and humor when I help parents reflect quietly on a scene in which they run around a room screaming and a small being of fifty or sixty pounds sits still and is unmoved.

At this juncture I am ready to begin genuine psycho"therapy" with the parents. It may take further discussions to demonstrate the futility of their wish that I straighten out their child (is the child bent?) or to clarify that I will not help them or try myself to "make" the child do as he "ought to." I try to get the parents to see that I will help them restore their family life as they would wish it to be. We shall work on how to communicate with one another and how to set up a democratic humanistic family and home.

I proceed with the parents in the same way as with any other patients. I work to help them understand the difference between judgments and descriptions. This is followed by discussions that relate the child's motivational structure to the rest of humanity's. Children are motivated by thoughts and feelings. I am always affected at how parents are surprised by the insight, even though on an informational level they already knew it to be true. I am also surprised at how effective Alice Miller's (1984) insights are concerning the degree to which fear and moral labeling detach us from any real knowledge of our own childhoods, let alone our children's.

I help parents understand that all authoritarian relationships are based on fear and that "the problem with children today" is that they do not fear adults as they used to. This usually leads to a discussion on the differences between fear and respect. I have long felt that as a child I had adults in my life whom I feared and respected, feared and disrespected, or respected without fear. I had some I neither feared nor respected. There is no correlation between the two psychological states. Most parents agree with me that we would much rather be respected without fear, especially by those we love. (I think there is a strong position correlation between love and respect as well as a negative correlation between love and fear. Fear seems most correlated with hate.)

To make my case I discuss ways of inducing genuine fear in children. I often suggest to parents, with obvious tongue in cheek, that if they break the recalcitrant child's kneecaps with a baseball bat, the child will listen to every order they bark at him or her. These children will not again question the orders of their "betters" or "commanders-in-parent". I also add, in genuine earnest, that if they use force on their children that they are not to tell me about it because I will label it abuse and will be sorely tempted to report them to the authorities. (I have to date never reported a parent for spanking a child on his bottom and am terrified at the speed with which newly trained social workers are willing to turn in parents to the state.)

As most parents laugh in horror at my suggestion of using a baseball bat, they immediately understand that they have no choice but to give up the nagging, threatening, and labeling that are the remnants of an authoritarian structure that no longer can function. Most parents (and citizens of our society) are committed to ideals of democracy but still function according to the demands of an authoritarian structure. I help parents reflect on the frustrations, worry, and sense of helplessness that motivate their yelling as well as on their identification with parents who used the same skills plus corporal punishment when they were children.

I then move the discussion to the role played by parents establishing a democratic, humanistic, scientifically psychological home life. This model helps parents be authoritative with their children rather than authoritarian. Discipline involves the use of positive reinforcers as well as punishments and giving the child meaningful choices, one of which can lead to praise and affection from the parents. I have parents draw up a comprehensive list of all the things they do for their children. I have them remove from the list all the things a parent must do, which includes feeding, clothing, sheltering, and providing medical care. I also try to help them see that their love for the child should be constant and not conditional upon desired behavior. I help them understand that being angry at a child does not mean that one does not love the child. Parents are delighted to discover how many things they routinely do for their children that are of vital importance to the children but need not be done unless the child agrees to various roles—or doing of chores. The ideas that a contract can be drawn with one's own children is often astounding and liberating to parents.

I wish that I had been more precise in keeping statistics since I began applying these procedures to my work with children. I will have to remain "sloppily clinical," however, in reporting my results, which happily are the most positive and effective of all the work I now do. Within six to eight weeks any parents who accept my premises and are able to reflect on its rationales and to develop and apply the skills required no longer experience much difficulty with their children. Most single parents and couples terminate therapy by eight to ten sessions, with my having spent only a session or two alone with their child.

Some parents are delighted with their new skills and stop treatment, feeling more in control of themselves and less in need of controlling their children. Family life has been improved, and from the parent's viewpoint that was all that was necessary. Many parents, however, remain in treatment, either individual or marital, as they develop the insights that the problems they experience with their children are really reflective of unhappiness with themselves or each other. The "therapies" that result have already been discussed in Chapter 11.

CONFIDENTIALITY

Psycho"therapy" is often a process in which two or more individuals bond and form an intense relationship. At other times it is a briefer interaction in which the patient receives information and acknowledgment from the therapist. In either case the effectiveness of the interaction depends on the ability of both individuals to perceive the other as worthy of respect and, perhaps more important, trust. A humanistic relationship cannot exist in a relationship in which the members of the relationship feel unrelated or betrayed in any significant way. Trust cannot develop if any of the members of a relationship, in this case specifically the patient, feels that his or her innermost secrets, emotions, and actions will not be held in confidence by the others in that relationship.

At the current time confidentiality does not exist in principle in our field, and thus one can do very little effective psycho"therapy." "In principle" means that a therapist is bound by rules of confidentiality in the same way as are priests and lawyers. No matter how awful, dangerous, or disgusting priests or lawyers find the thoughts and actions of an individual, they are bound by oath not to repeat what they have been told. A lawyer who, while acting as a client's attorney, reveals even the most heinous crime to the authorities can be disbarred for violating lawyer-client confidentiality. As an attorney put it, "I do not defend clients as much as the Constitution of the United States. I am bound by the constitution—not my personal relationship with the client." Priests are bound by a covenant with God. They do not hear a parishioner's confession as an individual person but as God's emissary.

Psycho"therapists" have only their personal relationships with patients to justify confidentiality, and our society has judged that this is not qualification enough. From the time of the *Tarasoff* case (*Tarasoff v. Regents of the University of California et al.* 1976. Al. 551 P 2nd 334) psychotherapists have been enjoined by the law not to keep the confidences of patients who are planning serious crimes, particularly murder. Psychotherapists who do so can be prosecuted and imprisoned as accessories to the crime. Psychotherapists have never fought the *Tarasoff* decision and could not, because we can claim no special basis for confidentiality other than that necessary for our work to be effective.

Most therapists I know are terrified of a patient's potential suicide. Suicide in our society is a crime and more important a major sin according to Judeo-Christian doctrines. Moreover, therapists are fair game for lawsuits because of their own use of the medical model. As suicide is mental illness and therapists are bound to cure mental illness, suicide represents a therapeutic failure. Therapists are regularly sued under malpractice statutes when clients succeed in (or even attempt) suicide. At a result, many therapists will report suicidal ideation or threats to the patient's family members, other mental health officials, or even the police.

One of our societies most vigorous attempts to undermine our constitution has involved protecting our children from abuse. Therapists are expected, under penalty of law, to report all cases of actual or suspected abuse to proper authorities. I have written elsewhere in this book how our accession to this demand has made us agents of the state instead of advocates of our patients. In addition, confidentiality has further eroded.

Still more inroads against confidentiality have been achieved in recent years as the courts and lawyers have been increasingly successful in getting psychotherapists to hand over their process notes and case files for use in court and criminal procedures. Finally, bureaucrats from all levels of government regularly examine the patient's case files in mental health clinics in order that the clinic be licensed or that public monies that pay for psychotherapy be justified.

I am often amazed to hear psychotherapists speak as if they assume complete confidentiality with their patients. They will state categorically that they maintain confidentiality even as they contend that they have reported suspected child abuse or possible patient suicide. It is as if confidentiality is not being defined and exists as a word and not a principled practice. Moreover, clients are shocked to discover that their fundamental rights to privacy exist only as an undiscussed assumption and not as a matter of practical reality.

Some time ago I worked with the husband of a married couple whose wife worked with my colleague. The patient was a Christian fundamentalist with whom I argued often over a number of issues, one of which was his principled belief that children are spoiled if one spares the rod. He and his wife occasionally spanked their children, who I believed were well loved and cared for. I argued that spanking children would only lead to negative unwanted consequences, but I was also prepared to do no more than to try to win him over to my viewpoint. When my colleague heard from the wife that they spanked their children, she demanded that they either cease and desist or she would report them.

My patient was astonished when I explained to him the law concerning child abuse in New York. He and his wife had assumed confidentiality. I considered this man to be a excellent patient and our relationship to be similarly fine. Our relationship was never the same after this incident, and though we both consider the therapy to have been successful (we still occasionally keep in touch), I believe it concluded prematurely and with less potential success because of the breach in trust created by the incident.

I now regularly tell patients about the bounds of confidentiality in our relationship. I explain that, as I am unwilling to go to jail to protect confidentiality, if they have committed or are contemplating a major crime they are not to tell me unless they want others to know about it. I have taken a strong principled stand on suicide. I agree with Szasz that to forcibly prevent suicide is to commit liberticide. It is no different than preventing persons from leaving their own countries if they so decide. I will report child abuse only if I feel a child's health or life is in jeopardy. Spankings, I believe, are morally wrong and counterproductive, but it will take many generations to convince people who love their children of this belief.

I have never had a patient commit suicide, although it has been threatened quite often. While I try to help my patients see life as worth living and have taken strong stands against their committing suicide while therapy is still in operation, I have, often with my heart in my throat, never reported any adult who threatened it and have maintained patient confidentiality. Similarly, I have held the confidences of a number of minor and not so minor crimes involving drugs, thievery, and the like. In recent years, my initial discussions with patients on confidentiality have lightened my moral burden, as patients are careful not to confide their criminal behaviors in me. One of the problems mentioned earlier involves patients' files. I am most judicious of what I put in a patient's file and never write anything that I am not completely comfortable showing to the patient. In principle, if the patient is not upset to have it written about then, although he or she might not like others knowing about it, he or she usually rests easier at the prospect of prying eyes reading the files.

One of the important issues of confidentiality involves the treatment of children. Therapists regularly promise children that they will not tell their parents what they are told, although I imagine that they exclude homicide, suicide, or serious drinking and use of drugs. I should like to discuss this issue in relation to my earlier exposition of child therapy. It seems to me that when therapists keep a child's secret from his or her parents they are damaging the functioning of that family.

Once therapists make it a goal to restore children to their parents and help the parents be people who can operate humanistically and scientifically with their children, then it must also be the therapists' goal to create conditions where children feel free to speak with their parents and the parents become capable of listening to their children. Children often say to me, "Don't tell my mother (father); she (he) will kill me." I have heard my own children speak the same words to their friends. Although in the overwhelming number of cases the child will not be killed or hurt, I believe this expression, so often used by children, has meaning. I believe the child is saying, "If I tell my parents this or that I will be so ashamed, guilt-ridden, or fearful that I will psychologically cease to exist."

Even if parents have not created the conditions of the children's fear (in most cases parents do create these conditions by yelling or reacting with dread or fear to their children's confessions and fears), I believe it is a goal of therapy to help parents overcome their children's reluctance to come to them first for confession, advice, direction, and the like. Whenever therapists say to a child, "You can tell me anything that you cannot tell your parents," they are not only taking over the parental role but also denigrating the role of the parent and accepting the status quo of family relationships that has inhibited unhindered communications in the first place.

By working with parents, as described earlier, I avoid problems of confidentiality with children. It is always my goal to help parents examine their own roles and those elements in the roles that inhibit the child's free expressions with them. Often parents are so afraid that if their children are unhappy it will reflect on their abilities to be "perfect" parents that they inhibit the child's communicating with them. At other times parents discipline their children for telling the truth and will say things such as, "Don't let me catch you doing (or saying) this again." I have found many of these problems quite manageable through therapeutic intervention, with the consequence of increased communication between parents and child.

I have not exhausted this topic by any means. Our field needs to debate such issues. Perhaps we do not wish ever to have a principle of complete confidentiality. Perhaps it is necessary for children to have neutral figures in whom to confide no matter how open relationships are with their parents. However, I maintain that unless confidentiality is established on some level with prospective patients there can be no psycho"therapy. If our field decides that psycho"therapy" or something like it is desirable, then we will have to battle with Congress and state legislatures for a binding law of confidentiality.

CLOSING REMARKS: THE MEDICAL MODEL REDUX

Recently my colleague Martha Habert (1993) presented a paper on how myths and fairy tales informed her therapeutic efforts. Drawing on the works of Bruno Bettelheim (1977), Carl Heinz Mallet (1984), and others she made clear that myths and fairy tales serve an enormous range of psychological functioning. Reality, suggests Spence (1987), is captured in myths and metaphors and serve as a basis for all scientific activity. The novelist Nicholas Mosely (1990: 26) writes, "What is true is usually in the form of a myth." Habert points out that myths allow her patients to explain, predict, and control the especially frightening situations in their lives and provide a mechanism for sharing the emotions of shame and guilt as well. May (1991) theorizes that our modern era has a hunger for myths that not only organize and give meaning to life but provide the basis of social order.

But myths also serve a defensive function. They not only can render the awfulness of experienced reality a little less awful but can create alternatives to experiencing reality at all. Myths help us disconnect ourselves from pain, alienating us from those aspects of life that require our immediate and intensive concern.

When individuals experience a myth as real by taking it literally and utilizing preoperational thinking they run the risk of being called mentally ill by the practitioners of our field. Throughout this book I have in effect been describing how myths experienced literally become the adaptive reality of individuals who see no other choice in how they satisfy needs and solve life's problems. Myths provide for them an alternative reality in which the individuals feel they can more easily function.

For most people, myths serve an intermediary function between the ideal of science and the ideal of an alternative reality. For most of us our myths create an experience of reality in which the world as it is and the world as we wish it to be become fused. We experience in one way or another that which is there to be experienced and that which we wish or believe should be there to be experienced. The myth of mental illness is no different from any other myth in its origins and in the function it is to serve. The myth of mental illness has, however, an unintended side effect that makes it intolerable for continued use:

It is a myth that is destructive of myth itself, or at the very least it is destructive to all myths but itself.

In my 1986 book I created a metaphor I called the "psychotic landscape." These experiences seem to demand the use of defenses and the creation of myths without whose protection we could not face or even begin to cope. Briefly these four types of situations or experiences:

1. involve the discovery that one is unloved by one's parents and the further discovery that one might be hated by a parent and one's parents might even wish to destroy one.

2. involve the discovery of one's mortality. Becker's *The Denial of Death* (1973) is mandatory reading to understand how myth protects one from the unacceptable and unexperienceable reality of death.

3. involve the discovery of evil and the potential for evil to triumph over good. Most of us seem not to be able to grasp that there are those who enjoy inflicting pain and destroying their fellow human beings. We cannot comprehend the ultimate expression of evil, which in our century is the Nazi Holocaust in Europe. Becker's (1975) treatise is indispensable reading.

4. involve the discovery that our lives may have no meaning except for the meanings that we create for it. To accept that our lives are not meaningful is to accept that life is lived in a world that is capricious and that accidents determine most of our happiness and unhappiness.

If we examine the myths and fairy tales of children, religion, and folk tales we see the above themes expressed over and over again and solutions provided to predict and control these events. No one of us can live in the face of these discoveries without a sustaining and defensive myth. Yet to do therapy, one must listen to people, day after day, as they tell stories in which the psychotic landscape is made manifest and real to anyone who can and will listen to the stories. We listen and then judge the myths that allow these people to function in the face of their horrors to be mental illness. To be cured they must give up the myths, which represent their best adaptations. How does one accept reality in the face of the following stories:

1. Three men, none of whom have met, tell similar stories to the same therapist. They all fought in Vietnam. One fired a rifle and killed a ten-year-old girl who was about to throw a bomb onto a truck of G.I.'s. The bullets hit her, and she fell "in two pieces."

   Another was a pilot in a helicopter gunship. He tells of firing a rapid-fire machinegun at a village. Everybody and everything below, people and animals, disappear before his power. He begins drinking heavily and misses a mission because he is hung over. His best friend covers for him and is killed on the mission.

The third soldier kills "too many people to count." He also "buries too many buddies to remember." All three drink heavily, live alternative lifestyles, and cannot relate to the families and friends they return to after their service ends.

2. A forty-year-old Korean woman tells of the first twelve years of her life, when her father regularly beat her, her three sisters, and her mother. She reports accepting the beatings for herself but being unable to bear the cries of the others. At age twelve she runs away to a large city and survives, along with hundreds of other children, many orphans of war, as a prostitute. At age fourteen she marries an American soldier who brings her to the United States and several months later abandons her. She survives by prostitution and ultimately lives on the street as a homeless person and in shelters.

She reports being beaten and raped more times than she can recall. One night, feeling more alone and frightened than ever before, her nose begins to bleed, her heartbeat becomes irregular, and the "voice of God" tells her that she is the "Ave Maria." She walks in heavy traffic to "heal the world" and is struck by a car. She spends the next and, according to her definition, the best years of her life in a mental hospital.

3. A woman in her sixties tells me that she has been "depressed" since spending three years in Auschwitz concentration camp. When she arrived it was with a large family that included her parents, brothers, sisters, aunts, uncles, nephews, and nieces. Some immediately went into the gas chambers. The rest went with her into slave labor. All died in the camps. She is the only survivor. She has not wanted therapy nor to tell her story to anyone.

To listen to one's patients is to listen to people unloved by mothers and fathers, abandoned by the human race, subjected to and participating in evils to which only our worst nightmare can give shape. They survive that which is created by the whim of tyrants and by the capriciousness of the fates. They tell of lives and deaths that have no meaning, of a universe in which the strong devour the weak, the rich the poor. They describe human beings destroying everything in their path including the earth itself.

The drinking, alienation, and myths of those people make their lives endurable. The myth of mental illness makes listening to them endurable. The victims are merely sick, suffering from chemical and neurological upset. These folks will feel better if they take the drugs prescribed. We will feel better for helping them and not feel ashamed of being human or terrified that we can be the next victims. The stories they tell are delusions and distortions, and indeed they brought it all upon themselves by being neurotic, irresponsible, and codependent. We can now differentiate ourselves from them and feel safe and superior. The myth of mental illness achieves all of this for us and more.

But like all defenses, our myth brings about the very thing it seeks to avoid. We have created meaninglessness out of meaning. We deny justice to those who cry out for it and fail to hold responsible (or at least bear witness against) those who need to be held accountable. I recently received a description of new books from a major publisher of psychoanalytic and psychotherapeutic literature. One of the books advertised was a joint effort by an M.D. and a Ph.D. claiming to have made the "definitive diagnosis" of Adolf Hitler. Were Hitler to be found alive, would the good doctors argue for his rehabilitation by psychotherapy and chemotherapy? Can we hold him responsible for his actions if he is mentally ill? And if the oppressor is not responsible for his actions and the victims are implictly responsible for their victimization, where then has our myth left us?

I agree with Jeffrey Masson (1988: 254) when he writes, "Recognizing the lies, the flaws, the harm, the potential for harm, the imbalance in power, the arrogance, the condescension, the pretension, may be the first stop in the eventual abolition of psychotherapy that, I believe, is one day inevitable and desirable." I suggest we begin by jettisoning our myth of mental illness. Although I recognize that new myths will have to replace it, I believe that psycho"therapy" may well help us do better in our endeavors.

REFERENCES

Ainsworth, Mary. 1985. "Attachment across the Life-Span." *Bulletin of the New York Academy of Medicine* 61: 792–811

———. 1989. "Attachments beyond Infancy." *American Psychologist* 44: 709–716.

Albee, George, G. W. Joffe, ; and J. M. Dusenbury, eds. 1988. *Prevention, Powerlessness and Politics: A Book of Readings on Social Change.* Newbury Park, Calif.: Page.

Asaad, Ghaszi. 1990. *Hallucinations in Clinical Psychiatry: A Guide for Mental Health Professionals.* New York: Brunner/Mazel.

Bandura, Albert. 1989. "Human Agency in Social Cognitive Theory." *American Psychologist* 44: 1175–1184.

Barnett, Lincoln. 1957. *The Universe and Dr. Einstein.* New York: William Morrow and Co.

Bateson, Gregory. 1978. "The Birth of a Matrix or Double Bind and Epistemology." In *Beyond the Double Bind,* edited by Milton Berger. New York: Brunner/Mazel, 1978.

Beck, Aaron. 1967. *Depression: Clinical, Experimental and Theoretical Aspects.* New York: Harper and Row.

Becker, Ernst. 1973. *The Denial of Death.* New York: Free Press.

———. 1975. *Escape from Evil.* New York: Free Press.

Beit-Hallahmi, Benjamin. 1974. "Salvation and Its Vicissitudes: Clinical Psychology and Political Values." *American Psychologist* 29: 124, 130.

Benjamin, Jessica. 1988. *The Bonds of Love.* New York: Pantheon.

Benson, Herbert, and Miriam Klipper. 1976. *The Relaxation Response.* New York: Avon Books.

Berger, Milton, ed. 1978. *Beyond the Double Bind.* New York: Brunner/Mazel.

Berger, P. I., and T. Luckmann. 1966. *The Social Construction of Reality.* New York: Doubleday.

Bettelheim, Bruno. 1977. *The Uses of Enchantment.* New York: Vintage Books.

Bevan, William. 1991. "Contemporary Psychology: A Tour inside the Onion." *American Psychologist* 46: 475–483.

Bowlby, John. 1969. *Attachment and Loss, Vol. 1: Attachment.* New York: Basic Books.

———. 1973. *Attachment and Loss, Vol. 2: Separation: Anxiety and Anger.* New York: Basic Books.

———. 1979. *The Making and Breaking of Affectional Bonds*. London: Tavistock.

———. 1980. *Attachment and Loss, Vol. 3: Losses: Sadness and Depression*. London: Hogarth Press.

———. 1988. *A Secure Base*. New York: Basic Books.

Braginsky, B. M, and D. D. Braginsky. 1974. *Mainstream Psychology: A Critique*. New York: Holt, Rinehart and Winston.

Bridgeman, Bruce. 1992. "Consciousness vs. Unconscious Processes: The Case of Vision." *Theory and Psychology* 2: 73–78.

Bridgman, P. W. 1927. *The Logic of Modern Physics*. New York: Macmillan.

Brofenbrenner, U., F. Kessel, W. Kessen, and S. White.1986. "Toward a Critical Social History of Development Psychology: A Propaedic Discussion." *American Psychologist* 41: 1218–1230.

Bronowski, Jacob. 1963. *The Common Sense of Science*. Cambridge, Mass.: Harvard University Press.

Bruner, Jerome. 1966. *Toward a Theory of Interaction*. Cambridge, Mass.: Harvard University Press.

Burgess, Anthony. 1978. *1985*. Boston; Little, Brown and Co.

Butt, T. 1990. "The Personal Historian: A New Model for P.C.P." Paper presented at the British Personal Construct Psychology Conference, York.

Campbell, Donald. 1975. "On the Conflicts between Biological and Social Evolution and Between Psychology and Moral Tradition." *American Psychologist* 30: 1103–1124.

Cattell, Raymond. 1987. *Beyondism: Religion from Science*. New York: Praeger Publishers.

Chein, Isidor. 1972. *The Science of Behavior and the Image of Man*. New York: Basic Books.

Chodorow, Nancy. 1978. *The Reproduction of Mothering: Psychoanalysis and the Sociology of Gender*. Berkeley, Calif.: University of California Press.

Cohen, I. Bernard. 1985. *Revolution in Science*. Cambridge, Mass.: Harvard University Press.

Cushman, Philip. 1980. "Why the Self Is Empty: Toward a Historically Situated Psychology." *American Psychologist* 45: 599–611.

Darnton, Nina. 1989. "Committed Youth." *Newsweek*, July 31.

Degler, Carl N. 1991. *In Search of Human Nature: The Decline and Revival of Darwinism in American Social Thought*. New York: Oxford University Press.

Dennett, Daniel. 1991. *Consciousness Explained*. New York: Little, Brown and Co.

Dewey, John. 1929. *The Quest for Certainty*. New York: G. P. Putnam Sons.

Diamond, Jared. 1992. *The Third Chimpanzee*. New York: Harper and Co.

Erdelyi, Matthew. 1985. *Psychoanalysis: Freud's Cognitive Psychology*. San Francisco: W. H. Freeman.

Erikson, Eric. 1968. *Identity, Youth and Crisis*. New York: W. W. Norton.

Eysenck, Hans J. 1952. "TheEffects of Psychotherapy: An Evaluation." *Journal of Consulting Psychology* 16: 319–324.

———. 1965. "The Effects of Psychotherapy." *International Journal of Psychiatry* 1: 97–168.

Fawcett, Jan. 1993. "Schizophrenia: The Glacier Is Moving." *Psychiatric Annual* 23: 100.

Fein, Melvin. 1992. *Analyzing Psychotherapy*. Westport, Conn.: Praeger Books.

Feldman, Carol Freigher. 1992. "The New Theory of Mind." *Human Development* 35: 107–117.

Feyerabend, Paul. 1988. *Against Method*. rev. ed. London: Verso.

Foucault, Michel. 1965. *Madness and Civilization*. New York: Pantheon Books.

Frankl, Victor. 1969. *The Will to Meaning*. London: Plume Books.

Freud, Sigmund. 1930. *Civilization and Its Discontents*. New York: Doubleday.

———. 1937. "Analysis Terminable and Interminable." In *The Standard Edition of the Complete Psychological Works of Sigmund Freud*. Translated and edited by James Strachey. London: Hogarth Press and the Institute of Psycho-Analysis.

——— . 1964. *The Future of an Illusion*. Edited by James Strachey. Garden City, N.Y.: Anchor Books.

Fridley, Mary. 1989. "Freud Never Had This in Mind: Therapists Canvas Door to Door." *National Alliance*, December 2.

Frijda, Nico H. 1986. *The Emotions*. Cambridge: University of Cambridge Press.

——— . 1988. "The Laws of Emotions." *American Psychologist* 43: 349–358.

Fromm, Erich. 1947. *Escape from Freedom*. New York: Holt, Rinehart and Winston.

——— . 1950. *Psychoanalysis and Religion*. New Haven, Conn.: Yale University Press.

——— . 1980. *The Greatness and Limitations of Freud's Thought*. New York: Harper and Row.

Fukuyama, Francis. 1992. *The End of History and The Last Man*. New York: Free Press.

Gergen, Kenneth. 1985. "The Social Constructionist Movement in Modern Psychology." *American Psychologist* 40: 266–275.

——— . 1988. "If Persons Are Texts." In *Hermeneutics and Psychological Theory: Interpersonal Perspective and Personality, Psychotherapy and Psychopathology*, edited by S. Messer, L. Sass, and R. Woolfolk. New Brunswick, N.J.: Rutgers University Press.

——— . 1991. "Emerging Challenges for Theory and Psychology." *Theory and Psychology* 1: 13–35.

Gilligan, Carol. 1982. *In a Different Voice: Psychological Theory and Women's Development*. Cambridge, Mass.: Harvard University Press.

Giorgi, A. 1970. *Psychology as a Human Science*. New York: Harper and Row.

Göncü, Artin. 1993. "Development of Intersubjectivity in Social Pretend Play." *Human Development* 36: 218–234.

Gordon, D. E. 1993. "The Inhibition of Pretend Play and Its Implications for Development." *Human Development* 36: 215–234.

Greenberg, Leslie S., and Jeremy D. Safran. 1987. *Emotions in Psychotherapy*. New York: Guilford Press.

Gross, Martin. 1978. *The Psychological Society*. New York: Random House.

Grunbaum, Adolf. 1984. *The Foundations of Psychoanalysis*. Berkeley, Calif.: University of California Press.

Guidano, Vittorio F., and Gianni Liotti. 1985. "A Constructivist Foundation for Cognitive Therapy." In *Cognition and Psychotherapy*, edited by Michael Mahoney and Arthur Freeman. New York: Plenum Press.

Habert, Martha. 1993. "The Uses of Fantasy and Myths in Psychotherapy." Paper presented to the staff of Flushing Hospital Mental Health Clinic.

Hacking, Ian, ed. 1981. *Scientific Revolutions*. Oxford: Oxford University Press.

Haley, Jay. 1976. *Problem Solving Therapy*. San Francisco: Jossey-Bass.

Hare-Mustin, Rachel T., and Jeanne Maracek. 1988. "The Meaning of Difference: Gender Theory, Postmodernism and Psychology" *American Psychologist* 43: 455–465.

Harré, Rom. 1984. *Personal Being: A Theory for Individual Psychology*. Cambridge, Mass.: Harvard University Press.

——— . 1986. *The Social Construction of Emotions*. Oxford: Basil Blackwell.

——— . 1991. "The Discursive Production of Selves" *Theory and Psychology* 1: 31–63.

——— . 1992. "What Is Real in Psychology: A Plea for Persons." *Theory and Psychology* 2: 153–159.

Hartmann, Heinz. 1958. "Ego Psychology and the Problem of Adaptation." Translated by D. Rappaport. *Journal of the American Psychoanalytic Association*. Monograph #1. New York: International Universities Press.

Helme, William. 1992. "Reformulating Psychology as a Human Science." *Theoretical and Philosophical Psychology* 12: 119–136.

Hofstadter, Richard. 1963. *Anti-Intellectualism in American Life*. New York: Alfred A. Knopf.

Holzkamp, Klaus. 1992. "On Doing Psychology Critically." *Theory and Psychology* 2: 193–204.

Horney, Karen. 1950. *Neurosis and Human Growth*. New York: W. W. Norton.

Howard, George S. 1985. "The Role of Values in the Science of Psychology." *American Psychologist* 40: 255–266.

———. 1991. "Cultural Tales: A Narrative Approach to Thinking, Crosscultural Psychology and Psychotherapy." *American Psychologist* 46: 187–197.

Husserl, Edmund. 1962. *Ideas: General Introduction to Pure Phenomenology*. Translated by W. R. Boyce-Gibson. New York: Collier Books.

Ibanez, Tomas. 1991. "Social Psychology and the Rhetoric of Truth." *Theory and Psychology* 2: 187–201.

Idhe, Don. 1986. *Experimental Phenomenology*. Albany, N.Y.: State University of New York Press.

Igbal, N., B. J. Schwartz, A. Cecil, I. Zahd, and C. Constantin. 1993. "Psychosocial Treatments of Schizophrenia." *Psychiatric Annual* 23: 216 – 221.

Izard, Carroll E. 1977. *Human Emotions*. New York: Plenum.

———. 1984. "Emotion-Cognition Relations in Human Development." In *Emotion, Cognition and Behavior*, edited by C. E. Izard, J. Kagan, and R. B. Zajonc. New York: Cambridge University Press.

———, ed. 1979. *Emotions in Personality and Psychopathology*. New York: Plenum.

Kagan, Jerome. 1984a. *The Nature of the Child*. New York: Basic Books.

———. 1984b. "The Idea of Emotions in Human Development." In *Emotion, Cognition and Behavior*, edited by C. E. Izard, J. Kagan, and R. B. Zajonc. New York: Cambridge University Press.

Kane, Steven, and Hans Furth. 1993. "Children Constructing Social Reality: A Frame Analysis of Social Pretend Play." *Human Development* 36: 199–214.

Kelly, George. 1955. *The Psychology of Personal Constructs in Theory of Personality, Vols. 1 and 2*. New York: W. W. Norton.

Kirk, Stuart. 1986. "A Last Dance with Freud." *Newsweek*, October 13, 1986, p. 15.

Klein, George. 1976. *Psychoanalytic Theory: An Exploration of Essentials*. New York: International University Press.

Kohlberg, Laurence. 1984. *The Psychology of Moral Development Vol. 2*. San Francisco: Harper and Row.

Kohut, Heinz. 1971. *Analysis of the Self*. New York: International University Press.

———. 1977. *The Restoration of Self*. New York: International University Press.

Kovacs, Arthur. 1988. "Shall We Take Drugs—Just Say No!" *Psychotherapy Bulletin* 23: 8–11.

Kuhn, Thomas. 1970. *The Structure of Scientific Revolutions*, 2d rev. ed. Chicago, Ill.: University of Chicago Press.

Laing, R. D. 1967a. *Knots*. New York: Pantheon.

———. 1967b. *The Politics of Experience*. New York: Pantheon.

———. 1969. *The Divided Self*. New York: Pantheon.

———. 1982. *The Voice of Experience*. New York: Pantheon.

Lazarus, Richard S. 1968. "Emotions and Adaptations: Conceptual and Empirical Relations." In *Nebraska Symposium of Motivation*, edited by W. J. Arnold. Lincoln: University of Nebraska Press.

———. 1982. "Thoughts on the Relation between Emotion and Cognition." *American Psychologist* 37: 1019–1024.

———. 1984. "On the Primacy of Cognition." *American Psychologist* 39: 124–129.

———. 1991. *Emotions and Adaptations*. New York: Oxford University Press.

Lerman, Hannah. 1986. *A Mote in Freud's Eye*. New York: Springer.

Lifton, Robert J. 1979. *The Broken Connection.* New York: Simon and Schuster.
——— . 1986. *The Nazi Doctors: Medical Killings and the Psychology of Genocide.* New York: Basic Books.
London, Perry. 1986. *The Modes and Morals of Psychotherapy,* 2d ed.. New York: Hemisphere Books.
Mahler, Margaret S. 1968. *On Human Symbiosis and the Vicissitudes of Individuation.* New York: International Universities Press.
Mahoney, Michael J. 1980. "Psychotherapy and the Structure of Personal Revolution." In *Psychotherapy Processes: Current Issues and Future Directions,* edited by M. J. Mahoney. New York: Plenum.
——— . 1985. "Psychotherapy and Human Change Processes." In *Cognition and Psychotherapy,* edited by M. J. Mahoney and A. Freeman. New York: Plenum.
——— . 1991. *Human Change Processes: The Scientific Foundations of Psychotherapy.* New York: Basic Books.
Mallet, Carl-Heinz. 1984. *Fairy Tales and Children.* Translated by Joachim Neugroschel. New York: Schocken Books.
Mandler, G. 1984. *Mind and Body: Psychology of Emotion and Stress.* New York: W. W. Norton.
Maslow, Abraham. 1986. *Toward a Psychology of Being,* 2d ed. Princeton, N.J.: Van Nostrand and Co.
Masson, Jeffrey Moussaieff. 1985. *The Assault on Truth: Freud's Suppression of the Seduction Theory.* New York: Penguin Books.
——— . 1988. *Against Therapy.* New York: Atheneum Press.
May, Rollo. 1991. *The Cry for Myth.* New York: W. W. Norton.
Mays, V. M., and G. W. Albee. 1992. "Psychotherapy: Its Relevance to Minorities." In *A History of Psychotherapy,* edited by D. K. Friedman. Washington, D.C.: American Psychological Association.
McClelland, D. C. 1953. *The Achievement Motive.* New York: Appleton-Century-Crofts.
McHugh, Paul. 1992. "Psychiatric Misadventures." *American Scholar* 61: 497–510.
Meichenbaum, Donald. 1974. *Cognitive Behavior Modification.* Morristown, N.J.: General Learning Press.
Merton, Robert K. 1968. *Social Theory and Social Structure.* New York: Free Press.
Miller, Alice. 1984. *Thou Shalt Not Be Aware: Society's Betrayal of the Child.* New York: Meridian.
Mills, C. W. 1956. *The Power Elite.* New York: Oxford University Press.
Morss, John R. 1992. "Making Waves: Deconstruction and Developmental Psychology." *Theory and Psychology* 2: 445–466.
Mosley, Nicholas. 1990. *Hopeful Monsters.* Elmook Park, Ill.: Dalkey Archives Press.
Omer, Haim, and Perry London. 1988. "Metamorphosis in Psychotherapy: End of the Systems Era." *Psychotherapy* 25: 171–185.
Orwell, George. 1949. *1984.* New York: New American Library.
Piaget, Jean. 1950. *The Psychology of Intelligence.* Translated by M. Piercy and D. E. Berlyne. London: Routledge and Kegan Paul.
——— . 1952. *The Origins of Intelligence in Children.* New York: International Universities Press.
——— . 1954. *The Construction of Reality in the Child.* Translated by M. Cook. New York: Basic Books.
——— . 1957. *Biology and Knowledge.* Chicago, Ill.: University of Chicago Press.
——— . 1973. *The Child and Reality.* New York: Grossman Publishers.
——— . 1975. *The Development of Thought.* New York: Viking Press.
——— . 1981. *Intelligence and Affectivity.* Palo Alto, Calif.: Annual Reviews.

228 *References*

Plutchik, Robert. 1977. "Cognition in the Service of Emotions: An Evolutionary Perspective." In *Emotions,* edited by D. Landland, J. R. Fell, E. Keen, A. Leshrer, R. Plutchik, and R. H. Tarpiz. Monterey Calif.: Brooks Cole.

———. 1980. *Emotions: A Psychoevolutionary Synthesis.* New York: Harper and Row.

Polanyi, Michael. 1958. *Personal Knowledge.* Chicago, Ill.: University of Chicago Press.

———. 1966. *Science, Faith and Society.* Chicago, Ill.: University of Chicago Press.

———. 1967. *The Tacit Dimension.* New York: Anchor Books.

———. 1969. *Knowing and Being.* Chicago: University of Chicago Press.

Pollster, Murray. 1987. *Every Person's Life Is Worth a Novel.* New York: W. W. Norton.

Popper, Karl. 1945. *The Open Society and Its Enemies.* Princeton, N.J.: Princeton University Press.

———. 1961. *The Logic of Modern Discovery.* New York: Science Editions.

Prilleltensky, Isaac. 1989. "Psychology and the Status Quo." *American Psychologist* 44: 795–802.

Prirogene, J., and I. Stengers. 1984. *Order Out of Chaos.* New York: Bantam Books.

Puhakka, Kaisa. 1992. "Discovery as Seeing: Lesson from Radical Empiricism and Meditative Practice." *Theoretical and Philosophical Psychology* 12: 48–58.

Reiff, Philip. 1966. *The Triumph of the Therapeutic.* New York: Harper and Row.

Reynolds, Emily M. 1992. "Socially Constructed Sexuality: Toward a Postmodern Theory of Sexual Intimacy." *Theoretical and Philosophical Psychology* 12: 38–46.

Rorty, Richard. 1979. *Philosophy and The Mirror of Nature.* Princeton, N.J.: Princeton University Press.

Rosen, Hugh. 1985. *Piagetian Dimensions of Clinical Relevance.* New York: Columbia University Press.

Rossman, Neil. 1991. *Consciousness: Separation and Integration.* Albany, N.Y.: State University of New York Press.

Rotman, Brian. 1977. *Jean Piaget: Psychologist of the Real.* Ithaca, N.Y.: Cornell Univesity Press.

Rotter, J. B. 1966. *Generalized Expectancies for Internal versus External Control of Reinforcement.* New York: International Universities Press.

Sampson, Edward E. 1981. "Cognitive Psychology as Ideology." *American Psychologist* 36: 730–743.

———. 1983. *Justice and the Critique of Pure Psychology.* New York: Plenum.

———. 1985. "The Decentralization of Identity: Toward a Revised Concept of Personal and Social Order." *American Psychologist* 40: 1203–1211.

———. 1989. "The Challenge of Social Change for Psychology." *American Psychologist* 44: 914–921.

Sarason, Seymour B. 1981. "An Asocial Psychology and a Misdirected Clinical Psychology." *American Psychologist* 36: 827–837.

Sarbin, Theodore R., and James C. Mancuso. 1980. *Schizophrenia: Medical Diagnosis or Moral Verdict?* New York: Pergamon Press.

Scarr, Sandra. 1985. "Constructing Psychology: Making Facts and Fables for Our Time." *American Psychologist* 40: 449–513.

Schafer, Roy. 1976. *A New Language for Psychoanalysis.* New Haven, Conn.: Yale University Press.

———. 1980. *Narrative Action in Psychoanalysis.* Worcester, Mass.: Clark University Press.

———. 1983. *The Analytic Attitude.* London: Hogarth Press.

Shanes, Morris. 1992. "Intentionality and the Problem of Discovery in Scientific Epistemology." *Theory and Psychology* 2: 5–28.

Sharif, Z., G. Gewirtz, and N. Igbal. 1993. "Brain Imaging in Schizophrenia: A Review." *Psychiatric Annals* 23: 123–134.

Shotter, John. 1991. "Rhetoric and the Social Construction of Cognition." *Theory and Psychology* 1: 495–514.

Simon, Laurence R. 1981. "The Therapist-Patient Relationship: A Holistic View." *American Journal of Psychoanalysis* 41: 213–225.

———. 1986. *Cognition and Affect: A Developmental Psychology of the Individual.* Buffalo, N.Y.: Prometheus Books.

Spence, Donald P. 1982. *Narrative Truth and Historical Truth.* New York: W. W. Norton.

———. 1987. *The Freudian Metaphor.* New York: W. W. Norton.

Sroufe, L. A. 1987. "The Role of Infant-Caregiver Attachment in Development." In *Clinical Implications of Attachment,* edited by J. Belsky and M. T. Nezworski. Hillsdale, N.J.: Erlbaum.

Stander, Philip. 1988. *Bertrand Russell: Educational Philosophy.* Manuscript in possession of the author.

Stern, Daniel. 1977. *The First Relationship: Infant and Mother.* Cambridge, Mass.: Harvard University Press.

Strenger, Carlo. 1991. *Between Hermeneutics and Science.* New York: International Universities Press.

Storr, Anthony. 1988. *Solitude.* New York: Free Press.

Sullivan, Harry Stack. 1953. *The Interpersonal Theory of Psychiatry.* New York: W. W. Norton.

Sykes, Charles J. 1992. "I Hear America Whining." *New York Times,* November 2.

Szasz, Thomas. 1973. *The Second Sin.* Garden City, N.Y.: Anchor Press.

———. 1974. *The Myth of Mental Illness,* rev. ed. New York: Harper and Row.

———. 1978. *The Myth of Psychotherapy.* Garden City, N.Y.: Anchor Press.

Tamney, Martin. 1992. Personal communication with the author.

Tetlock, Philip. 1992. "An Alternative Metaphor in the Study of Judgment and Choice: People as Politicians." *Theory and Psychology* 1: 451–475.

Thomas, A. S., S. Chess, and H. G. Birch. 1968. *Temperament and Behavior Disorders in Children.* New York: New York University Press.

Tolman, Edward C. 1932. *Purposive Behavior in Animals and Men.* New York: Century.

Tomacek, Odile. 1990. "A Personal Commentary on 'Schizophrenia as a Brain Disorder.'" *American Psychologist* 45: 550–551.

Viney, Linda. 1992. "Can We See Ourselves Changing: Toward a Personal Construct Model of Adult Development." *Human Development* 35: 65–75.

White, Robert W. 1959. "Motivation Reconsidered: The Concept of Competence." *Psychological Review,* 66.

Whitaker, Carl. 1976. "A Family Is A Four Dimensional Relationship." In *Family Therapy,* edited by P. J. Gueran. New York: Gardner Press.

Williams, Donna. 1992. *Nobody, Nowhere: The Extraordinary Autobiography of an Autistic.* New York: Times Books/Random House.

Winnicott, D. W. 1965. *The Maturational Process and the Facilitating Environment.* New York: International Universities Press.

Zajonc, R. B. 1980. "Feeling and Thinking: Preferences Need No Inferences." *American Psychologist* 33: 150–175.

———. 1984. "On the Primacy of Affect." *American Psychologist* 39: 117–123.

Zajonc, R. B., and H. Markor. 1984. "Affect and Cognition: The Hard Interface." In *Emotions, Cognition and Behavior,* edited by C. E. Izard, J. Kagan, and R. B. Zajonc. New York: Cambridge University Press.

Zilbergeld, Bernie. 1983. *The Shrinking of America: Myths of Psychological Change.* Boston, Mass.: Little, Brown.

INDEX

ABOUT THE AUTHOR

LAURENCE SIMON is Professor of Psychology at Kingsborough Community College of CUNY, Chief Psychologist at Flushing Hospital Mental Health Clinic, and in private practice. He has written several articles and books on psychotherapy and the development of human personality.

ISBN 0-275-94690-8

90000>

EAN

9 780275 946906

HARDCOVER BAR CODE